THE BOOK
OF THE
REVELATION

For Margaret

THE BOOK
OF THE
REVELATION
A COMMENTARY
Philip Edgcumbe Hughes

Inter-Varsity Press
Leicester, England

William B. Eerdmans Publishing Company
Grand Rapids, Michigan

INTER-VARSITY PRESS
38 De Montfort Street, Leicester LE1 7GP, England

Wm. B. EERDMANS PUBLISHING COMPANY
255 Jefferson S.E., Grand Rapids, MI 49503

First published 1990

British Library Cataloguing in Publication Data
Hughes, Philip Edgcumbe *1915–1990*
  The book of the Revelation.
  1. Bible. N.T. Revelation – Critical studies
  I. Title
  228.06

  ISBN 0-85111-748-1

Library of Congress Cataloging-in-Publication Data
Hughes, Philip Edgcumbe.
  The book of the Revelation: a commentary /
Philip Edgcumbe Hughes.
    p.   cm.
  ISBN 0-8028-3684-4
  1. Bible. N.T. Revelation — Commentaries. I. Title.
BS2825.3.H85   1990
228'.077 — dc20   90-44122
                                                       CIP

Set in Linotron Palatino
Typeset in Great Britain by Parker Typesetting Service, Leicester
Printed in the United States of America

*Inter-Varsity Press is the book-publishing division of the Universities
and Colleges Christian Fellowship.*

CONTENTS

INTRODUCTION

The fact that the book of Revelation is placed last in the New Testament does not mean that it is held to be less important than the other canonical books that precede it. For reasons that will become apparent later in this introduction its position at the end is entirely appropriate. No book could more fittingly bring not only the New Testament but the Bible in its entirety to a conclusion. Yet there are many who approach it with apprehension, and some who neglect it altogether. Regarded as difficult and unrewarding because of the strange mysteries recorded in its pages, the book is set aside. Nor can it be denied that there are parts that are hard to understand and visionary images that seem grotesque and fantastic. At the same time, however, there are numerous passages that are both readily comprehensible and also full of beauty and rich in spiritual truth. While it is true of all Holy Scripture that it should not be read hurriedly but studied and pondered, it is perhaps true of Revelation more than of any other biblical book. Its wealth is there to be mined by every believing mind and heart.

The title *The Apocalypse* by which this book is also known means simply (from its Greek original) 'The Unveiling' or 'The Revelation', and its significance is explained in the opening sentence of the book. The literary form or genre is that which is classified as Apocalyptic, and in this respect it is unique among the books of the New Testament. An apocalyptic writing discloses mysteries, generally with respect to the future – mysteries the import of which is sometimes plainly interpreted, but which frequently remain veiled in enigmatic figures and symbols. This holds good for the book of Revelation. (The visions of Ezekiel and Daniel are examples of apocalyptic writing in the Old Testament.)[1]

[1] Sections that are more or less apocalyptic in character are found in what are otherwise non-apocalyptic works; in the New Testament, for example, see passages such as Mt. 24, Mk. 13, Lk. 21.

REVELATION

The use of symbolism is a distinctive mark of apocalyptic literature. It is not surprising, therefore, that symbolism has an important role in Revelation, and in a serious work of this nature this is far from being just a conventional device or custom. There is a need for symbolism because the reality of the scenes revealed and recorded is transcendental in character. Vistas of eternity and infinity cannot be fully described by our human language which is finite and bound by time. But human language is our only medium for setting down and passing on disclosures of the transcendental realm; and so the seer must do his best to communicate what he has seen to others by means of analogical approximations and images which suggest and point beyond themselves to realities that far exceed all that can be said. The Lamb, who is so much the central figure in these visions, portrays the incarnate Son with reference to his offering up of himself as a substitutionary sacrifice to redeem sinful men and bring them back to God. Moreover, because of the symbolical character of the language, it is not incongruous or contradictory for the Lamb to be called the Lion of the tribe of Judah, for this designation declares the majestic power and supreme authority of the Son in the glory to which he has ascended. The whiteness of the robes of the redeemed signifies both the purgation of their sinfulness through the atoning sacrifice of the Son and also their conformity to his spotless purity in the glory for which they are destined. The surpassing beauty of the eternal realities witnessed by the Apostle is indicated by resorting to the inferior lustre of the lovely things of this present world, such as gold and precious stones and pellucid crystal.

The imagery of the sublime loveliness and perfection of the new heaven and earth is in radical contrast to the terrifying spectacle of earthquakes, darkness, thunder, lightning, hailstorms, and smoking devastation by which the horror of the final judgment of the impenitent is depicted. Strongly symbolical, also, are the four living creatures with their distinctive appearances and the dragon and the beast from the sea with their many heads and horns and diadems. And, further, the numbers that occur in the Apocalypse have a symbolical import. This is obviously the case with the mysterious number of the beast (13:18), but it holds good as a general principle throughout the book, as I endeavour to show in the commentary that follows. Because many of the symbolic expressions are left by the author without an interpretation (for example, the hidden manna and the white stone promised to overcomers in 2:17), it does not mean that they are incomprehensible; on the contrary, it is our responsibility to understand them as best we can, and particularly in relationship to the teaching of Scripture elsewhere. This principle of interpreting as far as possible the less clear places by the plain teaching found elsewhere in Scripture applies equally to those symbols that are explained in the text (for example, the information in 1:20 that the seven lampstands are the seven churches, for there remains the need to understand lampstands as an analogy for churches).

There has, indeed, been, and there continues to be, a wide variety of opinions regarding the over-all interpretation of the Apocalypse and the range or scope of its applicability to the fortunes of the Christian church. The preterists have wished to assign the fulfilment of the book's prophecies, for the most part, to the earliest age of ecclesiastical history. The historicists maintain that the Patmos visions portray the development of the church and its affairs in a sequence of periods that stretch successively from the beginning to the end of its history. The futurists, as the name indicates, hold that the focus of Revelation is neither on the past nor the present but on events that have yet to take place. It is only to be expected that the interpretation offered by any of these will be governed by the particular presupposition with which the text is approached. All too frequently history has been tortured on the rack of dominant suppositions to deliver confirmation of a cherished theory.

One area, or arena, in particular where the clash of conflicting opinions continues undiminished is that of the millennium or reign of a thousand years. Chapter 20 is the only place not only in the Apocalypse but in all Scripture where this thousand-year period is mentioned. This does not make it any less important. Moreover, there is a cryptic aspect of the passage which, as is usual with writings of an apocalyptic nature, helps to explain the different ways of understanding its meaning. Of the three schools of interpretation, the premillennialists hold that prior to his reigning for a thousand years on earth Christ's second advent will take place, the postmillennialists hold that Christ's return will be after the millennium which they envisage as a golden age of church prevalence and gospel fruitfulness throughout the world, and the amillennialists hold that the thousand years signify the duration of the present gospel era extending between the two comings of Christ, treating the number one thousand, in line with the other numbers of the book, as symbolical in significance. (To call the last named 'amillennialists' is somewhat misleading, since they do not reject the teaching concerning the millennium, but only the interpretation proposed by pre- and postmillennialists.) As the commentary on chapter 20 will show, the amillennial position is the one which I believe to be most compatible with the realities of the biblical revelation.

It is my firm judgment that the contents of this fascinating work are relevant and applicable to the church in every age, as is true of all the other books of the New Testament. Certainly to take an example, the letters to the seven churches in chapters 2 and 3 were addressed, in the first instance, to those particular churches to their contemporary situation, with special reference to the strengths and weaknesses and needs of each, and with the addition of appropriate warnings and promises. But these seven letters are messages also to every church in every generation and location. What the Lord says to them he says to all; for the state of the Asian churches of the first century is, so to speak, a cross-section of the state of the pilgrim church in its unfolding history of struggle: here fervent, there lukewarm, at one time full of joy and faith, at another dejected and unfruitful. So also the prophecies and promises and the warnings and exhortations throughout the length of the book are perennial in their significance and ever fresh.

This commentary, however, is not polemical in its thrust, but positive and straightforward. There are many things in St. John's Revelation whose meaning will be fully clear to us only when we see and experience the wonderful realities to which they point in the pure light of that glory which is hereafter. Meanwhile we must be content, like the Apostle Paul, to see but dimly and to know in part (1 Cor. 13:12), and with St. John to acknowledge that it does not yet appear what we shall be (1 Jn. 3:2); and by comparing scripture with scripture we must seek not only to increase our understanding and to avoid error and misinterpretation, but also, with the help of divine grace, to lay hold of the blessings made known to us through this book.

Although it is based on a study of the Greek text, the commentary that follows is 'popular' in the sense that it is free from academic technicalities, linguistic annotations, and critical discussions of terms and theories. In order to preserve the spirit and 'flavour' of the original I have kept the translation as close as possible to the form and sense of the Greek text. New Testament quotations are my own translation, unless stated otherwise. When quoting from the Old Testament I have followed the Revised Standard Version. It is not my purpose to provide a learned disquisition on questions concerning the date, authorship, background, and grammar of the Apocalypse. Excellent works that deal with such issues are readily available. Suffice it to say that I regard the evidence, both internal and external, that the Apostle John is the author as convincing (that is why I speak without hesitation of St. John both as the writer of this book and as the recipient of the visions recorded in it), and that I judge the arguments for a late date to be outweighed by those which place the composition of the Apocalypse prior to AD 70.

Finally, the Revelation of St. John rounds off the biblical canon. It brings the beginning to its authentic conclusion. This conclusion, however, is not a termination; it is itself a beginning in the sense that it is not only the renewal of the beginning but also the fulfilment that has no end, the completion that is perfect and everlasting. A key to the understanding of the Apocalypse is the Lord God's identification of himself as 'the Alpha and the Omega, the first and the last, the beginning and the end' (22:13; 1:8, 17; 21:6). This self-designation signifies the absolute existence of God from eternity to eternity and, moreover, it implies that what God starts he finishes. The last two chapters of this book reveal the consummation of creation, the end for which the created order was intended and designed, the omega-point that is the actualization of the potential that was contained, like a germ, in the alpha-seed. For the end was enclosed in the beginning like a promise, and the beginning is there in the end that is its completion.

The point is that what God begins he completes. If his will were frustrated and his purpose came to nothing he would not be God. Thus St. Paul speaks of 'the purpose of him who accomplishes all things according to the counsel of his will' (Eph. 1:11). Therefore the new creation of the Apocalypse must not be sundered from the original creation of Genesis. The connection is that of continuity and completion. When the Lord God says, 'Behold, I make all things new' (21:5), this indicates the abolition not of the order of creation but of the degradation and perversion it has suffered through the sinfulness of man. All things are made new by the thorough purgation of the existing order. This making new involves therefore the renewal of creation and the restoration of its pristine purity; but, more than that, it is the bringing of the original creation to the glorious destiny for which it was always intended – a destiny which consummates the purpose of the original. The end, then, not only restores but also fulfils the beginning, and in doing so transcends the glory of the beginning. The bond between the old and the new, the dynamism that achieves the end present in the beginning, is the will of Almighty God fulfilled through the redemptive mission to our world of the incarnate Son. It was God's good pleasure 'through him to reconcile to himself all things, whether on earth or in heaven, having made peace by the blood of his cross' (Col. 1:20).

The reconciliation of all things on earth and in heaven, the constituents, that is, of the existing creation, to God and therefore also to each other makes real the harmony and the enhancement of the whole, the bringing of the beginning to its predetermined fulfilment. Thus the biblical canon opens with the statement that in the beginning God created heaven and earth, and it ends with the disclosure to St. John of the new heaven and earth (Gn. 1:1; Rev. 21:1). The river flowing in Eden and watering the garden reappears at the river of the water of life proceeding from the throne of God and of the Lamb (Gn. 2:10; Rev. 22:1). The tree of life from which man because of his sinful rebellion was separated is once again freely accessible to the great multitude of the redeemed (Gn. 2:9; 3:22–24; Rev. 22:2). The curse that in his folly man brought upon his original blessedness is forever removed (Gn. 3:17–19; Rev. 22:3); and the intimate and unclouded communion of the creature with his Creator which was forfeited by man's turning away from God is recovered as in the renewed creation the redeemed joyfully serve the Lord and, stamped with his name, see his face (Gn. 3:8; Rev. 22:3f.). Thus the paradise that was lost is regained, and regained to a transcendental degree, in Christ. And this is the message not only of the last book of the Bible but of the scriptural canon in its entirety.

COMMENTARY

Introduction, 1:1–20

1. PROLOGUE, 1:1–3

The revelation of Jesus Christ, which God gave him to show to his servants the things which must soon come to pass; and he sent and signified it by his angel to his servant John, who bore witness to the word of God and to the testimony of Jesus Christ, even to all that he saw (1:1–2).

These words of introduction summarize the origin and purpose of this last book of the New Testament canon (last, that is, in position, though not necessarily in time).[1] It is a *revelation* in the sense, indeed, of a communication of truth, but also in the sense of a disclosure in the form of a vision or series of visions concerning ultimate realities. It is, further, a revelation *of Jesus Christ*, that is to say, about Jesus Christ, who is the central figure of the book and whose total victory over the hostile forces of evil is the dominant theme.[2] And it is a revelation *which God gave him*, namely Jesus Christ. Accordingly, God is the source of the revelation (that is why it is so important), and its first recipient is Jesus Christ, the incarnate Son who, one with God and one with us, is the authentic Mediator between God and men (1 Tim. 2:5), and who from the glory to which, still in union with our human nature, he is now exalted draws back the curtain to give his apostle glimpses of that glory which his redeemed are destined to share (Rom. 8:18; 2 Cor. 4:17).

The purpose for which the Son is given the revelation is *to show* it *to his servants*, in other words, to those who truly love and faithfully follow him as their Redeemer and Lord. There are, however, two other links in the chain of communication: *his angel* and *his servant John*, the former being *sent* to signify the revelation to the latter, who in turn records it in writing. There is no fuller identification of the angel, and it is sufficient to say here that the angelic function is essentially that of

---

[1] On the date of Revelation see p. 10 above.

[2] The phrase 'of Jesus Christ' could mean received *from* Jesus Christ, but it seems preferable to take it as an objective genitive.

15

being a messenger (which is the meaning of the term 'angel') who does God's will with special reference to those who through Christ are the heirs of salvation (*cf.* Ps. 103:20f.; Heb. 1:14). Thus from God, the source of the revelation, the sequence of communication is, first, to Jesus Christ, the incarnate and glorified Son, and from Jesus Christ through his angel to his servant John, and then through his servant John to his servants as a whole by the writing of this book.

The verb *signified* has a particular appropriateness here, for to signify means to communicate by means of signs or to explain the meaning of signs, and this writing is by its very nature a book of signs or symbols which are in themselves cryptic and dark, some more, some less, and which are clarified, at least partially, either by the context or by the addition of some words of explanation. For example, the 'seven candlesticks' are defined as 'seven churches' (1:20), but all that is declared of 'the number of the beast', 666, is that it is 'the number of man' (or 'of a man', 13:18). Because the book is permeated by the symbolism of images and numbers, those who seek to understand its message must grasp as far as possible the significance of these signs and symbols, not only by considering such clues as are given, but also by seeking light from Holy Scripture in its entirety.

John tells us that the revelation concerns *the things which must soon come to pass.* This information immediately injects the note of urgency into what he is writing. It should be heeded as in effect a warning that the Apocalypse is not a collection of puzzles and cryptograms for those who find such things amusing and diverting: the fearful judgments so graphically depicted in John's visions are real and they are impending. That they must take place *soon* accords with the teaching both of Christ himself and of his apostles regarding the *imminence* of the Day of the Lord. The message to the church in the first generation remains firm for the church in every generation: 'Watch therefore; for you know not when the Lord of the house will come' (Mk. 13:35).

If it is objected that the predictions of the book of Revelation have not taken place 'soon', since century follows century and there is still no final day, the reminder is needed that history is advancing in accordance with God's timetable, not man's, indeed that 'one day is with the Lord as a thousand years, and a thousand years as one day' (2 Pet. 3:8). There is, and there will be, no failure of fulfilment. That is why the events foretold in these visions *must* come to pass; there is no escaping them. Moreover, as the interval between the Lord's two comings is perceived as comprising the last days (Heb. 1:2; 1 Pet. 1:20) which are inexorably leading up to the Last Day (Mt. 24:50; Lk. 17:30; Acts 17:31; Rom. 2:16; 1 Thes. 5:2; 2 Pet. 3:10, 12), and the church is constantly under attack, it is right for Christians in every age to feel that they are living in the last hour and that the Day of the Lord is at hand (1 Jn. 2:18; 2 Thes. 2:2). The preview provided in these visions of the fulfilment of God's day of judgment (6:12ff.; 19:11ff.) lends intensity to the admonitions to the churches to be watchful and to persevere in faithfulness to their Lord (chapters 2 and 3) and to the announcement in the conclusion of the book that the Lord is coming quickly (22:7, 20).

In his own sufferings for the gospel as well as in setting down *all that he saw*, John *bore witness* in true apostolic fashion *to the word of God and to the testimony of Jesus Christ*, for this witness is borne by life and conduct no less than by word of mouth or by putting pen to paper. Thus it was 'on account of the word of God and the testimony of Jesus' that John had been banished to the island of Patmos (verse 9). And the same constancy in witness-bearing is the mark of all Christ's true followers, for it is against those who 'maintain their testimony to Jesus' that Satan makes war (12:17, NEB), it is for their 'testimony to Jesus and for the word of God' that the martyrs are put to death (20:4), and it is 'through the blood of the Lamb and through the word of their testimony' that God's people overcome their great enemy (12:11).

> *Blessed is he who reads and those who hear the words of the prophecy, and who keep the things written in it; for the time is near (1:3).*

John sends forth his book with a beatitude, declaring both *he who reads* and *those who hear the words of the prophecy* to be *blessed*. The reader is singular and the hearers plural because John envisages one person, perhaps an elder, reading aloud what he has written to the many persons who form the congregation; and with the public reading there was no doubt the further intention that copies should be made as the document was transmitted from church to church. The beatitude, however, is pronounced not merely on those who read and hear the prophecy (another way of referring to his book), but in particular on those who *keep the things* which are *written in it.* Reading or hearing is of course a preliminary necessity, but to heed the warnings and obey the precepts the prophecy contains is the essential response, apart from which all reading and hearing is worthless. The note of urgency, already sounded in the assertion that the predictions must shortly come to pass (verse 1), is reinforced here by the addition of the caveat, *for the time is near*, in other words, there is no time for trifling and insincerity.

2. SALUTATION, 1:4–8

> *John to the seven churches that are in Asia: Grace to you and peace from him who is and who was and who is to come, and from the seven Spirits who are before his throne, and from Jesus Christ the*

> *faithful witness, the firstborn of the dead, and the ruler of the kings of the earth (1:4–5a).*

This salutation indicates that the book was despatched like a letter, though otherwise its form can hardly be classified as epistolary. It is addressed to **the seven churches** that are the recipients of the letters written, in chapters 2 and 3, at the Lord's command, the churches, namely, in Ephesus, Smyrna, Pergamum, Thyatira, Sardis, Philadelphia, and Laodicea. These churches are **in Asia**, which in the geography of the first century denoted the Roman province of Asia and is now part of the territory of Turkey. As previously observed, the apocalyptic character of Revelation justifies the supposition that the numbers found in it have some symbolical significance; so here the number seven is probably intended to convey a notion of completeness,[1] to the effect that these seven churches stand for all churches in the first and in every subsequent century. This understanding is, if anything, confirmed by the declaration that the message conveyed in each letter to a particular church is 'what the Spirit says to the churches' (2:7, 11, 17, 29; 3:6, 13, 22), that is, to the churches, or the church, as a whole.

Though **grace and peace** occur together as words of greeting used in most of the New Testament letters, they are far from being a superficial formality, but belong rather to a salutation sincerely founded on the grace and peace of the gospel which flow to us from God. This is clearly spelled out here as grace and peace from the Triune God, Father, Spirit, and Son (in that order). They came firstly, **from him who is and who was and who is to come**, designating, as the context requires, God the Father, though it could equally apply, because of their union and consubstantiality with the Father, to the Son and to the Holy Spirit, and also to God without reference to the trinitarian differentiation (*cf.* 1:8; 4:8, and comparable designations in 1:17f.; 11:17; 16:5, also Heb. 13:8), descriptive as it is of the eternal existence of the Deity. They come secondly, **from the seven Spirits who are before his** (the Father's) **throne**, designating the Holy Spirit, the number seven here being symbolical of divine perfection (see 3:1; 4:5; 5:6). And thirdly, **from Jesus Christ**, the Second Person of the Trinity, thus named because he is the incarnate Son, who as such is our Saviour (Jesus, Mt. 1:21) and the Lord's Anointed One (Christ, Acts 4:26f.).

As the Word of God and therefore the absolute Truth (19:13; Jn. 1:1; 14:6) Jesus Christ is **the faithful witness** (*cf.* 3:14; Jn. 3:11; 8:14; 18:37), altogether trustworthy, who throughout his earthly mission set us an example by unfailingly maintaining a faithful witness in the face of antagonism, suffering, and death (*cf.* Heb. 5:8f.). He is, furthermore, **the**

---

[1] The completion of creation in seven days is an example of the association of the number seven with the concept of completeness.

firstborn of the dead by virtue of his resurrection on the third day (*cf.* Col. 1:18; Rom. 8:29; 1 Cor. 15:20), and therefore 'the Living One' who was dead and is alive for evermore (verse 18) and in whom we belong to the 'church of the firstborn who are enrolled in heaven' (Heb. 12:23; 1 Cor. 15:22). And, his mission to earth completed, he is **the ruler of the kings of the earth**, exalted as Lord above all (Phil. 2:8–11), joyfully served and worshipped by his redeemed, and the righteous Judge and Destroyer of every enemy (5:9f.; 11:17f.; 17:14; 19:16; *cf.* Ps. 89:27). This brief portrait of Jesus Christ thus depicts his witness as Word, his work as Redeemer, and his dominion as Lord.

> *To him who loves us and freed us from our sins by his blood and made us a kingdom, priests to his God and Father, to him be the glory and the dominion for ever and ever. Amen (1:5b–6).*

This ascription of praise and gratitude to the Redeemer follows on naturally and spontaneously from what John has just written, and it also relates harmoniously to all that he will yet write in the ensuing pages. The liberation from our sins flows from the unique event of Christ's death on the cross, which is the supreme expression of his love for us; but his love is constant and ever-present, it precedes the cross and it continues after the cross, it embraces us in our sin before we are believers and it remains with us to the end (Rom. 5:8; 1 Jn. 4:10; Jn. 13:1) – hence the present tense of the verb, **loves**.

One consequence of this redeeming love is that we who believe are constituted **a kingdom**; united to Christ, we share in his kingship (*cf.* 2 Tim. 2:12), who reigns for ever and ever (22:5; *cf.* Lk. 22:29f.). Our true citizenship is not here but in the glorious realm of the new heaven and earth; in the meantime we are strangers and pilgrims on the earth, our eyes fixed on the better country and the incorruptible inheritance of God's promise (Heb. 11:13, 16; 1 Pet. 1:4).

Another consequence of this saving grace is that we have become **priests** who constitute, as the Apostle Peter says, 'a holy priesthood' set apart 'to offer up spiritual sacrifices, acceptable to God through Jesus Christ' (1 Pet. 2:5). Now that Christ, who is our sole High Priest, has offered up the one perfect and all-sufficient sacrifice to bring us back to God (Heb. 9:11 – 10:25; 2 Cor. 5:21; 1 Pet. 2:24f.; 3:18), the function of our priesthood is to offer up such sacrifices as express the response of our gratitude for the wonderful redemption that is ours by virtue of his propitiatory sacrifice of himself in our stead. In sum, we are to offer the 'sacrifice of praise to God continually' (Heb. 13:15), proceeding indeed from our lips, but lived out with constancy in our lives. Because it is the logical response to the saving grace of God in Christ Jesus, it is 'our reasonable service' as priests to 'offer our bodies as a living sacrifice, holy, acceptable to God' (Rom. 12:1). The motivation and the 'movement' of our priestly offering is *to his* (our incarnate Lord's) **God and Father.** Christ's total self-offering at infinite cost for our everlasting redemption calls forth our total self-offering in his service, which is our response of eucharist or thanksgiving: 'We offer and present unto thee, O Lord, ourselves, our souls and bodies, to be a reasonable, holy, and living sacrifice unto thee' (*Book of Common Prayer*).

The note of priestly praise and thanksgiving resounds throughout St. John's book because it belongs to our reasonable, holy, and living service not only here and now but throughout eternal ages. The concept of God's people as a kingdom and priests is found early on in Exodus 19:6: 'You shall be to me a kingdom of priests and a holy nation'; and it is echoed in St. Peter's assertion: 'You are a chosen race, a royal priesthood, a holy nation' (1 Pet. 2:9; *cf.* Is. 61:6). The royal and priestly status of the company of the redeemed is even now a present reality, but its consummating fulfilment will be experienced in the perfection of the new heaven and earth as the innumerable white-robed multitude serve God ceaselessly in his temple (7:15). The ascription proper that now follows, *to him be the glory and the dominion for ever and ever. Amen*, is itself an outpouring of priestly praise; for, since we owe everything to God, the blessing of our creation, the grace of our redemption, and his providential care of our every need, all the praise and glory is due to him and none at all to ourselves. Our glorying is always and only in the Lord (1 Cor. 1:30). The occurrence of *Amen* here and in the next verse, and also in 5:14, 7:12, 19:4, 22:20, 21, points to its liturgical usage in the first century. On the significance of the term see comments on 3:14 below.

> *Behold, he is coming with the clouds, and every eye will see him, and those who pierced him; and all the tribes of the earth will mourn over him. Even so, Amen (1:7).*

Much of St. John's language reflects the imagery of the book of Daniel. Thus the first clause here recalls the declaration of Daniel 7:13: 'Behold, with the clouds of heaven there came one like a son of man'; and the similarity is even more apparent in 14:14, where St. John writes: 'And I saw, and behold, a white cloud, and seated on the cloud one like a son of man'. **The clouds** intended here are not dark storm-clouds which presage divine judgment (true though it is that the Lord's coming spells wrathful judgment for the unrepentant, as passages elsewhere in Revelation indicate), but the bright clouds of his transcendental glory. They stand for the *shekinah* glory of God's presence which caused the face of Moses to shine with supernatural brilliance after speaking with God at Sinai or in the sanctuary (Ex. 34:29ff.; 2 Cor. 3:7ff.); and they are to be identified with the 'bright cloud' of Christ's divine glory witnessed by Peter, James, and John on the mount of transfiguration (Mt. 17:5), and with the cloud which received him out of the apostles' sight at his ascension, followed by the assurance that 'this Jesus, who was received up from you into heaven, shall so come in like manner as ye beheld him going into heaven' (Acts 1:9–11). This association of the clouds of Christ's coming with his glory is plainly made in Matthew 24:30, where he declares that 'all the tribes of the earth . . . shall see the Son of Man coming on the clouds of heaven with power and great glory' (*cf.* 16:26f.; 26:64). Accordingly, his coming with the clouds is the equivalent of his coming again with glory, as professed, for example, in the Nicene Creed.

Because *every eye will see him* there will be no escaping or hiding from the resplendent majesty of his coming; every knee will bow in submission to him and every tongue will acknowledge his lordship (Phil. 2:10f.; Rom. 14:11; Is. 45:23). It is true that at the time of Christ's crucifixion those who pierced him looked upon him as he suffered and died on the cross to which they had nailed him (Jn. 19:37; Zc. 12:10); but the reference here is to the coming in glory of him who proclaims, 'I was dead, and behold, I am alive for evermore' (verse 18), and this coming will be witnessed not just by a few in a particular locality but by *all the tribes of the earth.* The number of those who pierced him will not then be limited to those who were responsible for his crucifixion and the ones who drove the nails through his hands and feet, but it will include all persons of every nationality and every generation whose sins, so to speak, fixed him to the cross. The universal mourning will be the anguished lamentation of all who have impenitently rejected the grace that flows from that cross as now the wrath of divine judgment overwhelms them (*cf.* 6:15–17). The confirming expression *Even so, Amen* is a combination of the Greek and Hebrew affirmatives, *Nai, Amen,* and as such strengthens the note of universality: what has been said applies neither just to Gentiles nor just to Jews, but to both, that is, to all without distinction. It also emphasizes the inescapability of the Last Day and its mourning for all who continue in unrepentance. Too late then for them, with change of heart, to acknowledge: 'Who was the guilty? Who brought this upon thee? Alas, my treason, Jesus, hath undone thee. 'Twas I, Lord Jesus, I it was denied thee: I crucified thee.'[1]

> *I am the Alpha and the Omega, says the Lord God, who is and who was and who is to come, the Almighty (1:8).*

Alpha is the first letter and *Omega* the last letter of the Greek alphabet; thus the self-identification 'I am the Alpha and the Omega' is the same as 'I am the First and the Last' (as in 22:13; *cf.* 21:6; 1:17; 2:8). The title designates God's absolute uniqueness and self-sufficiency which both Old and New Testaments consistently and emphatically affirm. 'Before me no god was formed, nor shall there be any after me', the Lord declared

---

[1] From Johann Heermann's hymn (1630), translated by Robert Bridges.

through his prophet Isaiah; 'I am the first and I am the last; besides me there is no god' (Is. 43:10; 44:6; *cf.* 41:4; 48:12). This means, not that God had a beginning and will have an end, but that he is before all and after all. The statement is always in the present tense of his eternal being, without beginning and without end: 'I AM the Alpha and the Omega, the beginning and the end' (21:6). It is clear from the explanatory relative clause, *who is and who was and who is to come*, that God's past (who was) and his future (who is to come) must be understood in the light of the eternal present of his being (who is), which significantly is in the first place. The great name by which God revealed himself to Moses was the name I AM: 'This', he insisted, 'is my name for ever, and thus I am to be remembered throughout all generations' (Ex. 3:14f.).

God is the Alpha, too, the First, the Beginning, in the sense that he has brought the whole order of creation into existence (cf. Jn. 1:1–3), and the Omega, the Last, the End, in the sense not only that he brings the ungodly to destruction but also that he brings his creation to the glorious consummation for which it was formed – two of the major themes of Revelation. God who had the first word will also have the last word, and this is so because of the everlasting presentness of his sovereign existence. And that is why he alone can designate himself *the Almighty*, the omnipotent Lord who wields all power and whose purposes can never come to nothing, and why he alone in his trinitarian majesty is the recipient of all true worship (4:8; 11:17; 15:3; 16:7; 19:6; *cf.* Mt. 4:10; Dt. 6:13). All this, moreover, is implicit in the fact that he is known as *the Lord God.*

As the seed is to the harvest, so the omega (destiny) is already present in the alpha (origin), for it is both the promise and the achievement, both the potential and the goal, the end that lies hidden in the beginning; and the unbreakable line that connects the first to the last is 'the purpose of him who accomplishes all things according to the counsel of his will' (Eph. 1:11). The uniqueness of God in his being, his power, and his purpose is in itself the rebuttal of atheism and likewise of polytheism and idolatry in all its forms, and also of pantheism, which confuses the Creator with the creation. Our contemplation of God should evoke the spontaneous exclamation of doxology: 'for from him and through him and unto him are all things – to him be glory for ever and ever!' (Rom. 11:36).

3. THE APOSTLE ON PATMOS, 1:9–20

I John, your brother and partaker with you in the tribulation and kingdom and patience, in Jesus, was on the island called Patmos on account of the word of God and the testimony of Jesus (1:9).

The majesty of God has been proclaimed in accordance with his self-disclosure and his redeeming grace extolled, and now the author, who hitherto has made no more than a bare mention of his name (verse 4), is free to communicate something regarding himself and the occasion that led him to set pen to paper. He introduces himself as *John, your brother*, that is, your fellow believer in Christ. The basis of this brotherly relationship is union with Christ, for those who through faith are one with the incarnate Son are brothers, first of all with him, and then and for that reason with each other (see Heb. 2:11–14).

The reality of the brotherhood that bound St. John to the members of the seven churches he is addressing (verse 4) is, if anything, intensified by the consideration that he is able to describe himself as *partaker* with them in the costliness of personal affliction which is inseparable from the true brotherhood of the faith, or, as he puts it here, *in the tribulation and kingdom and patience, in Jesus.* 'Tribulation . . . kingdom . . . patience' is at first sight a sequence in which 'kingdom' looks like an ill-fitting companion of 'tribulation' and 'patience'. In any case, placing it at the end instead of in the central position might have been considered more appropriate, in the light of the apostolic assertions that 'through many tribulations we must enter into the kingdom of God' (Acts 14:22) and that 'if we endure we shall also reign with him' (2 Tim. 2:12). But future fullness does not rule out what is a present reality. Here and now Christian believers are members of Christ's kingdom, and it is their allegiance to Christ as their king that involves them in the necessity to suffer and endure. With this understanding the awkwardness of 'kingdom' being included, and even being centrally placed between 'tribulation' and 'patience', disappears.

The same association is discernible in the desire expressed by St. Paul that the members of the Colossian church should be 'strengthened with all power . . . unto all patience and longsuffering with joy, giving thanks unto the Father . . . who delivered us out of the power of darkness and translated us into the kingdom of his beloved Son' (Col. 1:11–13); and, it is evident, again, in the manner in which he relates the persecutions and afflictions endured by the Thessalonian believers to their being 'counted worthy of the kingdom of God, for which you also suffer' (2 Thes. 1:5).

Nor should it be overlooked that the inclusion of 'kingdom' by St. John is justified and elucidated by the fact that just previously he has stated that the exalted Son has 'made us to be a kingdom' (verse 6): as a participant in that kingdom St. John is also a participant in the sufferings endured by his fellow participants. Whether, on the author's part, the placing of 'kingdom' centrally between 'tribulation' and 'patience' was studied or not, it is true to say that tribulation in Christ's cause is patiently accepted by his followers because belonging to his kingdom is already the central reality. It is important also to observe that the participation in both kingship and suffering of which St. John is writing is *in Jesus*, whose road to the crown was through his suffering for us. Mere earthly suffering in itself has no more eternal significance than does mere earthly kingship. As Christ himself taught, the affliction that is blessed is affliction borne *for his sake*; only to this affliction is the 'reward in heaven' attached (Mt. 5:11f.)

St. John informs his readers that he **was on the island called Patmos** when he received the visions and communications that are recorded in this book. Patmos, a small island in the Dodecanese group off the south-west coast of Asia Minor, was the place to which, according to a firm tradition in the early church, St. John was banished by order of the Roman emperor. He says nothing about banishment here, only that he **was** on Patmos (the past tense of the verb may indicate that either the whole or this introductory section of the book was written after he had been permitted to return to the mainland); and the reason for his being there is given as being **on account of the word of God and the testimony of Jesus**. This means that it was because of his witness to the gospel elsewhere that he was sent to Patmos;[1] an experience which, no doubt with many other experiences of hardship, justified his calling himself a partaker with other Christians in affliction (*cf*. 6:9 and 20:4 where St. John refers to those who suffered martyrdom for this same reason; also verse 2 above). The rigors and cruelties of St. John's exile on Patmos belonged to the baptism of suffering with which his Lord had said he would be baptized (Mk. 10:38f.)

> *I was in the Spirit on the Lord's day, and I heard behind me a loud voice like a trumpet, saying, Write what you see in a book and send it to the seven churches: to Ephesus and to Smyrna and to Pergamum and to Thyatira and to Sardis and to Philadelphia and to Laodicea (1:10–11).*

To be **in the Spirit** is to be under the control of the Holy Spirit, an experience that distinguishes the authentic from the false seer (see also 4:2; 17:3; 21:10; *cf*. Ezk. 3:12, 14; 11:1, 5; 37:1). Though spirituality is certainly involved, St. John is not speaking here of a state of being constantly 'filled with the Spirit' (Eph. 5:18) but of an intermittent experience connected with the visions and revelations he records in this book. This follows from his assertion that it was **on the Lord's day** that he was in the Spirit, with particular reference to the vision of the glorified Redeemer and the instructions received from him which he goes on to describe. The Lord's day here must not be confused with the eschatological Day of the Lord (6:17; 16:14; 1 Thes. 5:2; 2 Pet. 3:10).[2] It designates

---

[1] St. John's contemporary Pliny the Elder says that Patmos was one of the islands on which the Romans had located penal settlements (*Hist. Nat.* iv, 12, 23).

[2] In Greek the Lord's day, *hē kyriakē hēmera*, which occurs only here in the New Testament, contrasts with the Day of the Lord, *(hē) hēmera (tou) kyriou*. Being potentially synonymous, the former assumes its particular meaning in relation to the context and the usage of the early church.

the first day of the week, the day of the Lord's resurrection from the dead, which for this reason became the weekly Christian day of worship in place of the Jewish Sabbath (*cf.* Acts 20:7; 1 Cor. 16:2) – an observance which dates back to the earliest times. Unable, because of his isolation, to enjoy the privilege of worshipping with fellow Christians, on this day commemorative of Christ's triumph over death, St. John is granted the special grace of a vision of the Risen Lord himself.[1]

The *loud voice* heard by St. John resounded with a *trumpet-like* authority (*cf.* 4:1). Whether it was the voice of the Lord (*cf.* verses 17ff.) or of an angel (*cf.* the seven angels with seven trumpets, 8:2, 6ff.) is not clear; if the latter, it was the word of the Lord which the angel proclaimed. The message conveyed by this utterance was that St. John was to *write in a book*, that is, a papyrus roll, the vision he was about to see and then to *send* the book *to the seven churches* which are identified by the names of the cities in which they are located. (In verse 4 they were mentioned without being named.) As previously observed (on verse 4), the number seven carries the implication that these churches were representative of the church in its entirety. Not all those named belonged to the top seven in respect of size or, from the human viewpoint, importance; but they illustrated, because of the variety of their failings and attainments, the goals and the pitfalls before the church as a whole, as we shall see when we come to the exposition of the letters to the seven churches (chapters 2 and 3).

> *And I turned to see the voice that was speaking to me; and on turning I saw seven golden lampstands, and in the midst of the lampstands one like a son of man, clothed with a robe down to the feet and girded with a golden girdle round his breast (1:12–13).*

The voice St. John had heard was behind him (verse 10); now he *turned to see the voice that was speaking* to him – not that he could see a voice: it is a compact way of saying 'to see the person whose voice he had heard speaking to him'. The first thing he saw, however, was not the speaker but *seven golden lampstands* or candlesticks. Whether each of these had but one light or, like the *menorah* of tabernacle and temple, seven lights (Ex. 25:31ff.) is not stated. As is explained in verse 20 below, the candlesticks represent or symbolize the seven churches. It is *in the midst* of them that St. John sees the person who had addressed him, whose appearance is *like a son of man*, that is to say, whose form was that of a human being. This figure, beyond doubt, is Christ, the incarnate Son now resplendent in the glory that is properly his. There are affinities here, as also elsewhere in Revelation, with the visions of

---

[1] It is of course possible that all the visions and communications of this book were seen and heard by the Apostle on this one Lord's day.

Daniel, who saw 'one like a son of man' coming 'with the clouds of heaven' (*cf.* verse 7 above) to whom everlasting 'dominion and glory and kingdom' were given (Dn. 7:13f.; *cf.* one like a son of man seated on a white cloud and wearing a golden crown, 14:14 below). In other words, it is the Son of Man[1] who presents himself to the eyes of the seer, and his position in the midst indicates that he is the true centre and focus of the church. Though he is now glorified, he is still the incarnate Son, one with us in our humanity; and this means that our humanity, which he took to himself to redeem, is already exalted and glorified in and with him.

The full-length robe, no doubt resplendently white as on the occasion of his transfiguration (Mk. 9:3; *cf.* 3:4 below), and the **golden girdle** designate him as a person of the highest dignity.

His head and his hair were white as white wool, white as snow; and his eyes were like a flame of fire (1:14).

Whiteness in general throughout Revelation, and of head and hair here, denotes absolute purity and integrity. As in Isaiah 1:18, **wool** and **snow** are earthly symbols of such spotlessness. In Daniel 7:9 it is said of 'one that was ancient of days' that 'his raiment was white as snow, and the hair of his head like pure wool', and that to him 'one like a son of man' came (verse 13) – the coming, that is, of the incarnate Son to the Father. There is, however, no conflict of descriptions; that similar language can be used of both Father and Son is a pointer to their consubstantiality or identity of essence, as the First and Second Persons of the one trinitarian God. To the same effect, what is said of Almighty God in 1:8 is said of Christ in synonymous terms in 1:18 and 22:13. Some of the patristic authors supposed, mistakenly in our judgment, that the whiteness of head and hair was a mark of great antiquity indicating the Son's eternal pre-existence.

The likeness of the Son's **eyes** to **a flame of fire** (so also in 2:18 and 19:12) is indicative of the burning, penetrating vision of the Lord from which there can be no concealment: 'There is no creature that is not manifest in his sight; but all things are naked and laid open before the eyes of him with whom we have to do' (Heb. 4:13). The language, once again, is reminiscent of Daniel's prophecy in which he saw 'a man clothed in linen, whose loins were girded with gold of Uphaz' and whose eyes were like flaming torches (Dn. 10:5f.).

---

[1] The phrase 'like a son of man' is anarthrous (*i.e.* without the definite article), but it could also be translated 'one like the Son of Man', the noun 'son' being defined by the accompanying genitive. The link with Christ's frequent description of himself as the Son of Man is hardly open to question.

And his feet were like burnished brass, as though refined in a furnace; and his voice was like the sound of many waters (1:15).

The similarities with Daniel's vision continue, for the man seen by Daniel had arms and feet that gleamed like burnished bronze and a voice like the sound of a multitude (Dn. 10:6; cf. Ezk. 1:7, 24; 8:2; 43:2; also 14:2; 19:6 below). The form revealed to St. John is one of indescribable beauty and splendour and strength; but his description in terms of earthly phenomena and analogies falls far short of the reality, because human language is the only medium of expression at his command. It is for the eye of faith to penetrate to the truth beyond the imagery. Indeed, to attempt to portray the figure of St. John's vision in a painting would only be to obscure the truth and to fashion a hopelessly inadequate caricature; for the person he describes is both man and very much more than man – man as the incarnate Son who is in his essential self the divine Son from all eternity. *Burnished brass* is no more than a pointer to his glorious perfection, and *the sound of many waters*, like the sonorous thunder of a mighty waterfall, approaches without coming near to the awe-inspiring majesty of the authority of his speaking.

And in his right hand he held seven stars; and from his mouth a sharp two-edged sword proceeded; and his face was like the sun shining in its strength (1:16).

The *seven stars* held *in his right hand* are interpreted as the angels of the seven churches in verse 20 (on which further comments are offered below). Suffice it to say here that the right hand is a symbol of power and that this imagery teaches that Christ is Lord of the church. The *sharp two-edged sword* issuing *from his mouth* (see also 2:12, 16; 19:15) symbolizes the Word of the Lord. As God's prophet, Isaiah declared: 'He made my mouth like a sharp sword' (Is. 49:2; cf. 11:4); and the Apostle Paul wrote of 'the sword of the Spirit which is the word of God' (Eph. 6:17). Once again, the earthly analogy falls short of the spiritual reality; thus in Hebrews 4:12 we read that 'the word of the Lord is living and active and sharper than any two-edged sword', penetrating as it does to the innermost heart of our being. Such sharpness far surpasses the sharpness of any man-made sword. That the sword which is the Lord's word has two edges means that it never fails to cut. If it does not cut with the edge of salvation it cuts with the edge of condemnation; for the word of redemption to all who believe is at the same time the word of destruction to those who refuse to believe, as in 2:16 and 19:15 (see in particular Jn. 12:47f.).

How should not the *face* of him who is the Sun of Righteousness (Mal. 4:2; cf. Ps. 84:11; Is. 60:1) shine *like the sun*? The brilliant glory radiating from his face is the same glory that suffused his countenance on the mount of transfiguration (Mt. 17:2), which itself was a glimpse of the glory that was his before the creation of the world (Jn. 17:5) and is his to all eternity. But, as with all the other analogies, the brightness of the sun is a creaturely analogy which cannot possibly match the transcendental splendour of the reality, for his is the absolute glory, 'above the brightness of the sun', which instantly blinded Saul of Tarsus on the road to Damascus (Acts 26:13ff.). And it is into the likeness of him who is the true Image of their creation that his redeemed people are being changed from glory to glory (2 Cor. 3:18; 4:6), with the assurance that in the new heaven and earth they will 'shine forth as the sun in the kingdom of their Father' (Mt. 13:43).

> *And when I saw him I fell at his feet as though dead. And he laid his right hand on me, saying, Fear not; for I am the first and the last, and the Living One; and I was dead, and behold, I am alive for evermore, and I have the keys of Death and of Hades (1:17–18).*

Any encounter with the Lord in his glory must be a stupendous experience which drives mortal man to the ground. So it was with St. Paul at his conversion (Acts 9:3f.; 22:6f.) and with the seers Ezekiel and Daniel (Ezk. 1:28; 3:23; 43:3; 44:4; Dn. 10:7ff.). Special grace is needed for the human frame to sustain the impact of so glorious a spectacle. Thus here the Lord *laid his right hand* on the apostle, who had fallen at his feet *as though dead*, and enabled him to rise and face the brilliance of his presence. Otherwise no man can see God and live (Ex. 33:20). Yet the expectation of every Christian believer is that he will see God (Jb. 19:26f.), when his own glorification has become a reality, which will be the completion of his sanctification. This will be the attainment of the glorious destiny for which mankind was created. Then we shall see face to face (1 Cor. 13:12), and, seeing the Lord even as he is, we shall be like him (1 Jn. 3:3) as his glory becomes ours as well (Jn. 17:22, 24).

The Lord's *right hand*, as in the preceding verse, is a symbol of his power, here to raise his servant, whom he now addresses, person to person, with the reassuring words, '*Fear not*' (*cf.* Dn. 8:18; 10:10; Mt. 17:6f.). The Lord then identifies himself as *the first and the last*, which is the equivalent of the divine self-identification as 'the Alpha and the Omega' in verse 8 above, a designation of his eternal power and existence (see on verse 8). His deity is disclosed, further, by his self-disclosure as *the Living One*. As such, he is in an absolute sense the Life (Jn. 14:6) and the source of all created life (Jn. 1:1–3; 6:57; 10:10; Heb. 3:12; 9:14; 10:31; 12:22; Mt. 16:16). If this seems to be contradicted by the fact that he *was dead*, that is, he actually experienced death, it is important to understand that his coming to us was for the express purpose of dying the death that is our due and then rising from the grave. As the Good Shepherd who came to lay down his life for the sheep, he declared: 'I lay down my life that I may take it again. No one takes it away from me, but I lay it down of myself. I have power to lay it down and I have power to take it again' (Jn. 10:11, 15, 17f.). This is precisely what he did, thereby demonstrating that he is indeed the Living One, for only the Living One could, as the incarnate Son, conquer death and the devil in this way (Heb. 2:14f.). Not only, then, does he say, 'I was dead', but he also exclaims, *and behold, I am alive for evermore*. Only he who is truly the Living One can reveal himself by deeds that verify his claim to be the Lord of life and power in an absolute sense.

Moreover, only the Living One could make the additional claim: *I have the keys of Death and of Hades*. The keys are a symbol of the power and authority which he wields by reason indeed of his being the divine Second Person of the Blessed Trinity, but still more particularly by virtue of his victory over Death and Hades through the death, burial, and resurrection he experienced as the incarnate Son. Death and Hades are virtually coterminous, the latter being the grave or the state of the dead.[1] By his dying and burial Christ invaded Death and Hades; by his rising from the grave he proved that he has the keys of Death and Hades, showing that, though alien to his kingdom which is the kingdom of life, they are not immune to or excluded from his power and authority. This will be demonstrated, further, at the end of the age when Death and Hades must give up all the dead that they have held, both the impenitent to judgment and destruction and the regenerate to life and glory as the great harvest of which Christ himself, through his resurrection, is the first fruits; and then also Death and Hades themselves, as though personified, will with all that is ungodly be cast into the lake of fire, which is 'the second death', that is, the death of death, the total elimination of death from God's creation (20:11–15). This will be the ultimate manifestation of the Lord's possession of the keys of Death and Hades.

Write therefore the things you saw, both the things that are and the things that will come to pass hereafter (1:19).

St. John is now instructed to **write** down **the things** he **saw**, and the book of Revelation is the result (*cf.* verse 3). The same voice, which was the voice of the Lord, has told him to write what he sees (verse 11), that is, it would seem, what he was about to see, though it could mean what he had just seen; the command here, to write what he saw, could be proleptic, with the sense, 'when you have seen what is to be revealed to you write it down', or the force could be to write down what he had already seen. The question at issue is simply whether St. John wrote

---

[1] The Greek *Hades* is the equivalent of the Hebrew *Sheol*.

down the visions successively as they were shown to him or whether the writing was done at the very end, when the revelation was completed; or, otherwise stated, whether the command to write was uttered before or after the reception of the visions. It is not, however, a question of importance. We should take notice of the instruction given to St. John that the things seen have a twofold temporal reference. As **the things that are**, such as the heavenly glory and lordship of the incarnate Son and the prevailing state of the church disclosed in the letters to the seven churches in Asia, they are present. As **the things that will come to pass hereafter**, that is, at the end of these last days, namely, final judgment and the elimination of all evil from the world, and the consummating perfection of the new heaven and earth, towards which human history is inexorably moving, they are future. Meanwhile we do not yet know things as we shall know them and as they are already known to God. The unveiling of St. John's revelations is but a partial manifestation. Only in the event itself of the Lord's appearing and in the unshadowed light of the eternal day will everything be fully clear to us. And so even what is communicated to us through the writing of St. John is shrouded in the language of mystery and symbolism: it was the only medium available to him for the transmission of the transcendental realities which surpass the finite scope of our comprehension here below.

> *The mystery of the seven stars which you saw in my right hand, and the seven golden lampstands: the seven stars are the angels of the seven churches, and the seven lampstands are the seven churches* (1:20).

In this place we are favoured with the interpretation of two symbols. **The seven lampstands**, or candlesticks, are **the seven churches** already mentioned in verse 11. As such, the churches are intended to let their light shine brightly in the world darkened by sin (*cf.* Mt. 5:14–16) and their witness is to be focused on the incarnate Son who is in their midst (verse 12 above). **The seven stars** held in his right hand are **the angels of the seven churches**, and it is to these angels that the seven letters that follow are addressed. But who in fact these angels were is not at all clear.

The Greek noun corresponding to the term 'angel' means a messenger, and in the New Testament it is sometimes used in this simple sense (for example, as applied to John the Baptist, Mt. 11:10, quoting Mal. 3:1; see also Lk. 7:24; 9:52). As such, the angels could have been delegates of the seven churches, perhaps sent to visit St. John on the island of Patmos by their respective churches, like the 'apostles of the churches' in 2 Corinthians 8:23 who were sent out for a particular purpose (the Greek noun from which 'apostles' is derived means literally 'sent ones'). To each of these angels or messengers a letter could have been given by St. John to take back to their churches. Another possibility is that the angels here designated persons of authority in these churches, such as their respective bishops, to each of whom a letter could have been directed. Most frequently throughout Scripture the term 'angels' denotes those non-human spirits who serve God as his ministers and messengers (*cf.*, for example, Ps. 103:20; Heb. 1:4ff.), and, leaving aside the angels of the churches referred to here and in the seven letters (chapters 2 and 3), the seventy or so remaining references to angels in Revelation are to these ethereal beings. Though it is possible to conceive of a guardian angel being assigned to each church, it is unlikely that the letters would have been written or addressed to these spirits. To understand these angels as human beings, whether local church leaders or appointed delegates, is therefore more satisfactory.

The letters to the seven churches,
2:1 – 3:22

1. TO THE CHURCH IN EPHESUS, 2:1–7

To the angel of the church in Ephesus write: These things says he who holds the seven stars in his right hand, he who walks in the midst of the seven golden lampstands (2:1).

That **the church in Ephesus** should be the first to be addressed is of interest because the biographical information available to us from the second and third centuries associates St. John closely with the city of Ephesus. He is reputed to have lived and taught there during the latter part of his life and also to have died there in extreme old age. It may well be that he was exiled from Ephesus to Patmos, a distance of some sixty miles by sea. As the administrative centre of Roman government in the province of Asia, Ephesus was a city of importance, graced with splendid buildings and boulevards, and a melting-pot of nationalities and exotic cults. The Christian church in that city had been founded by St. Paul when, accompanied by Aquila and Priscilla, he arrived there from Corinth (*c.* AD 52, on his second missionary journey), and subsequently he had returned and spent more than two years in the work of building up the Corinthian church (Acts 18:18ff.; 19:1ff.; 20:17ff.). Christ himself who **holds the seven stars in his right hand** (see 1:16) and who is **in the midst of the seven golden lampstands** – signifying his centrality in the life of the church and his authority over the 'angels' of the churches (see 1:20) – is the author of this message to the church in Ephesus. That Christ is seen, further, to be **he who walks in the midst** indicates that his lordship is active and dynamic, bestowing grace and dispensing judgment, and that he is directly interested in and aware of the condition of the churches.

I know your works, and your toil and patience, and that you cannot bear evil men, and tested those who call themselves apostles, and they are not, and found them false (2:2).

The Lord who walks in the midst of his churches has a full knowledge of all that is going on in them. In five of the seven letters he says, '*I know your works*' (here in the letter to Ephesus and in those to Thyatira, Sardis, Philadelphia, and Laodicea), and in the two other letters he also says, 'I know . . .', to Smyrna, 'I know your tribulation . . .', and to Pergamum, 'I know where you dwell . . .' (2:9, 13, 19; 3:1, 8, 15). Not only, as the Good Shepherd, does he know his own sheep (Jn. 10:14, 27), but also, as St. John recorded in his Gospel, 'he knew all men . . . and had no need for any one to bear witness concerning man, for he himself knew what was in man' (Jn. 2:24f). In the words of the communion collect in the *Book of Common Prayer*, he is the one 'unto whom all hearts be open, all desires known, and from whom no secrets are hid'. As these letters confirm, it is not only some works but *all* works that he knows – bad works as well as good works, in accordance with the affairs and circumstances of each particular church. 'O Lord, thou hast searched me and known me', the psalmist exclaimed. 'Thou knowest when I sit down and when I rise up; thou discernest my thoughts from afar . . . Even before a word is on my tongue, lo, O Lord, thou knowest it altogether' (Ps. 139:1–4); and similarly St. Peter: 'Lord, thou knowest all things!' (Jn. 21:17).

In the case of the Ephesian church, though there is a critical admonition (verses 4f.), the tone is in the main commendatory. It has not been easy for the Ephesian Christians; perseverance for them has required **toil and patience** as they have met with hardship and hostility. Praiseworthy, too, is the manner in which they have shown that they **cannot bear evil men** who have presented themselves as friends of the gospel, and especially *those who call themselves apostles*. These impostors who, very likely, had come from Jerusalem claiming to have apostolic authority, they had *tested* and found to be *false*, presumably by comparing their teaching and conduct with the teaching and conduct of Christ and his apostles – a comparison which plainly demonstrated that *they are not* what they profess to be.

The church in every century, including the apostolic church of the first century, has had its survival threatened by the infiltration of deceivers whose persuasive rhetoric has made them appear to be what they are not. Christ himself warned his disciples that false prophets, and even false Christs, would arise (Mk. 13:22; Mt. 7:10; 24:11, 24). St. Paul had to contend with 'deceitful workers, disguising themselves as apostles of Christ', and he warned Timothy against 'the hypocrisy of men that speak lies' (1 Tim. 4:2). St. Peter wrote of 'false teachers who will privily bring in destructive heresies' (2 Pet. 2:1). St. John also declared elsewhere that many antichrists had already appeared (1 Jn. 2:18), and stressed the necessity of putting to the test all who claimed to bring authentic teaching. The denial that Jesus Christ had come in the flesh, that is to say, the denial of the incarnation which was characteristic of the dualistic heresy that threatened to cut the tap-root of the gospel in the early church, was teaching stamped with the mark of the antichrist. Therefore any persons who denied that Jesus was the Christ, the truly incarnate Son of God, were false teachers who failed to pass the test of Christian authenticity (1 Jn. 4:1–3). The same test holds good today. So, in the verse before us, the Christians in Ephesus are commended because they put to the test some who came to them professing to be imparters of apostolic truth and showed them to be imposters.

> *And you have patience and endured for my name's sake, and you have not grown weary (2:3).*

This resumes and confirms the commendation of the preceding verse: the genuineness of their faith is proved by their patient endurance and perseverance; they have not abandoned the struggle under the stress of painful opposition and affliction. The secret of their constancy was that all their suffering had been *for my name's sake*. Had it been for their own sake, they would soon have given up. They were Christ-centred, not self-centred. They willingly suffered because the Redeemer had a claim on them, not because they imagined that their sufferings placed God in their debt. They were expressing gratitude, not accumulating merit. Moreover, they were learning that there is blessing in the endurance of hardship and indignity for the Lord's sake. 'Blessed are you', Christ himself had declared, 'when men revile you and persecute you and utter all kinds of evil against you falsely *on my account*' (Mt. 5:11). The apostles, after being beaten for preaching the gospel, 'rejoiced that they were counted worthy to suffer dishonour *for the name*' (Acts 5:41). To suffer and endure for the sake of him who was obedient even to the death of the cross for our salvation may mean to follow a hard uphill path, but it is a path that leads to incomparable glory (Phil. 2:8; Rom. 8:18; 2 Cor. 4:17).

> *But I have this against you, that you have left your first love (2:4).*

Praise is followed by reproof, for the state of the churches is, as we have seen, a matter of deep concern to the Lord who walks in their midst (verse 1). To withhold rebuke or turn away from discrimination is not the mark of genuine love. The Bridegroom desires his bride the church to be sanctified and without blemish (*cf.* Eph. 5:25–27; 2 Cor. 11:2). The cooling down of the *first love* of the Ephesian church is a sure indication that all is not well. That it can lead to disastrous consequences is illustrated by the history of the Israelites: 'I remember the devotion of your youth, your love as a bride, how you followed me in the wilderness, in a land not sown', the Lord said to them. 'Israel was holy to the Lord . . . What wrong did your fathers find in me that they went far from

35

me?' (Je. 2:2–5). Perseverance in the midst of hardships must not be divorced from love; indeed, it should be motivated by love, for otherwise it becomes joyless and introverted. The evaporation of love was at the root of the problems and aberrations by which the Corinthian church was plagued (*cf.* 1 Cor. 1:10ff.; 13:1ff.). The first love of which St. John speaks is the original spontaneous love of total commitment to the Lord; it is the logical response to his total love for us (Rom. 12:1; 1 Jn. 4:19); and it is a theme that governs the mind of St. John in his exhortation:

> Beloved, let us love one another, for love is of God, and every one who loves is born of God and knows God; for God is love ... Herein is love, not that we loved God, but that he loved us, and sent his Son to be the propitiation for our sins. ... God is love, and he who abides in God abides in love, and God abides in him *(1 Jn. 4:7, 10, 16).*

The diminishing of first love, therefore, is an indicator of decrease in godliness.

> *Remember therefore from whence you have fallen, and repent, and do the first works; or else I will come to you and will move your lampstand out of its place, unless you repent (2:5).*

Departure from first love is a falling; it is symptomatic of a decline in practice as well as in devotion, for first love and **first works** belong together: the latter spring naturally from the former. Consequently, the disappearance of the first love entails the disappearance also of the first works, which are works distinguished by selfless zeal and joyful dedication. To recapture the first love is to return to the first works, and this is what the church in Ephesus needs to do if it is to recover its well-being before God. Although still toiling and enduring in the Lord's cause, the Ephesian church is in a state of decline, and culpably so. Hence the admonition to **remember** the original intensity of zeal and devotion from which it has **fallen** and to **repent** of its declension and return to that first intensity.

The Lord adds the warning that if the Ephesian church remains unrepentant he **will come** and **will move** its lampstand. Here again, as we have said before, the church must be distinguished from the churches: no power will ever be able to prevail against the church of Christ (Mt. 16:18); but, as we learn from this warning, this does not mean that a church in a particular place cannot lapse into the darkness of extinction. Ephesus, in fact, is one of the many places where the light of the local church that burned brightly in the early centuries is no longer to be seen. But the bright light of the church's witness is an inextinguishable light that continues to shine through all the centuries; for it is

God's light, shining indeed in the darkness, but which the darkness is powerless to overcome (Jn. 1:5).

What is said here is that the lampstand of the Ephesian church will be moved, unless there is repentance, *out of its place*. This gives us to understand that the lampstand or candlestick with its light will be transferred elsewhere: a locality where before there was light may be left in darkness, but the light will not cease to burn and its brightness will enlighten others. The defection of a church is indeed a tragedy, both for the church and also for the local population on whom it should be beaming the light of the gospel. God's work continues, however, and he will raise up other churches to shed forth the light of his truth.

> *But this you have, that you hate the works of the Nicolaitans, which I also hate* (2:6).

To the credit of the Ephesians is their intolerance of evil men who pose as apostles (verse 2), and now they are commended further for hating *the works of the Nicolaitans*. The identity of these 'Nicolaitans' and particularly of their leader or founder, whose name, presumably, was Nicolaus, is unknown to us. In the second and third centuries some expressed the opinion that they took their name from the proselyte of Antioch called Nicolaus (or Nicolas) who was one of the seven 'deacons' mentioned in Acts 6:5; but there is no solid evidence to support this view. What is evident is that there was a party or sect known as Nicolaitans whose presence in the apostolic church threatened to destroy the integrity and purity of Christian faith and conduct. They had gained adherents also (as verses 14f. show) among the members of the church in Pergamum, where their teaching, like that of Balaam, viewed with approval the eating of food sacrificed to idols and the practice of immorality – misconduct which (in verse 20), in connection with the church in Thyatira, is also associated with Jezebel. Thus this permissive teaching appears to have found its way into three of the seven churches of Asia, and there is a probability that the three designations, 'Nicolaitans', 'Balaam', and 'Jezebel', refer to the same cult, whose libertarianism was in conflict with the decrees of the Council of Jerusalem (Acts 15:29). In their hatred of the works of the Nicolaitans the Ephesian Christians were at one with the Lord (*which I also hate*).

> *He who has an ear, let him hear what the Spirit says to the churches. To him who overcomes I will give to eat of the tree of life which is in the paradise of God* (2:7).

To *have an ear* is to be attentive, not wilfully deaf, and to *hear* is to hear to good purpose, that is, to hear in such a way as to understand and obey. Responsible hearing is imperative because it is God the Holy Spirit who is speaking.

The admonition, moreover, is addressed to all the churches (see 2:11, 17, 29; 3:6, 13, 22), from which we conclude that what the Holy Spirit says to one he says to all, not just those churches in a particular geographical area in the first century, but to all the churches throughout the world in each successive century. Christ used a similar formula in the application of his teaching to individuals (Mk. 4:9, 23, *etc.*); and it is clear from verse 1 above (and also from the opening words of the six letters that follow) that what the Spirit says is at one and the same time what the Lord says to the churches. The office of him who is the Spirit of truth is to bear witness to the Son who is the Truth, teaching what he has taught, and glorifying him by declaring to us what is his (Jn. 14:6, 26; 15:26; 16:14). Thus the harmonious unity of the Second and Third Persons of the Holy Trinity is attested. As each church is composed of individuals, so it is the responsibility of each individual (*he who has an ear*) to heed the divinely given message.

So, too, the challenge to persevere and gain the victory is addressed to the individual members of the church: *to him who overcomes*. Moreover, the challenge is given in the form of a gracious promise which is made not only here to the members of the Ephesian church, but, with a varied wealth of symbolism, to the members of all the churches (see 2:11, 17, 26–28; 3:5, 12, 21). In this way the warning about the consequences of impenitence are tempered by words of hope and encouragement, indicating that it is not too late for recovery and reconstruction.

To speak of *the tree of life which is in the paradise of God* is plainly to refer to the garden in which man was placed at his creation with unimpeded access to the tree of life at the centre of that garden (Gn. 2:9). It was from that garden and particularly from the approach to that tree that man was driven when he fell into sin (Gn. 3:22–24). Now, through Christ, the power of death, the dire consequence of man's sin, is nullified (Rom. 5:12ff.; 6:23) as access to the tree of life is restored. Man's destiny, forfeited in Adam, is realized in Christ. Paradise regained, indeed, is greater and more glorious than paradise lost, just as the fulfilment is more than the promise and the harvest than the seed. As the conclusion of this book of Revelation shows, in the renewed and glorified creation the tree of life will be unfailingly fruitful and the multitude of the redeemed will freely partake of its plenty (21:1ff.; 22:1f). Thus is symbolized the fullness of that everlasting life in Christ which God's faithful ones are given to inherit.

2. TO THE CHURCH IN SMYRNA, 2:8–11

> *And to the angel of the church in Smyrna write: These things says the first and the last, who was dead and lived again (2:8).*

Smyrna (now Izmir), situated some thirty-five miles to the north of Ephesus, was another flourishing metropolis of importance in the province of Asia. It is not mentioned elsewhere (apart from 1:11) in the New Testament; but according to one ancient account St. Paul, when travelling back from Galatia to Jerusalem, stayed in Smyrna with Strataeas, who was Timothy's brother and whom he had previously instructed in Pamphylia.[1] Polycarp, the celebrated bishop of Smyrna who suffered a martyr's death in the middle of the next century, had in his youth enjoyed the friendship of the Apostle John and others who had seen the Lord and received instruction from them.[2] For the Lord's self-designation as **the first and the last, who was dead and lived again** see the comments above on 1:17f., where he identifies himself in a corresponding manner. How appropriate and full of significance this introduction is for a church whose members, as this letter shows, have come face to face with persecution and the threat of death.

> *I know your tribulation and your poverty (but you are rich) and the blasphemy of those who say they are Jews, and they are not, but are a synagogue of Satan (2:9).*

The Lord knows all about the **tribulation** that has come upon those who belong to the church in Smyrna, for his is not a detached knowledge but a knowledge of compassion. He who has drunk to the last drop the cup of suffering and passed through the baptism of blood for our sakes has the fullest fellow-feeling for us in the trials and adversities we endure as his servants (*cf.* Mk. 10:38f.; Heb. 4:15). He who became poor for our sakes knows all about the **poverty**, the deprivation of worldly goods and wealth, to which his followers have been driven in Smyrna, a city proud of its worldly prosperity and abundance. Yet, he reassures them, '**You are rich**': rich in the treasures of eternity, blessed with spiritual abundance entirely by virtue of the self-impoverishment he voluntarily accepted (2 Cor. 8:9). They have learnt that 'a man's life does not consist in the abundance of the things he possesses' but in being 'rich toward God' (Lk. 12:15, 21). So, accordingly, St. Paul found that it is no loss at all, but infinite wealth, to suffer the loss of all things, and to count them but dung, in order to gain Christ (Phil. 3:8). Likewise, St. James testified

---

[1] *Life of Polycarp* 2.
[2] Irenaeus, *Against Heresies* III, iii, 4; Letter to Florinus, quoted in Eusebius, *Church History* v, 20.

that God has chosen those who are poor in the world's judgment to be 'rich in faith and heirs of the kingdom which he has promised to them that love him' (Jas. 2:5). Moses of old 'reckoned the reproach of Christ greater riches than the treasures of Egypt' (Heb. 11:26); and the believers to whom the Epistle to the Hebrews was addressed joyfully accepted the plundering of their possessions since they knew that they had 'a better possession and an abiding one' (Heb. 10:34). Those who are called upon to suffer for their Redeemer discover the infinite difference between treasure on earth and treasure in heaven (Mt. 6:19–21).

Those referred to here **who say that they are Jews** are no doubt Jews by birth and ancestry, but Jews **they are not** in the radical spiritual sense. This is because they reject Jesus as their promised Messiah and Redeemer, and wilfully blind themselves to the truth that all the promises of God are Yes in him (2 Cor. 1:20). Yet all the first believers were Jews whose lives had been transformed by the grace of the gospel. The **blasphemy** of these violent enemies of the church in Smyrna consisted in their obstinate rejection of all that God had done in and through his incarnate Son in fulfilment of the Hebrew Scriptures. Their denunciation as **a synagogue of Satan** suggests that they were propagators of a perverted, pseudo-Christian gospel which was in reality no gospel at all (*cf.* Gal. 1:6ff.; 2 Cor. 11:3f.; 1 Tim. 1:3f.).

It was Jews not only who were the first converts but also who were the first persecutors of the Christian faith. The point is not that Jews were worse or more wicked than non-Jews, but that as the privileged recipients of God's oracles and promises they should have been the first to welcome the new covenant mediated by Christ as the actualization of all the blessings predicted by Moses and the prophets (Heb. 8:6; 9:15; 12:24). Thus St. Paul's practice was to proclaim the gospel to the Jew first, and then to the Gentile; and he told the hostile Jews in Pisidian Antioch, who were filled with jealousy and contradicted his message and blasphemed, that it was necessary that the word of God should first be spoken to them, but that by thrusting it from themselves they had judged themselves unworthy of eternal life (Acts 13:44–46).

John the Baptist had advised the Pharisees and Sadducess: 'Think not to say within yourselves, We have Abraham as our father; for I say to you that God is able to raise up children to Abraham from these stones' (Mt. 3:9). 'For he is not a Jew who is one outwardly', St. Paul explained, 'neither is that circumcision which is outward in the flesh; but he is a Jew who is one inwardly, and circumcision is that of the heart, in the spirit, not in the letter, whose praise is not of men, but of God' (Rom. 2:28f.). As he assured the Galatian believers, in the unity which is ours in Christ Jesus there is neither Jew nor Greek; indeed, 'if you are Christ's, then you are Abraham's seed, heirs according to promise' Gal. 3:28f.) – and this is what he means by 'the Israel of God' (Gal. 6:16). By contrast, those who are not Christ's, but his enemies, constitute themselves in their hostility *a synagogue of Satan*. In a similar manner Jesus told his Jewish opponents, who boasted of having Abraham as their father, that, because of their deeds, they were of their father the devil (Jn. 8:33–44). The synagogue worshippers in Smyrna should have been the first to welcome the gospel, but instead they, or their leaders, turned against it with fierce animosity.

> *Do not fear the things which you are about to suffer: behold, the devil is about to throw some of you into prison, that you may be tested; and you will have tribulation ten days. Be faithful unto death, and I will give you the crown of life* (2:10).

The severe affliction that awaits the faithful in Smyrna will include imprisonment and death; but, painful though this will be, it is not something that they should fear. In the New Testament, Christian believers are exhorted many times to be unafraid of what the enemies of Christ and his gospel may do to them. 'Do not be afraid of those who kill the body, but are not able to kill the soul', Christ himself said to his disciples; 'but rather fear him who is able to destroy soul and body in hell' (Mt. 10:28). Three good reasons why they are not to fear the impending persecution emerge. First, it will be overruled by God to be a time of testing (*that you may be tested*) by which their faith will be purified and strengthened, and thus, contrary to appearances, be turned into an occasion of victory for them and of defeat for *the devil* whose malevolence instigates this assault on the church in Smyrna. This aspect of suffering endured in the cause of the gospel is admirably presented by St. Peter's exhortation to scattered Christians:

> Guarded through faith by the power of God for salvation ready to be revealed in the last time, you greatly rejoice, though now for a little while, if need be, you have been distressed in manifold trials, so that the genuineness[1] of your faith, being more precious than perishable gold which is proved genuine by fire, may be found to praise and glory and honour at the revelation of Jesus Christ *(1 Pet. 1:5–7)*.

Once again, suffering for Christ's sake is crowned with glory (Rom. 8:18).

Second, the *tribulation* through which they pass will be of limited duration: it will last for *ten days*. This means that everything continues to be constantly under God's control. God will not fail to bring blessing out of the persecution of his saints; in itself, however, persecution is ungodly, and its agents will not be permitted to exceed the bounds

---

[1] The Greek term (*to dokimion*) denotes the proof of genuineness that results from testing.

prescribed by the will of God. The sovereignty of Almighty God over the history not only of his saints but also of the ungodly enemies of his will, indeed over the whole of his creation, is one of the key themes of the Apocalypse. (*Cf.* 13:5, where the 'beast' is allowed to exercise authority for a period symbolically defined as forty-two months.) The ten days here symbolize a limited and comparatively brief duration of persecution. However long and intense affliction may seem to be, it shrinks into insignificance when viewed in the light of eternity. Thus St. Paul, who appeared to have so little relief from his sufferings as an apostle, described his affliction as light and as lasting but for a moment in comparison with the 'eternal weight of glory' to which it was the road (2 Cor. 4:17).

Third (and this follows on closely from what we have just said), the Lord promises **the crown of life** to those who are *faithful unto death*, thus turning what seems to be loss into gain. So glorious a prize shows how insignificant and momentary imprisonment and martyrdom really are. It shows how in fact they may even be welcomed. For the incarnate Lord it had been first the cross and then the crown, and, as he himself taught, 'it is enough for the disciple that he be as his master' (Mt. 10:24f.). Accordingly, Christians when passing through the severe testing of persecution are urged to look away to Jesus, 'who for the joy that was set before him endured the cross' and is now enthroned in glory, and, lest they become weary or faint-hearted, t • 'consider him who endured such hostility of sinners against himself' (Heb. 12:2f.). To the same effect St. James pronounced blessed the person who is tested by affliction, for when he has passed the test and been proved genuine 'he will receive the crown of life which the Lord has promised to them that love him' (Jas. 1:12). This is the explanation of St. Paul's confident serenity as the hour of his martyrdom was about to strike: 'I have fought the good fight, I have finished the course, I have kept the faith', he wrote; 'henceforth there is laid up for me the crown of righteousness, which the Lord, the righteous Judge, will give me on that Day, and not only to me, but also to all who have loved his appearing' (2 Tim. 4:6–8). All who in Christ's cause are faithful unto death, whether by martyrdom or not, have the assurance that there awaits them the crown of life – that is, the all-transcending joy and blessedness of fullness of life, never again to be terminated by death, in the glorious presence of their own crowned and enthroned Lord and Redeemer.

> *He who has an ear, let him hear what the Spirit says to the churches. He who overcomes will not be hurt by the second death (2:11).*

The admonition is present in each of the seven letters (see on verse 7 above), and each contains a promise to the person *who overcomes*. Here the assurance is given that the overcomer, whom the preceding verse defines as the one who is faithful unto death, **will not be hurt by the second death**. This 'second death', as we learn from 20:6, 14 and 21:8, is the final destruction awaiting the devil and all his followers. It denotes total and endless exclusion from life and from the incomparable glory and perfection of the new heaven and earth. From this appalling end the Lord's redeemed have been saved. Moreover, the significance of being untouched by the second death is identical with that of receiving the crown of life (preceding verse) and eating from the tree of life (verse 7).

3. TO THE CHURCH IN PERGAMUM, 2:12–17

And to the angel of the church in Pergamum write: These things says he who has the sharp two-edged sword (2:12).

The city of Pergamum, situated some fifty miles to the north of Smyrna, was another place where the Christian church fought to survive in the midst of a diversity of pagan cults which included emperor-worship. Concerning the description of the Lord as **he who has the sharp two-edged sword** see the comments above on 1:16. The somewhat ominous overtone of impending judgment it seems to convey is justified by the seriously compromised state of the church in Pergamum revealed in this letter.

I know where you dwell, even where Satan's throne is, and you hold fast my name, and did not deny my faith, even in the days of Antipas my witness, my faithful one who was killed among you, where Satan dwells (2:13).

The presence of a church **where Satan's throne is** gives some indication not only of the devil's sway in Pergamum but also of the power of the gospel in a satanic milieu. If the opposition to the gospel was mainly Jewish in Smyrna (and in Philadelphia; see the designation 'synagogue of Satan', verse 9 above and 3:9), in Pergamum it appears to be mainly pagan in origin (as the reference in the next verse to the sacrifices and the licentiousness associated with the worship of idols suggests). Pergamum was a place where it looked as if Satan's throne was superior to the throne of Christ, but, no matter how contrary the appearances, the truth was that the power and authority of Christ are incontestably supreme over all, including Satan. This truth is fully established in the visions recorded in this book (*cf.* 11:15ff.; 19:1ff.). Even so, in a city like Pergamum only genuine faith empowered by divine grace (*cf.* 2 Cor. 12:9) could withstand the ungodly forces of evil that were active on all sides. To say this, of course, is to say what is generally true of all times and all situations; but there always have been occasions and places where, because of prevailing superstition and antipathy to the gospel, it is more noticeably true.

Unlike the church in Smyrna, which was about to enter a time of severe persecution (see verse 10 above), the church in Pergamum had already experienced the cruel excesses of satanic hostility to the Christian message. The constancy with which the Christians in Pergamum had borne the test of persecution earned them the Lord's commendation: *you hold fast my name, and did not deny my faith*. They had remained firm even at the cost of the forfeiting of life for Christ's sake. *Antipas* who is named here (but is otherwise unknown to us) may well have been their bishop or leader. He, perhaps in company with others, had been put to death. The Lord praises him by calling him *my witness*[1] and *my faithful one who was killed among you, where Satan dwells*. We may suppose that his martyrdom had been intended to be a lethal blow to the church by depriving it of its spiritual leader and terrifying its members. But their spirit was undaunted and they had refused to deny the Lord by the shedding of whose blood they had been redeemed.

To be approved as 'my witness, my faithful one' is to be accepted as essentially Christlike, for Christ himself is supremely 'the faithful witness' (1:5). Moreover, if the faithful witness of Antipas shone forth all the more brightly in Pergamum 'where Satan's throne is', immeasurably more brilliant was the faithful witness of him who is the Light of the world (Jn. 8:12; 9:5) where universally Satan has set up his throne (*cf.* Jn. 14:30; 16:11; 2 Cor. 4:4), and who by his atoning death has overthrown Satan's sway over the world (*cf.* Jn. 16:31; 1 Jn. 3:8).

> But I have a few things against you, because you have there some
> that hold the teaching of Balaam, who taught Balak to cast a
> stumbling-block before the children of Israel, to eat things sacri-
> ficed to idols, and to commit fornication (2:14).

Constant though the members of the church in Pergamum have been under affliction and persecution, the Lord, who knows all about them, finds it necessary to rebuke them for tolerating some inconsistencies of doctrine and conduct in their midst. The *few things* he has against their church are related to idolatry and sexual immorality, of which *some*, not all, are guilty. There had been a failure to take steps to correct these aberrations or to remove their perpetrators (*cf.* 1 Cor. 5:1ff.), who in

---

[1] The Greek word translated 'witness' here is the same word as our *martyr*, which of course is taken over from the Greek. There may be an early evidence here of the transition of the term from meaning a witness in a general sense to the narrower sense of a witness who has suffered the loss of life for the faith he professes (*cf.* 17:6).

principle were following *the teaching of Balaam*. In the account of the dealings of the prophet Balaam with *Balak* the king of Moab (Nu. 22 – 24), Balaam, though constrained to speak the word of the Lord, seems to have been a somewhat unwilling messenger. He was in the end put to death by the forces under Moses' command, ostensibly for causing the Israelites 'to act treacherously against the Lord' (Nu. 31:8, 16). Their treacherous conduct involved immoral relationships with Moabite women and the idolatrous worship of the pagan god Baal (Nu. 25:1ff.). Thus here Balaam is described as the one *who taught Balak to cast a stumbling-block before the children of Israel, to eat things sacrificed to idols, and to commit fornication*. It is worthy of remark that among the practices proscribed by the Council of Jerusalem were the pollutions of idols and fornication (Acts 15:20, 29) as ungodly and incompatible with Christian faith and conduct. Elsewhere in the New Testament, Balaam is denounced as one 'who loved the dishonest gain of wrong-doing' (2 Pet. 2:15; *cf.* Jude 11).

> *So you also have some who hold the teaching of the Nicolaitans in like manner* (2:15).

The Ephesian church was commended for hating the works of the Nicolaitans, which the Lord also hates (verse 6); the church in Pergamum, however, displeased the Lord because of its accommodating attitude to *some who hold the teaching of the Nicolaitans*. As the phrase *in like manner* indicates, the Nicolaitan teaching was apparently similar to that of Balaam by reason of its association with idolatrous and immoral practices. (See the comments above on verse 6.)

> *Repent therefore; or else I will come to you quickly, and I will make war against them with the sword of my mouth* (2:16).

As with the Ephesian Christians (verse 5), so also with the church in Pergamum: it is not too late to repent and to put right what is dishonouring to God and his truth. But the warning is added that if they fail to set things in order the Lord himself will *come quickly* and will himself *make war against them*, that is, against the Balaamites and Nicolaitans, wielding *the sword of* his *mouth* (see verse 12 above and comments on 1:16). This is spiritual warfare: the Lord will smite these perverters of his word with the very word that they have perverted (*cf.* Jn. 12:48). Here again, as in all these letters, we perceive Christ's intense concern for the well-being and integrity of his church.

> *He who has an ear, let him hear what the Spirit says to the churches* (2:17a).

We are reminded, once more, that what the Holy Spirit says to one church he says to all the churches, and that what he says is to be heeded and acted upon.

> *To him who overcomes I will give of the hidden manna, and I will give him a white stone, and upon the stone a new name written which no one knows but he who receives it (2:17b).*

In the Old Testament the manna was the sustenance provided by God from above for his people as they journeyed through the wilderness, described as 'bread from heaven' (Ex. 16:4; Ps. 78:23f.). The measure of wilderness manna which was preserved in a golden urn in the tabernacle sanctuary (Ex. 16:32–34; Heb. 9:4) could be regarded as **hidden manna** which was both a symbol and a promise of the true Bread of Life that was yet to be given. The promise symbolized by the manna was fulfilled in Christ, as he himself taught, declaring that he was the true Bread from heaven, the Bread of God that gives life to the world (Jn. 6:31–33). 'I am the Bread of Life', he declared. '. . . I am the Living Bread that came down from heaven; if any man eat of this bread, he will live for ever; yea, and the bread which I will give is my flesh, for the life of the world' (Jn. 6:35, 48, 51). The incarnate Son who was crucified for us is now the risen and ascended Christ, removed indeed from our physical sight now that he has entered into the heavenly sanctuary (Heb. 9:11f., 24). It is he, then, who is the Hidden Manna that sustains and strengthens us on our pilgrimage to the celestial city, while at the same time, because he is our Life, we have the assurance that our life is 'hid with Christ in God' (Col. 3:3).

To him who overcomes the gift is promised not only of hidden manna but also of *a white stone*. In the ancient world a white stone was a ballot of approval and a token of admission, whereas a black stone denoted rejection and exclusion, comparable to the practice of blackballing the names of uncongenial applicants for membership of a club. Accordingly, the white stone promised here to the person who overcomes signifies acceptance by the Lord and a rightful place among the company of his redeemed. The **new name** that is **written upon the stone** has been taken by some to mean a secret divine name. The Lord states in 3:12, for example, that he will write the name of his God and his own new name on the one who overcomes; in 14:1 the 144,000 have the name of the Lamb and the name of his Father written on their foreheads; and in 22:4 it is said that the name of the Lord will be on the foreheads of his servants in the new heaven and earth. Those who are thus stamped with the divine name are demarcated as precious to God and his special possession.

Here, however, it is not the person but the white stone that is marked with a name – a name, moreover, *which no one knows but he who receives it* – and this indicates not a divine name, but, rather, a divinely given name to each person who overcomes. The white stone thus inscribed conveys not only the assurance of God's approval and acceptance but also the message that God does not view the multitude of the redeemed as an undifferentiated mass. The name known only to the recipient indicates the uniqueness of each individual before God and the distinctness of the interpersonal relationship of each with him. There will be no confusion of names in the mind of God. As the name is given by the Lord, it also, of course, signifies that the recipient of the white stone is precious to him and his possession. What is revealed to St. John here is really the fulfilment of the age-old promise: 'You shall be called by a new name which the mouth of the Lord will give' (Is. 62:2; *cf.* 65:15; 43:1). The Good Shepherd, as Jesus said of himself, 'calls his own sheep by name . . . and the sheep follow him, for they know his voice' (Jn. 10:3f.). In the new creation every name will be a new name which because of its uniqueness establishes a sacred bond between the Lord God and its recipient; no two names will be the same. This means, in other words, that the significance of the image of God in which each person is made, and which is stamped upon the very heart of each one's being, will find at last full and actual expression.

4. TO THE CHURCH IN THYATIRA, 2:18–29

And to the angel of the church in Thyatira write: These things says the Son of God who has eyes like a flame of fire and whose feet are like burnished brass (2:18).

The city of Thyatira, located, somewhat inland, some forty miles southeast of Pergamum, was a busy trading centre long famous for its purple dye. St. Paul's first convert in Europe was Lydia,[1] 'a seller of purple from the city of Thyatira' (Acts 16:14). The speaker identified himself as **the Son of God**; this is, in fact, the only place in the book of Revelation where this designation is used by or of the Lord, but it is completely in harmony with those places where God is declared to be his Father (1:6; 2:27; 3:5, 21; 14:1). The description of his **eyes** as **like a flame of fire** and his **feet** as **like burnished brass** is resumed from 1:14f. (see the comments there). It conveys the impression of his absolute justice and inflexible integrity.

I know your works and your love and faith and ministry and patience, and that your last works are more than the first (2:19).

[1] 'Lydia' in Acts 16:14 may be a geographical identity-label, signifying 'a woman from Lydia', the domain in which Thyatira was located, rather than this lady's proper name.

He whose all-seeing eyes are like a flame of fire says with absolute authority to the church in Thyatira, as to all the churches, '*I know your works*', for he infallibly discerns what is deserving of commendation and what of reproof. The essential importance in the Christian life of *love* and *faith* is plain from the whole of the New Testament. Love heads the list of virtues which comprise the fruit of the Spirit (Gal. 5:22; see also, for example, 1 Cor. 13 and 1 Jn. 4:7ff.), and it is by faith that the Christian lives and in faith that he dies (Heb. 11). Here, by implication, it is the *constancy* of the love and faith in the church of Thyatira that is approved – in contrast to the church in Ephesus which had departed from its first love (verse 4 above). Commendable also is the *ministry* of the believers in Thyatira, the selflessness of their service. The wide range of meaning of the term 'ministry' (*diakonia*) in the New Testament includes the particular ministry of the clerical office (Acts 6:4; 20:24; 21:19; Rom. 11:13; 2 Cor. 4:1; Col. 4:17; 1 Tim. 1:12; 2 Tim. 4:5), administration in a more general sense (Acts 6:1; 1 Cor. 12:5; 2 Cor. 3:7ff.; Eph. 4:12; Heb. 1:14), and service in the sense of charitable giving and care for the poor (Acts 11:29; Rom. 15:31; 2 Cor. 8:4; 9:1, 12, 13). The 'ministry' of the members of the church in Thyatira was the practical manifestation of their love and faith in the service of God and their fellow men; and inseparable from their love, faith, and ministry was their *patience*, their steadfast endurance of calumny and affliction for the sake of Christ. Indeed, there has been an intensification in their zeal, with the result that their *last works* were *more than the first*. That is no small commendation!

> *But I have this against you, that you tolerate the woman Jezebel who calls herself a prophetess and teaches and seduces my servants to commit fornication and to eat things sacrificed to idols (2:20).*

There is need for rebuke as well as occasion for commendation. The church in Thyatira had shown itself to be accommodating to *the woman Jezebel* who claimed to be *a prophetess* but in fact *seduced* them to indulge in practices associated with immorality and idolatry. In this major respect there was an affinity between the cult of Jezebel and the cult of the Nicolaitans and Balaamites (see verses 6 and 14f. above), and it is possible that it was but one cult under different guises by which the churches of that area were being troubled. Jezebel is almost certainly a code-name intended to indicate an ideological affinity with the heathen wife of Ahab, king of Israel, named Jezebel who taught the Israelites the degrading worship of Baal which was marked by immorality and idolatry (1 Ki. 16:29ff.). The likelihood is that here 'Jezebel' designates an actual woman who posed as a prophetess and was advocating this heathen conduct within the ranks of the Thyatiran church. Assuming that Jezebel, the Balaamites, and the Nicolaitans were representatives of the same cult under different forms, it may be observed that the Ephesians *hated* this cult (verse 6), the Pergamene Christians *had* them (verses 14f.), perhaps disliking them but not directly opposing them, and the Thyatirans *tolerated* them without being disturbed by their evil influence.

> *And I gave her time that she should repent, and she is unwilling to repent of her fornication* (2:21).

'Jezebel' had at first, presumably, professed the true faith with every appearance of being regenerate, but then, with hard-hearted defiance, had rejected the light, trampling the Son of God under foot, profaning the blood of the covenant, and outraging the Spirit of grace (Heb. 10:29). Her will had become immutably fixed against repentance. Her spirit, in short, was one of apostasy. Christ's lament over Jerusalem might well have been spoken over this 'Jezebel': 'I was willing . . . and you were unwilling' (Mt. 23:37).

> *Behold, I cast her into a bed and those who commit adultery with her into great tribulation, unless they repent of her works* (2:22).

The bed of lust becomes a bed of sickness. Just as unbridled licentiousness and unnatural vice lead to diseases of the most dreaded and horrible kind, so, too, ungodly faithlessness brings one to **great tribulation**. Unlike 'Jezebel', however, whose heart is hardened against repentance, there is still time for those she has led astray to **repent of her works**, that is, of the works she has taught them to do. If, as seems to be the case, 'Jezebel' had induced them to commit adultery that was physical and carnal, this was at the same time a symptom of deep spiritual unfaithfulness. The unity of human nature is such that the body cannot be isolated from the spirit. Dishonourable passions proliferate in the soil of ungodliness (*cf.* Rom. 1:24f.), and the Lord, as St. Paul warned the Thessalonians, 'is an avenger in all these things', since 'God called us not for uncleanness, but in sanctification' (1 Thes. 4:6f.). And again, as he expostulated when writing to the Corinthians, who were in danger of the same sort of seduction: 'Do you not know that your body is a temple of the Holy Spirit? . . . You are not your own, for you were bought with a price: glorify God therefore in your body' (1 Cor. 6:19f.). That is an admonition, too, for the admirers of 'Jezebel'.

> *And I will kill her children with death, and all the churches shall know that I am he who searches the reins and hearts; and I will give to each of you according to your works* (2:23).

The *children* of 'Jezebel' are those who, so to speak, have been begotten or brought into being by her teaching and have given themselves over to her evil practices. To 'kill with death' is an Old Testament expression which means to kill with a deadly plague or affliction. Should they continue unrepentant, this dire judgment which they bring upon themselves will make plain not merely to the church in Thyatira but to *all the churches* how concerned the Lord is for the purity and integrity of his church. It will also be a startling reminder that nothing can be hidden from him *who searches the reins and hearts*, that is to say, the innermost recesses of each person's being and character (*cf*. Heb. 4:12f.): the internal organs, 'reins (kidneys) and hearts', standing for the unseen centre and source of the human will and affections (see Pss. 7:9; 26:2).

The children produced by spiritual adultery are bastard children who, because of their impenitence and ungodliness, do not belong to the family of God. Thus God declared through his prophet Isaiah that the unfaithful people of Judah were 'sons of the sorceress, offspring of the adulterer and the harlot, . . . children of transgression, the offspring of deceit' (Is. 57:3f.). And the incarnate Son denounced the hard-hearted society in Jerusalem as 'an evil and adulterous generation' (Mt. 12:39; 16:4); for he is 'the Son of God, who has eyes like a flame of fire' (verse 19), and who, consequently, sees what man covers over and knows what man wishes to remain unknown. Only he, from whom no secrets are hidden, is competent to declare, '*I will give to each of you according to your works*'. It was in virtually identical terms that God had asserted by the lips of the prophet Jeremiah, 'I the Lord search the mind and try the heart, to give every man according to his ways, according to the fruit of his doings' (Je. 17:10; *cf*. 11:20; 20:12). The verdict of the Lord unfailingly accords with absolute justice: no one will be unjustly commended by him, no one unjustly condemned.

> **But to the rest of you in Thyatira, as many as do not hold this teaching, who do not know what they call the deep things of Satan, I do not lay on you any other burden** (2:24).

The rest of you in Thyatira, who are now addressed, specifies those who have not allowed themselves to be seduced by the self-styled prophetess 'Jezebel' and have not been deceived by the **deep things** that she claimed to teach. These so-called 'deep things' were doubtless presented as the revelation of profound mysteries, perhaps of esoteric knowledge (*gnosis*).[1] Far from being authentically Christian, however, they were the deep things **of Satan**, falsehoods from the abyss, not truth from above. Very possibly St. Paul's assertion that through the Spirit

---

[1] The gnostic leaders in the second century liked to advertise themselves as the communicators of 'the deep things'.

'the deep things of God' are revealed to us (1 Cor. 2:10) was cited as justifying this spurious indoctrination. It was 'knowledge' which those who had a right understanding of apostolic teaching refused to accept (*who do not know* being the equivalent here of 'who reject as knowledge' the 'deep things' that 'Jezebel' pretended to communicate).

To these faithful and discerning Christians the Lord says, '*I do not lay on you any other burden*' – that is, other than to shun the evil precepts and practices advocated by 'Jezebel'. The language here is strongly reminiscent of the decree of the Council of Jerusalem, at which St. John was present: 'It seemed good to the Holy Spirit and to us to lay no further burden on you than these necessary things', which included abstention from meat sacrificed to idols and from fornication (Acts 15:28f., note verse 20 above). Earlier at this same council St. Peter, insisting that salvation is 'by the grace of the Lord Jesus', had spoken against 'putting a yoke upon the neck of the disciples which neither our fathers nor we were able to bear' (Acts 15:10); and this in turn calls to mind Christ's denunciation of the scribes and Pharisees for laying 'heavy burdens, grievous to bear', on men's shoulders (Mt. 23:4). So here the Lord has no intention of weighing down the Christians in Thyatira with unnecessary and useless demands.

Only hold fast what you have until I come (2:25).

To shun all that is associated with idolatry and immorality and to **hold fast** are two sides of the same coin: the one implies the other; the negative is balanced by the positive requirement. **What you have** refers to the things they possess that are good and genuine: the authentic doctrine they have received, obedience to the Lord's commands, and the pursuit of holiness, in short, the love, faith, ministry, and patience for which they have been commended (verse 19). To hold fast to these essentials is not to stand still or to be self-protective but progressively to advance more and more in evangelistic zeal, the service of others, and likeness to Christ. Moreover, the imminence of the Lord's return should be an extra incentive to godly living; hence their Master encourages them to hold fast '*until I come*'. They, and we, are to live daily in the expectation of his coming, not in fear but in joyful anticipation of seeing him face to face and of entering into the perfection of glory which he will bring. Christ pronounced blessed the faithful and wise servant whom at his coming he finds doing his will (Mt. 24:45f.). Such a one has confidence and will not be ashamed before the Lord when he appears; indeed, the person whose hope is truly fixed on Christ and whose longing is to be like Christ 'purifies himself as he is pure' (1 Jn. 2:28; 3:2f.). It is of ultimate importance, then, to hold fast until he comes.

> *To him who overcomes and keeps my works to the end I will give authority over the nations, and he shall rule them with a rod of iron, as the vessels of the potter are broken in pieces, even as I have received authority from my Father (2:26–27).*

He *who overcomes and keeps my works to the end* is just another way of saying he who holds fast what he has until the Lord comes (preceding verse). What is promised to the overcomer here is really union with Christ in his universal authority, as is plain from the explanation *even as I have received authority from my Father*. The basis of the promise is, in fact, the declaration prophetically addressed to the incarnate Son: 'Ask of me, and I will make the nations your heritage, and the ends of the earth your possession. You shall break them with a rod of iron, and dash them in pieces like a potter's vessel' (Ps. 2:8f.). By virtue of their oneness with him, the power of the redeemed is identified with the power of the Redeemer; his glory becomes also their glory; in his rule they rule. Thus to the same effect as here St. Paul affirms: 'If we endure, we shall also reign with him' (2 Tim. 2:12) 'Do you not know', he asks the Corinthians, 'that the saints shall judge the world?' (1 Cor. 6:2). Similarly those who overcome are given the assurance that they will sit with the Son on his throne (in the letter to the Laodiceans, 3:21 below). That the Lord's authority is absolute and his sovereignty supreme over the whole of creation is one of the great themes of this book (*cf.* 12:5; 19:15). Those who are his will be made one with him in this sovereign authority.

> *And I will give him the morning star (2:28).*

The morning star is the herald of the new day as the darkness of the long night is dispelled (2 Pet. 1:19). This is the promise to the overcomer of participation in Christ's glory in that kingdom where there will be no night (Rev. 21:25). More than that, it is the possession of Christ himself, for he says: 'I Jesus . . . am the bright morning star' (22:16). Thus to be given the morning star is to be given the Son himself, in comparison with whom there is no other gift worth having. Accordingly, in the night of his affliction St. Paul was only too willing to suffer the loss of all things that he might gain Christ (Phil. 3:7f.). The wonderful joy conveyed in this promise of the morning star is not, however, without an overtone of urgency, as we see so clearly in the zeal and earnestness of St. Paul. 'The night is far spent, and the day is at hand', he admonished the Christians in Rome: 'let us therefore cast off the works of darkness, and let us put on the armour of light; let us walk honestly, as in the day' (Rom. 13:12f.).

In the present night of this fallen world the light of the eternal day has already dawned in the hearts of those who by faith have received him who is the morning star into their lives. His coming at Bethlehem was the advent of 'the dayspring from on high . . . to give light to those who sit in darkness and in the shadow of death' (Lk. 1:78f.). Satan's purpose is to prevent the light of the glory of Christ from dawning in the minds of unbelievers; but God in his sovereign power, who at creation caused light to shine out of darkness, has in the renewal of creation 'shined in our hearts to give the light of the knowledge of God in the face of Jesus Christ' (2 Cor. 4:4, 6). Consequently, those whose hearts are illumined by this celestial grace find that 'the path of the righteous is like the light of dawn, which shines brighter and brighter until the full day' (Pr. 4:18). For them the morning star that now gleams afar will then be known in all its fullness, which is none other than the fullness of the Son and his glory.

He who has an ear, let him hear what the Spirit says to the churches (2:29).

See comments on verse 7 above.

5. TO THE CHURCH IN SARDIS, 3:1–6

And to the angel of the church in Sardis write: These things says he who has the seven Spirits of God and the seven stars: I know your works, that you have a name that you live, and you are dead (3:1).

Sardis, some thirty miles south-east of Thyatira, was the ancient capital of Lydia and a hub of the woollen and dyeing industries. It was also a stronghold of the cult of the pagan goddess Cybele and had a reputation as a hotbed of hedonism. The earliest work known to us on the book of Revelation was written by Melito, bishop of Sardis, in the latter part of the second century. He *who has the seven Spirits of God and the seven stars* is the Lord Jesus Christ (see comments above on 1:4, 16, 20). He alone is able to say, with unerring percipience, '*I know your works*', not only to the church in Sardis but to every single church. In this address to the Christian community of Sardis there is no word of general commendation, but only of rebuke. The condition of their church is alarmingly unhealthy. It has indeed *a name*, that is, a reputation, for being a live and active church, but the reality is that it is *dead*. Its supposed vitality is but a façade which covers over the rottenness at its heart. Its membership as a whole is no better than the scribes and Pharisees, whom Christ denounced for being 'like whitewashed tombs, which outwardly appear beautiful, but inwardly are full of dead men's bones and of all uncleanness', since 'outwardly they appeared righteous to men, but inwardly were full of hypocrisy and iniquity' (Mt. 23:27f.; *cf.* 1 Tim. 5:6, a widow who is pleasure-seeking 'is dead even while she lives'). They are indistinguishable from the mere formalists whose lives are a denial of the power of the godliness they appear to retain (2 Tim. 3:5).

> *Be watchful and strengthen the things that remain which are about to die, for I have not found your works fulfilled in the sight of my God* (3:2).

Despite the general state of spiritual necrosis, there is still a remnant of life; hence the challenge to arouse themselves from stupor and to salvage and fortify what otherwise must soon die. If everything were beyond repair, there would be no point in addressing the church in Sardis in this or in any other way. To the eyes of men all may seem to be well (preceding verse), but *in the sight of my God*, who sees things as they really are, this church's **works**, no doubt enthusiastically begun, are *unfulfilled*, and thus stultified by the blight of incompletion. It is now full time, and perhaps the last chance, for its members to wake from sleep (Rom. 13:11) and to lift their drooping hands and strengthen their weak knees (Heb. 12:12). How deplorable for them if, as in the parable of the fig tree, the Lord should come seeking fruit and find none! And so he is saying to their church in effect: 'If it bears fruit next year, well and good; but if not, cut it down!' (Lk. 13:7-9). That it is not too late for them to be spiritually reinvigorated and to bring their works to completion is implicit in the admonition to **be watchful** and to **strengthen the things that remain**. Indeed, it is an evidence of the divine forbearance and merciful concern that the Lord seeks their restoration rather than their rejection.

> *Remember therefore how you have received and heard, and hold fast and repent. If therefore you will not be watchful, I will come like a thief, and you will not know at what hour I will come upon you* (3:3).

The Lord's admonition continues in a manner similar to that given to the Ephesian church (2:5). The Christian community in Sardis is urged to **remember** the message they first **heard** and the teaching they then **received** and welcomed; and, instead of being distracted by alien voices, or preferring ease to hardship, to **hold fast** to that truth in a spirit of repentance for their delinquency. Their neglect of the truth originally communicated to them is inexcusable. To the same purpose St. Paul exhorted the elders from Ephesus to be watchful and to keep in remembrance the teaching they had received from him (Acts 20:31), and encouraged Timothy to 'hold the pattern of sound words' which he had heard from him and to guard the truth which had been entrusted to him by the Holy Spirit (2 Tim. 1:13f.). Similarly he instructed Titus that it was necessary for a bishop to 'hold fast to the faithful word which is according to the teaching, in order that he may be able both to give encouragement in sound doctrine and also to refute those who speak against it' (Tit. 1:9).

Should the church members in Sardis fail to respond to the call to *be watchful*, the Lord warns them that he *will come* to them suddenly *like a thief* at an hour when they are unprepared because of their slothful self-indulgence to meet him. It is a simile which occurs frequently elsewhere in the New Testament with reference to the Lord's second coming (*cf*. Mt. 24: 42-44; Mk. 13:33-37; Lk. 12:39f.; 1 Thes. 5:2, 4; 2 Pet. 3:10; also ch. 16:15 below). The point, of course, is that a thief comes unannounced, without forewarning, when he is not expected, and while people, instead of being watchful, are sleeping. The coming threatened by the Lord here could be that of his second coming, which is always imminent; but in the meantime it could be a provisional visitation in the form of a judgment comparable to that against which the Ephesian church was warned: 'I will come to you and will move your lampstand out of its place' (2:5). The light of life which suffers neglect is transferred for the benefit of others who will welcome its rays.

> But you have a few names in Sardis who did not defile their garments; and they shall walk with me in white, for they are worthy (3:4).

In the darkening situation at Sardis these *few names* constitute a remnant of faithful individuals who have kept *their garments*, that is, their personal lives, undefiled by turning away from the enticements on all sides to indulge in degrading immorality and spiritual infidelity. Through the ardour of their witness God's light continues to burn as they 'hate even the garment spotted by the flesh' (Jude 23). The Lord's promise, '*they shall walk with me*', signifies the restoration of redeemed mankind to that sacred fellowship with the Creator of all which was enjoyed in the garden before the fall, when the Lord God walked and conversed in personal friendship with the man and the woman formed in his image. This walking together is the expression of the perfect harmony of will and affection between the Redeemer and his redeemed (*cf*. Am. 3:3). It is the regaining of the paradise that was lost, a reality that is denoted by the recovery of access to the tree of life (2:7; 22:2, 14, 19).

Moreover, it is *in white* that they will walk with their Lord, that is to say, clothed with the spotless purity of the Redeemer as they take their place in that great company of those 'who have washed their robes and made them white in the blood of the Lamb' (7:9, 14); *for*, it is added, *they are worthy*. Their worthiness, however, does not consist in any meritorious virtue of their own, nor is there a basis here for a doctrine of self-justification in the presence of God. The essential precondition for the restoration of the pristine fellowship of man with his Maker is the total cleansing away of the alienating defilement of our sinful ungodliness, and this is effected by the blood of the Lamb, which means the atoning death of the incarnate Son in our place on the cross. Worthiness here is attributed to those who have gratefully received the grace of forgiveness and reconciliation freely offered in the gospel; and that is to say that the Christian believer is worthy not in himself or herself but in Christ. Thus in the parable of the wedding banquet those who rejected the king's invitation 'were not worthy' (Mt. 22:8). Nor does mere obedience establish a claim to worthiness: 'When you have done all that is commanded you', Christ taught, 'say, "We are unworthy servants; we have only done what was our duty"' (Lk. 17:10). Again, in the episode recorded in 5:1ff. below, concerning the scroll with seven seals, when the question is asked, 'Who is worthy to open the scroll and to loose its seals?', John 'wept much because no one was found worthy', until he was assured that the Lamb was worthy. Accordingly, in the coming glory the whole creation unites in proclaiming the worthiness, not of the redeemed, but of the Redeemer (4:11; 5:9, 12).

While, however, worthiness in the sense of self-justification is totally excluded; for those whose justification before God is in Christ and his work, there is a form of worthiness inherent in the Christian life that is distinguished by constant faithfulness. In this connection worthiness is synonymous with what is fitting or appropriate. To revert to the sinful ways from which one has been redeemed is plainly inappropriate to one's standing in Christ and inconsistent with one's profession to be a Christian whose life has been transformed by the gospel. To do so is utterly unworthy. Justification by grace does not absolve one from responsibility. It is not improper for a Christian to desire to hear his Master's commendation: 'Well done, good and faithful servant!' (Mt. 25:21). Accordingly, St. Paul exhorted the Ephesians to 'lead a life worthy of the calling' to which they had been called (Eph. 4:1), and the Philippians to let their 'manner of life be worthy of the gospel of Christ' (Phil. 1:27), and the Colossians to 'lead a life worthy of the Lord, fully pleasing to him, bearing fruit in every good work, and increasing in the knowledge of God' (Col. 1:10; *cf.* 1 Thes. 2:12; 2 Thes. 1:5). It is in this sense that the few in Sardis who did not defile their garments are called worthy. Yet even this worthiness, which is the response of gratitude and devotion to God for the new life in Christ, is inseparable from divine grace, for it is through and in that grace that it finds expression: 'It is God', St. Paul affirmed, 'who is at work in you, both to will and to work for his good pleasure' (Phil. 2:13); and of himself he testified: 'I worked harder than any of them; yet it was not I, but the grace of God which was with me' (1 Cor. 15:10).

He who overcomes shall be arrayed in white garments, and I will in
no wise blot his name out of the book of life, and I will confess his
name before my Father and before his angels (3:5).

To *be arrayed in white garments* is the same as to walk with the Lord in
white (preceding verse), and the fulfilment of the promise is seen in the
great multitude of the redeemed in glory, arrayed in white robes which
have been washed in the blood of the Lamb (7:9, 14). *The book of life*, in
which are written the names of those to whom the grace of eternal life
has been given, symbolizes the truth that the names of his elect whom
he has redeemed are all known to the Lord and that their persons are
cherished by him. (It is mentioned again in 13:8; 17:8; 20:12, 15; and
21:27; see also Phil. 4:3.) Christ counselled the seventy who had
returned from their mission with joy because even the demons were
subject to them in his name: 'Do not rejoice that the spirits are subject to
you, but rejoice that your names are written in heaven' (Lk. 10:17–20). In
a similar way the author of the Epistle to the Hebrews speaks of 'the
firstborn who are enrolled in heaven' (Heb. 12:23). The imagery must
not be interpreted literalistically: to *blot out* a name signifies that that
name has no place among those who have received eternal life, because
the person whose name it is is an unrepentant sinner and rejector of the
gospel (*cf.* Ex. 32:33; Dt. 9:14; 29:19f.). It would be altogether wrong to
imagine an activity of constant book-keeping in heaven, involving not
only the registration of new names but also the removal of names
previously entered and the restoration of names previously removed.
Such a conception could only be conducive to insecurity on the part of
God's people (whose names might be in his book today and out tomor-
row) and to uncertainty even in the mind of God himself regarding the
ultimate outcome of his redemptive action, which is unthinkable.

It is precisely 'every one whose name had not been written in the book
of life of the Lamb slain from the foundation of the world' who worships
the beast (13:8); whereas the Good Shepherd says of his sheep: 'I give
them eternal life, and they shall never perish, and no one shall snatch
them out of my hand' (Jn. 10:28). As those who have been 'chosen in
him before the foundation of the world' (Eph. 1:4) their inheritance,
'reserved in heaven' for them, is 'imperishable, undefiled, and
unfading' (1 Pet. 1:4). Were this not so, the eternal life possessed by the
redeemed (Jn. 3:16; 5:25, *etc.*) could turn out to be not eternal after all but
only for the time being, dependent on man rather than God, with the
consequence that the promises of God would be open to falsification,
which again is unthinkable.

The Lord's further promise, to *confess* the *name* of the conqueror
before my Father and before his angels, is a repetition and a confirmation of the promise recorded in the Gospels to those who steadfastly
confess him before men and who, rather than deny the gospel, willingly

suffer persecution for his name's sake (Mt. 10:32; Lk. 12:8). The name confessed by the Son is at the same time the name written in his book of life.

> *He who has an ear, let him hear what the Spirit says to the churches* (3:6).

See comments on 2:7 above.

6. TO THE CHURCH IN PHILADELPHIA, 3:7–13

> *And to the angel of the church in Philadelphia write: These things says he who is holy, he who is true, he who has the key of David, he who opens and none shall shut, and who shuts and none opens* (3:7).

The city of Philadelphia was less than thirty miles south-east of Sardis. Situated in a territory of vineyards, it was a centre of the cult of Dionysius. The letter is free from rebuke, even though the church in Philadelphia would seem not to have been a strong church. The Lord **who is holy** and **who is true** addresses its members (the same adjectives are applied to him in 6:10), and his followers are called to be holy in all their conduct as he is holy and to be obedient to the truth (1 Pet. 1:15f., 22). His further designation as **he who has the key of David**, and **who opens and none shall shut, and who shuts and none opens** is virtually a quotation of Isaiah 22:22, where the reference is to Eliakim, who was over the household of Hezekiah (2 Ki. 18:18, 37). Christ, having been appointed 'head over all things for the church' (Eph. 1:22) and invested with 'all authority' (Mt. 28:18), is 'faithful over God's household' (Heb. 3:6). **The key** placed in his charge is the symbol of trust and authority; and it is the key **of David** because he is the promised son of David, the throne of whose kingdom is established for ever (2 Sa. 7:13, 16; Is. 9:7; *cf.* ch. 22:16 below). Accordingly, the angel Gabriel announced to the Virgin Mary regarding the son to whom she was to give birth: 'He shall be great and shall be called the Son of the Most High; and the Lord shall give him the throne of his father David, and he shall reign over the house of Jacob for ever, and of his kingdom there shall be no end' (Lk. 1:32f.). The absolute supremacy of his authority is indicated by the assertion that what he opens **none shall shut** and what he shuts **none opens**. Even death, which to us seems so final and so invincibly annihilating, is not proof against his key. For, as we have already been assured, he wields the keys of death and of Hades (1:18); and this means that the ultimate power is his, both as Redeemer and as Judge (*cf.* Jn. 5:22, 25–29).

I know your works – behold, I have set before you an open door, which none can shut – that you have a little power, and that you kept my word and did not deny my name (3:8).

As with all the churches, the Lord knows all about their spiritual condition and their trials, their strengths and their weaknesses. Continuing the thought of the preceding verse, he now declares that he has **set before** the Philadelphian church **an open door**, that is, a door which he has opened and which, precisely for that reason, **none can shut**. In similar manner God had announced of old that he would open doors before Cyrus and gates that would not be closed (Is. 45:1). The door opened for the Philadelphians was a door of present opportunity, rather than of ultimate salvation (true though the latter may be): in the midst of testing circumstances the door stands open for witness to the power of the gospel. To the same effect Paul and Barnabas explained to the Christians in Antioch how God had 'opened a door of faith to the Gentiles' (Acts 14:27). The Corinthians were informed by St. Paul that in Ephesus 'a great and effectual door' had been opened for him (1 Cor. 16:9), and, later, that in Troas a door was opened for him in the Lord (2 Cor. 2:12); and the Colossians were requested by him to pray 'that God may open to us a door for the word' (Col. 4:3). Now in Philadelphia, where there was fearsome opposition, God has opened a door which no hostile power can shut.

It is not the case that the Philadelphian church is stronger than others; it is in fact weak, with but *a little power*. But human weakness is no hindrance to the power of God; on the contrary, by unmistakable contrast, it provides the setting for the manifestation and the magnification of God's power. The Lord assures his faithful servants that it is not our ability but his grace that is sufficient to meet our need, 'for', he says, 'my power is made perfect in weakness'. Consequently, the church can and should affirm with St. Paul: 'Most gladly therefore will I rather glory in my weaknesses, that the power of Christ may rest upon me; for the sake of Christ, then, I take pleasure in weaknesses, insults, hardships, persecutions, and distresses, for when I am weak then I am strong' (2 Cor. 12:9f.).

Small though their strength was, to be told by the Lord '*You kept my word and did not deny my name*' is high commendation, and approbation of which every church should strive to be worthy. The members of the Philadelphian church exemplify the truth that God chooses the weak things of the world in order to put to shame the strong (1 Cor. 1:27); for in the end what really matters is not powerfulness before men but faithfulness before God (*cf.* 1 Cor. 4:1f.). Physical hardship and ideological assault had failed to breach the ranks of the Lord's forces in Philadelphia. Consequently, as the next verse shows, it is not they but the opponents of the gospel who will be brought into submission.

> *Behold, I will cause those of the synagogue of Satan – those who say that they are Jews and are not, but lie – behold, I will make them come and bow down before your feet so that they may know that I have loved you (3:9).*

On *the synagogue of Satan* composed of those who claim to be *Jews and are not* see comments above on 2:9. The Lord's declaration that he *will make them come and bow down* before the feet of his faithful witnesses in Philadelphia, and acknowledge that it is they whom he has loved can be interpreted in two ways. It may mean either that they will be forced to abase themselves as vanquished enemies or that they will humbly, under the Lord's hand, join the ranks of the believers whom previously they had persecuted. They will be brought either to judgment or to salvation. The latter sense is implicit in the context of Isaiah 60:14, which seems to be in mind here: 'The sons of those who oppressed you shall come bending low to you . . . and . . . shall bow down at your feet'. In the prophecies of the Old Testament it is the coming and submission of the Gentiles that is foretold; here it is the coming and submission of those who, calling themselves Jews, oppose the gospel. In both of these perspectives it is the triumph of the gospel that is envisaged, and the supremacy of Jesus Christ that will be acknowledged, whether it be willingly or unwillingly. For ultimately submission to the authority of Jesus will be universal: at the name of Jesus every knee will bow, and 'every tongue will confess that Jesus Christ is Lord, to the glory of God the Father' (Phil. 2:10f.).

In contrast to the futility of believing the promises of Satan and joining his 'synagogue' (*cf.* Mt. 4:9f.), the indefectibility of the love of God for his faithful people will be made unmistakably plain to all – *'that they may know'*, he says, *'that I have loved you'*. He who has said, 'You are precious in my eyes . . . and I love you' (Is. 43:4) and 'I have loved you with an everlasting love' (Je. 31:3) is the Lord who, as St. John has already reminded his readers, has demonstrated his love, at infinite cost to himself, by freeing us from our sins by his blood (cf. 1:5). He is also the one who, as St. John wrote in his Gospel, 'having loved his own who were in the world, . . . loved them to the end' (Jn. 13:1). So, together with St. Paul, the believers in Philadelphia in the first century, and in every place and age, have the assurance that there is absolutely nothing, not even Satan or affliction or death, that is able to separate them from the love of God in Christ Jesus our Lord (Rom. 8:35–39).

> *Because you have kept my word of patient endurance, I also will keep you from the hour of trial which is coming upon the whole world to try the dwellers on earth (3:10).*

Struggling with adversity for their Lord's sake, the Philadelphian Christians have *kept* his *word of patient endurance*, that is, his exhortation to endure hardship with patience (or, as the Greek may be rendered, 'the word of my patient endurance', that is, the exhortation to endure patiently as he did, as in Hebrews 12:1f.: 'Let us run with patient endurance the race that is set before us, looking to Jesus the pioneer and perfector of our faith, who for the joy that was set before him endured the cross, despising the shame'). They are given the assurance that he *will keep* them *from the hour of trial which is coming upon the whole world*, by which the universal ordeal of final judgment is intended. Those who have persisted in impenitence and unbelief will be *the dwellers on earth* who are overwhelmed by the terrors of this hour of trial (*cf.* 6:14ff.). Those, however, who thankfully receive the grace of God that flows to them from the cross, where Christ bore the punishment of their sins, are safe in him from this final ordeal, and are secure in the knowledge that their present trials are but for the time being. The final judgment of their sins has already taken place on the cross. Just as the incarnate Son was nailed to a cross which was prepared for someone else, so his 'hour of trial' at Calvary was in their place. By it they are delivered from the judgment impending over the whole unregenerate world.

> *I am coming quickly; hold fast what you have, so that no one may take your crown* (3:11).

The Lord's coming will be sudden and it is always imminent; hence the need for constant earnestness and vigilance. Nothing could be more lamentable than to lose the crown of life that is promised those who are faithful to the end (*cf.* 2:10). No anguish could be more intense than to see the crown that might have been one's own presented to someone else, and to hear the Lord say, 'I do not know you!' (Mt. 25:12). There is no suggestion here that God's work of grace may fail in the end and come to nothing; far from it! The emphasis is on the need for us to be sincere and unhypocritical in our profession of faith and to be undaunted as we persevere in the midst of trials and afflictions; and to be this there is unceasing need for the strengthening and edifying grace of God. Grace does not begin and end with our justification in Christ; for all from beginning to end is of grace.

> *I will make him who overcomes a pillar in the temple of my God, and he will never again go out of it; and I will write on him the name of my God and the name of the city of my God, the new Jerusalem, which comes down out of heaven from my God, and my own new name* (3:12).

The pillars of a magnificent edifice, such as a great cathedral, are fitting symbols of strength and stability and permanence. Moreover, they belong inseparably to the whole structure. So here the Lord's promise that the overcomer will be *a pillar in the temple of my God* is a promise of full and abiding power and dignity in the cosmic spiritual sanctuary that he is raising up. That this will be the overcomer's true and proper position, unblighted by the ephemeral character of the honours and dignities of our fallen secular age, is made clear by the further assurance that *he will never again go out of it* – a pillar, by its nature and function, is not removable! The Psalmist rejoiced in the same assurance when he confidently declared, 'I shall dwell in the house of the Lord for ever' (Ps. 23:6; *cf.* 27:4).

The temple of which St. John is writing, because it is *God's* temple, is not a man-made structure of this world; nor are its materials the materials of this world. Its component parts are Christian believers, described by St. Peter as 'living stones' who are being 'built up to be a spiritual temple' (1 Pet. 2:5), or, as St. Paul puts it, are 'growing into a holy temple in the Lord', with 'Christ Jesus himself being the chief corner-stone' (Eph. 2:20–21; *cf.* Heb. 3:6). Thus bonded together in the eternal glory the multitude of the redeemed will be 'a habitation of God the Spirit' (Eph. 2:22), and, as those who by grace constitute the Lord's temple, they will serve before the throne of God unceasingly in his temple (7:15 below).

If, meanwhile, individuals such as the apostles James and Peter and John could be described as pillars of the church because of the authenticity of their teaching and their firm leadership (Gal. 2:9), it is also of interest to find that even the building itself could, by a widening of the metaphor, be described as a pillar, or the pillar. Thus in 1 Timothy 3:15 'the church of the living God' is defined by St. Paul as 'the pillar and bulwark of the truth': that is, the pillar collectively of all those faithful witnesses, from generation to generation, who are being built into the temple of God.

The overcomer receives the further promise that a special name with a threefold significance will be written on him. It will be, firstly, *the name of my God*, signifying divine ownership with its implication of eternal security under God's care and preciousness to God. Thus in the high-priestly blessing pronounced over the people of Israel there is implicit the central assurance: 'So shall they put my name upon the people of Israel, and I will bless them' (Nu. 6:22–27). And to the same effect, as though in confirmation of this promise, in 14:1 and 22:4 below St. John observes that those who form the company of the redeemed are marked with the name of their God.

It will be, secondly, *the name of the city of my God, the new Jerusalem, which comes down out of heaven from my God*. This naming represents the stamp of the overcomer's authentic citizenship.

By his repudiation of this age and its values and his devotion to the crucified Saviour, now risen from the dead and enthroned in glory, he declares to the world that he is a stranger and a pilgrim on the earth, that he has here no abiding city, and that he is journeying to the city which is to come (Heb. 11:13, 16; 13:14). The stamp of this name announces that his citizenship is in heaven, from where he awaits a Saviour (Phil. 3:20). Knowing that 'the Jerusalem above is free and is our mother' (Gal. 4:26), there is no uncertainty as to where his first loyalty lies; indeed, when the Lord's people finally come home it is to 'the city of the living God, the heavenly Jerusalem' that they come (Heb. 12:22). In the climactic vision of this book St. John sees the coming down of the new Jerusalem from God out of heaven (21:1, 2, 10), by which is signified the full harmony of heaven and earth as at last all God's purposes in their creation are brought to fulfilment in the establishment of the new heaven and earth where his people dwell joyfully with him.

And, thirdly, it will be *my own new name*, that is, the Lord's own new name, the name of him who is the overcomer's Redeemer and Lord. This name is the seal of his indefectible salvation in Christ, who redeemed him at the infinite cost of his own precious blood, to whom therefore he belongs, and, belonging, in whose love and grace he is secure for ever and ever (1 Pet. 1:18f.; 1 Cor. 6:19f.; ch. 7:14ff. below). Such is the blessedness that is symbolized by the threefold naming of those who overcome.

> *He who has an ear, let him hear what the Spirit says to the churches (3:13).*

See comments on 2:7 above.

7. TO THE CHURCH IN LAODICEA, 3:14–22

And to the angel of the church in Laodicea write: These things says the Amen, the faithful and true witness, the beginning of the creation of God (3:14).

Laodicea, some fifty miles south-east of Philadelphia, was an important commercial and manufacturing centre. The Hebrew root of the term *Amen* signifies what is firm and true. Particularly distinctive was the manner in which Christ introduced utterances of special importance with a double 'Amen': 'Truly, truly, I say to you . . .' (Jn. 1:51, *etc.*; in the synoptic Gospels it is a single 'Amen'). It is because all the promises of God are affirmative in Christ that we add our 'Amen' in him to the glory of God in our worship (2 Cor. 1:20; *cf.* also the 'Amens' in Rev. 1:6, 7, 18;

5:14; 7:12; 19:4; 22:20, 21). A parallel designation of God as 'Amen' is found in Isaiah 65:16, where 'Elohim' and 'Amen' occur twice in conjunction as 'Elohim Amen'. This is rendered in most versions as 'the God of truth', but the New English Bible conveys the force of the striking combination more effectively as follows: 'He who invokes a blessing on himself in the land shall do so by the God whose name is Amen, and he who utters an oath in the land shall do so by the God of Amen'. Christ's designation of himself here, in an absolute manner, as **The Amen** implies the deity of him who is absolute Truth (Jn. 14:6). The additional self-declaration as **the faithful and true witness** is fully consonant with and explanatory of the meaning of his name 'The Amen'; it also combines the description of Jesus Christ as 'he who is true' in verse 7 above and 'the faithful witness' in 1:5.

Furthermore, the Son declares himself to be **the beginning of the creation of God**. This appellation is not unrelated to those which denominate him 'the First and the Last', 'the Alpha and the Omega', and 'the Beginning and the End' elsewhere in this book (1:8, 17; 2:8; 21:6; 22:13), for what he who is The Amen begins cannot fail to attain to its predestined fulfilment. But what are we to understand by his being called 'the beginning of the creation of God'? It must be insisted, to begin with, that the whole context not only of Revelation but also of the New Testament rules out the possibility that this means that the Son was the first of God's creatures, that in the world of creation God began by creating the Son. Thus to interpret the expression would be only to revive ancient heresy. The Son's pre-existence is inseparable from his present power and his future coming (*cf.* 1:4, 8, 17, *etc.*). The term 'beginning' in this expression must not, then, be treated as a passive noun, meaning the first being created by God, but as an active noun, meaning the dynamic agent of God's creation, the One through whom the created order was brought into existence.

St. Paul speaks of Christ not only as 'the beginning' (Col. 1:18) but also as 'the firstborn of all creation' (Col. 1:15) in a passage, however, that makes it perfectly plain that, far from meaning that Christ is the first of creatures, his theme is the absolute pre-eminence of Christ over all creation. The existence of the Son prior to creation and his active role in the work of creation are free from all doubt and ambiguity: 'For', the Apostle writes, 'in him were all things created, . . . all things have been created through him and unto him, and he is before all things, and in him all things hold together, . . . that in all things he might have the pre-eminence' (Col. 1:16–18). What is true of him who is the firstborn of all creation applies with identical force to him who is the beginning of the creation of God. St. John wrote precisely to the same effect in the opening sentences of his Gospel: 'In the beginning was the Word, and the Word was with God, and the Word was God . . . All things were made by him, and without him was not anything made that has been made' (Jn. 1:1, 3). Moreover, and most appropriately, it is through him, through whom all things were made, that God is reconciling all things to himself, 'having made peace by the blood of his cross' (Col. 1:20; *cf.* Eph. 1:10). The fact that the Son is the beginning of all created things is the guarantee and assurance of the indefectibility of God's purposes in creation.

> *I know your works, that you are neither cold nor hot. Would that you were cold or hot! So, because you are lukewarm, and neither hot nor cold, I will spew you out of my mouth (3:15–16).*

As with all the other churches, the Lord says, '*I know*'. He knows the true inner state of each church: he knows where there is strength and where there is weakness, where there is faithfulness and where failure. He who as the Amen is altogether true lays bare all that is false and hypocritical. The condition of the Laodicean church is extremely unhealthy. Its members have lost all zeal and commitment: if they are not actually against Christ's cause, their attitude betrays no concern for it. Immobilized by accidie, their posture is characterized by languor and boredom. *Neither hot nor cold*, their tepidity makes God sick! Better extreme coldness than this carefree unconcern, for the *lukewarm* church is a church stamped with contradiction. Lukewarmness is totally incongruous in comparison with the unrestrained self-giving of God the Father, 'who did not spare his only Son but delivered him up for us all' (Rom. 8:32), and of God the Son, who 'came to give his life a ransom for many' (Mk. 10:45). To present oneself as 'a living sacrifice, holy and acceptable to God' is the logical response to the divine self-giving for us (Rom. 12:1). The Lord's total self-renunciation for our redemption should unfailingly inspire our total self-renunciation in his service (Lk. 14:26, 33). He who had left all and endured all, including the cross, for our sakes had the fullest justification for announcing: 'He who does not take his cross and follow me is not worthy of me' (Mt. 10:38). Because of their lukewarmness the members of the Laodicean church were not worthy of the Master with whose name they were associated. As the next verse shows, self-satisfaction had been allowed to take the place of self-renunciation; cross-bearing had been driven out by complacency.

> *Because you say, I am rich and prosperous and have need of nothing, and you do not know that you are wretched and pitiable and poor and blind and naked (3:17).*

The Laodicean spirit of self-adequacy and self-congratulation, which in fact is self-deception, is reminiscent of the boast of Ephraim: 'Ah, but I am rich, I have gained wealth for myself!', which evoked the prophetic rejoinder that 'all his riches can never offset the guilt he has incurred'

(Ho. 12:8). The church in Corinth, puffed up with self-esteem because of the wealth of their charismatic and philosophical competence, had lapsed into a position comparable to that of the Laodicean church. In fact, their Apostle found it necessary to ask them pointedly: 'What do you have that you did not receive?', and then to add: 'If you then received it, why do you boast as if it were not a gift?' (1 Cor. 4:7f). They were closing their eyes to the truth that every good and perfect gift comes from above (Jas. 1:17).

Like the Corinthians, the Laodiceans had been blessed by God; but their self-preoccupation, which was a symptom of ingratitude, showed that they had yet to learn that spiritual pride is a wasting disease. The attitude of self-sufficiency severs the relationship with God as the source of all our sufficiency and induces spiritual atrophy. The true condition of the members of the Laodicean church was quite the opposite of what they had persuaded themselves to believe. Through self-inversion they had actually ceased to know themselves (*you do not know that you are wretched and pitiable and poor and blind and naked*); indeed, they imagined themselves to be the opposite of what in reality they were. Far from being *rich* and *prosperous* and in *need of nothing*, and therefore, as they thought, secure and unthreatened, their state was one of the greatest danger. But it was not yet beyond repair; hence the counsel that follows.

> *I counsel you to buy from me gold refined by fire, that you may become rich, and white garments, that you may be clothed and that the shame of your nakedness may not be displayed, and salve to anoint your eyes, that you may see* (3:18).

The Laodiceans were putting their trust in riches that in the end would prove to be counterfeit and would never pass the test of human persecution or divine judgment, for genuineness of faith is immeasurably more precious than all the perishing commodities for which our fallen society barters its soul (1 Pet. 1:7; Mt. 16:26). The only ultimate and imperishable wealth is to be rich toward God (Lk. 12:21), to lay up treasure not on earth but in heaven (Mt. 6:19f). Christ, who is the concentration of all riches, is the believer's true treasure (Col. 2:3; Mt. 13:45f.). In the light of eternity all else is worthless (Phil. 3:7f.). Moreover, this priceless wealth is offered free of charge, simply because the infinite cost has been met by the incarnate Son of God 'who loves us and loosed us from our sins by his blood' (Rev. 1:5); consequently, the counsel to *buy gold refined by fire*, that is, authentic wealth, corresponds to the invitation issued through the prophet Isaiah 'to buy without money and without price' (Is. 55:1), as is clear also from the appeal in the closing section of this book: 'Let him who is thirsty come, let him who is willing take the water of life freely' (22:17).

The *white garments* represent the covering of *the shame* of their unholy self-righteousness, which is their *nakedness* before God, with the spotless righteousness of the incarnate Son. Thus clothed, they are able to walk with the Lord in white (see verses 4f. above), living holy lives and enjoying the enriching bliss of his fellowship (*cf.* 19:8).

Their blindness is the self-induced consequence of their complacency. Turned in upon themselves, they have closed their eyes to the will of the Lord and to the needs of the society in which they are placed, with the result that their own urgent need is for the healing *salve* of divine grace and forgiveness to enable them to *see* things as they really are. Their cry should be that of the psalmist: 'Open my eyes, that I may behold!' (Ps. 119:18). The spiritual significance of the counsel given here in metaphors to the Laodiceans is well expressed in St. Paul's prayer for the members of the church in Ephesus: 'that the God of our Lord Jesus Christ, the Father of glory, may give you a spirit of wisdom and revelation in the knowledge of him, having the eyes of your heart enlightened, that you may know what is the hope of his calling, what are the riches of the glory of his inheritance in the saints' (Eph. 1:17f.)

> *As many as I love I reprove and chasten; be zealous therefore and repent* (3:19).

Stern words of reproof and admonition are not incompatible with affection, but are rather an expression of the deep concern of genuine love. The aberrations of the loved one cannot be viewed by the lover with complacency. The assurance given here recalls the declaration of Proverbs 3:12, that 'the Lord reproves him whom he loves, as a father the son in whom he delights' (see also Heb. 12:5f.). The purpose of the Lord's chastening, or discipline, is positive, not hostile; it is designed 'for our profit, that we may be partakers of his holiness' (Heb. 12:10). The affectionate appeal in the next verse must not, then, be dissociated from the rebuke that precedes it. Moreover, the exhortation to *be zealous therefore and repent* indicates that there can still be a bright future for the church in Laodicea. 'Be zealous' in fact means be hot, fervent, on the boil,[1] and, by implication, cease being lukewarm (*cf.* verse 15); and the demand for repentance advises the Laodiceans that it is not too late for them to turn and mend their ways (see on 2:5 and 3:3 above).

> *Behold, I stand at the door and knock; if any one hears my voice and opens the door, I will come in to him and dine with him, and he with me* (3:20).

---

[1] The adjective 'hot' (*zestos*) in verses 15f. and the verb 'be zealous' (*zēleue*) here in verse 19 have a common root which may be seen in the verb *zeō*, 'boil'.

Though frequently used in evangelism, this appeal is not addressed to outsiders but to church members. It is an exhortation to the latter to rouse themselves from apathy and lukewarmness and to open their lives unreservedly to Christ so that the pre-eminence may be his alone. In their complacency the Laodiceans have in effect been closing the door against him. Self has subtly usurped the place of Christ. There is also an eschatological overtone: spiritual apathy is an indicator that one is neglecting to live in the light of the Lord's return. St. James, for example, warned Christians who were selfishly grumbling against each other that 'the coming of the Lord is at hand' and that 'the Judge is standing at the doors' (Jas. 5:8f.). The thrust is that of the teaching of Christ himself:

> Let your loins be girded and your lamps burning, and be like men waiting expectantly for their master, . . . so that when he comes and knocks they may open to him at once. Blessed are those servants whom the master finds watching when he comes; truly I say to you, he will gird himself and make them sit down to dine, and he will come and serve them (*Lk. 12:35–37*).

The appeal to the Laodiceans is an appeal to the church whose lukewarmness has made it careless and unwatchful.

To *hear* the Lord's voice is to be receptive and obedient to what he has to say. Those who hear in this way and open the door to him are his true sheep (Jn. 10:3, 16). 'Every one who is of the truth hears my voice', Christ said (Jn. 18:37). To open the door is to invite him to come in, and his coming is to be at home with us and we with him: 'If a person loves me', he declared, 'he will keep my word, and my Father will love him, and we will come to him and make our home with him' (Jn. 14:23). Our home becomes his home; the lordship we had assumed becomes his lordship; the guest we invite in proves to be the true host: his dining with us becomes our dining with him. For it is only through his abiding in us that we truly abide in him: the one abiding is inseparable from the other (a distinctively Johannine doctrine! – *cf.* Jn. 6:56; 14:20; 15:4, 5; 1 Jn. 3:24; 4:13, 15, 16).

> *I will grant to him who overcomes to sit with me on my throne, as I also overcame and sat with my Father on his throne* (3:21).

The Lord's promise *to him who overcomes* that he will sit with him on his throne is founded on the reality of the believer's status in Christ and therefore his union with Christ. It is indeed a present reality in that the incarnate Son, who has been raised from the dead and exalted to the transcendental glory, now sits, enthroned, at the Father's right hand in the heavenly places; for this means that all that has happened to him has also happened to our human nature which he took to himself to redeem and glorify. That is why St. Paul affirms that God has 'raised us up with him and made us sit with him in the heavenly places in Christ Jesus' (Eph. 1:20; 2:6) and that our life 'is hid with Christ in God' (Col. 3:1–3). His enthronement is the enthronement of his redeemed who are one with him. In him our glorification is even now a reality. But the promise indicates that there is also a future dimension to this reality: that while our salvation is already complete in Christ there is even so a *not yet* as well as an *already*. For there is a meantime in which the Christian is a stranger and a pilgrim in this fallen world as he journeys onwards to the celestial city (Heb. 11:13–16; 1 Pet. 2:11). His gaze is fixed on the glory yet to be revealed. Assured that 'if we endure we shall also reign with him' (2 Tim. 2:12), he presses on 'towards the goal for the prize of the upward call of God in Christ Jesus' (Phil. 3:14). And he longs to experience the fulfilment of the incarnate Son's prayer that those given him by the Father may be with him to behold his glory (Jn. 17:24).

The promise given here to the overcomer of participation with Christ in his enthronement and dominion is of a piece with the constitution of his people as a kingdom (1:6; 5:10), with their reception of the crown of life (2:10), and with their being granted power over the nations (2:26).

> *He who has an ear, let him hear what the Spirit says to the churches* (3:22).

What the Spirit says to the churches has been said in these seven letters – and said, as we have previously observed, to the churches of every place and every age, and therefore to us in our day and place.

A door opened in heaven, 4:1–11

After this I saw, and behold, a door opened in heaven, and the first voice which I heard speaking to me like a trumpet said, Come up hither, and I will show you the things that must take place after this (4:1).

In his vision the Apostle exiled on the island of Patmos now sees *a door opened in heaven* which enables him to perceive what are otherwise mysteries hidden from men. Ezekiel in his day had written similarly: '. . . the heavens were opened, and I saw visions of God' (Ezk. 1:1); and St. Paul, referring to visions and revelations he had received, spoke of having been caught up to the third heaven where he 'heard things that cannot be told' (2 Cor. 12:1–4). For St. John, too, seeing was accompanied with hearing. What he hears now is *the first voice* and it has the sound of *a trumpet*, that is, it is a voice of authority. The reference is evidently to the 'loud voice, like a trumpet' heard by him at the beginning (1:10). The authority of the voice is the authority of the Lord himself. What the apostle hears is the invitation, '*Come up hither*', that is, to enter through the open door, so to speak, and to become a spectator on the spot, not from a distance, as he is shown *the things that must take place after this*. The instruction given at first was to commit to writing both 'the things that are' and also 'the things that shall come to pass hereafter' as they were revealed to him (1:19). The first three chapters largely cover what is present, namely, the power and glory of the exalted Redeemer and the state of the churches; but from now on the revelations depict in the main what is future, and in particular the realities of final judgment and the blessed perfection of the new heaven and earth. To the same effect Daniel had learnt that 'there is a God in heaven who reveals mysteries' and who makes known 'what shall be hereafter' (Dn. 2:28f., 45): a God, in other words, who exercises sovereign control over his creation and its history.

At once I was in the Spirit; and behold, there was a throne set in heaven and one seated on the throne, and he who sat there was in appearance like a jasper stone and a cornelian, and around the throne was a rainbow in appearance like an emerald (4:2–3).

71

On hearing the trumpet-like voice St. John *at once* sensed that he was *in the Spirit*, an awareness continuing or corresponding to his experience referred to in 1:10, 'I was in the Spirit on the Lord's day'. There is no reason to doubt that he was in the Spirit throughout the time that he was the recipient of the revelations recorded in this book; but here it is being in the Spirit, perhaps to an intensified degree and for an immediate purpose, that enables him to respond to the invitation, 'Come up hither', and to describe what he saw and heard after passing through 'the door opened in heaven'. There he gazes on the majestic spectacle of *a throne*, which is really the throne above all thrones, the seat of ultimate power and authority so prominent in this book, and of the Lord God Almighty, *seated on the throne* as the prophet Isaiah had seen him 'high and lifted up' (Is. 6:1), in sovereign majesty ruling the universe. How was St. John to describe the transcendental glory of him who reigns from the throne and the dazzling brilliance of this exalted scene? The finite language of this earthly sphere is incompetent to define and depict the infinite realities that he saw before him. Yet it was the only language at his command; hence his use of earthly similitudes, but always with the understanding that the heavenly reality far surpasses the earthly symbol. And so the comparison he offers is with the flashing splendour of precious stones and the polychromatic lustre of the rainbow. The magnificence of it all is indescribably awesome and beautiful. The spectacle set before the Apostle corresponded with the vision granted to the prophet Ezekiel (Ezk. 1:26–28), and the impression conveyed is not only one of loveliness but also of majesty and holiness and authenticity that are as absolute and ultimate as the pallid relativities here below are transient and fallible.

> *Around the throne were twenty-four thrones, and seated on the thrones were twenty-four elders arrayed in white garments with crowns of gold on their heads (4:4).*

Central to all is *the throne*; the *twenty-four thrones* that surround it are subsidiary thrones and *seated* on them are *twenty-four elders*. These elders represent the totality of redeemed mankind. The ancient interpretation of the number twenty-four makes good sense, namely, that it signifies the twelve patriarchs of Israel plus the twelve apostles, who together stand for the saints of both the Old and the New Testament eras, or, in other words, the church universal (*cf.* 21:12f.). As elsewhere, their *white garments* symbolize the spotless holiness of Christ with which they are covered (*cf.* 3:4f., 18; 7:9, 14; 19:8, 14), and the crowns of gold symbolize their reigning with Christ (see on 3:21 above; *cf.* 2 Tim. 2:12 and on 22:5 below). Accordingly, in 5:8–10 below, they worship the Lamb who has ransomed them 'from every tribe and tongue and people and nation' and has 'made them a kingdom' to reign with him.

And from the throne proceed lightnings and voices and thunders; and burning before the throne are seven lamps of fire, which are the seven Spirits of God; and before the throne is as it were a sea of glass, like crystal (4:5–6a).

The *lightnings and voices and thunders* are indicative of the awe-inspiring dignity of him who from the central throne judges the world in righteousness. The vision is reminiscent of the terrifying occasion of the law-giving at Sinai, which took place to the accompaniment of 'thunders and lightnings, and a thick cloud upon the mountain, and a very loud trumpet blast, so that all the people who were in the camp trembled' (Ex. 19:16; *cf.* 1 Sa. 2:10; Jb. 37:1–5). See 8:5, 11:19, and 16:18 below for similar terminology depicting the terror of divine judgment.

St. John interprets *the seven lamps of fire* that are *burning before the throne* as meaning *the seven Spirits of God*, which have already been mentioned in 1:4 and 3:1 and will be mentioned again in 5:6. Seven being the divine number, the seven Spirits stand for the Holy Spirit, the Third Person of the Holy Trinity, from whom, with the Father and the Son, grace and peace flow to the churches (note 1:4f). Fire is in a special way associated with the Holy Spirit, for to be baptized with fire is to be baptized with the Holy Spirit (Mt. 3:11; *cf.* Acts 2:3f., *etc.*). Fire, moreover, is symbolical of purification, as in the testing of fine gold (1 Pet. 1:7), and also of judgment and destruction, as consuming all that is worthless (1 Cor. 3:12ff.); 'for', as the author of the Epistle to the Hebrews reminds his readers, 'our God is a consuming fire' (Heb. 12:29; *cf.* Dt. 4:24; 9:3; Ex. 24:17; Ps. 50:3; Is. 10:16ff.; 29:6; 30:27; 30; Zp. 1:18).

Also before the throne there is what looks like *a sea*, not of water but *of glass*, indeed of translucent *crystal*, that is, a transparent expanse of crystalline beauty and purity (*cf.* 21:11, 18, 21; 22:1). Human analogies, again, are inadequate to describe the full wonder of the scene on which the Apostle was privileged to gaze; they are but finite pointers to an infinite reality. The similitude here could well have been linked to the appearance of the expanse of the Aegean Sea viewed on a still, clear day from the hills of Patmos. The picture is one of immense distance and serenity, undisturbed by 'the lightnings and voices and thunders' which, once final judgment has been executed, will cease for ever.

And in the centre, around the throne, were four living creatures, full of eyes in front and behind. And the first living creature was like a lion, and the second living creature like a calf, and the third living creature had the face of a man, and the fourth living creature was like a flying eagle (4:6b–7).

The *four living creatures* represent the whole order of animate creation. Thus the one *like a lion* represents the wild beasts, of which the lion is king; the one *like a calf* or bull represents the domesticated beasts, of which the ox is king; the one *like a flying eagle* represents the birds of the air, of which the eagle is king; and the one with *the face of a man* stands for the king of all animate nature, to whom dominion over the earth was entrusted (Gn. 1:28). The order, lion, calf, man, eagle, is unstudied (otherwise we would have expected man to be given the first place); no doubt it reflects the order in which the living creatures were seen by St. John.

The statement that the living creatures were *full of eyes in front and behind* may be taken to signify the conscious awareness and constant vigilance of the diverse members of the animate creation, particularly in relation to the service in their respective orders of the Creator and his will. 'O Lord, how manifold are thy works!', the psalmist sang. 'In wisdom hast thou made them all; the earth is full of thy creatures' (Ps. 104:24). The ordered harmony of creation is glorifying to God by whose beneficent wisdom and power all was brought into being. The number of these living creatures, namely *four*, is a further indication that the sum of the animate creation is intended, for four is the number of universality, a symbol of that which is global. Hence in daily speech we refer to the four quarters of the earth (*cf.* 20:8), the four winds (*cf.* 7:1; also Mt. 24:31; Mk. 13:27), and the four cardinal compass points (*cf.* Lk. 13:29; Ps. 107:3).

> And the four living creatures, each of them with six wings, are full
> of eyes around and within; and day and night they say without
> ceasing, Holy, holy, holy is the Lord God Almighty, who was and
> who is and who is to come (4:8).

St. John perceives, further, that the four living creatures have **eyes** not only **around** but also **within**. This may indicate that the divine will in the formation of his creatures extends beyond their outward comeliness and competence deep down into the innermost heart of their faculties and energies. By his creative hand their whole being, in all its multiple diversity, is as it were illumined with a plenitude of eyes.

He observed also that each of the living creatures had **six wings**. Each of the seraphim seen by Isaiah in his vision had six wings: 'with two', we are told, 'he covered his face, and with two he covered his feet', symbolizing humility and self-veiling in the transcendental glory of God's presence; 'and with two he flew', symbolizing willing obedience and swift mobility in the Lord's service. We take the six wings of each living creature in St. John's vision to have a similar significance. There are also some interesting affinities with Ezekiel's description of the vision he received, as well as certain differences. The four living creatures seen by Ezekiel were in the form of men, and each had four faces, whereas here in Revelation each has one face. Otherwise the faces in Ezekiel, those of a man, a lion, an ox, and an eagle, correspond to those seen by St. John. In Ezekiel each living creature has four wings, in Revelation each has six wings; in Ezekiel the wheels associated with the living creatures are full of eyes, whereas in Revelation the creatures themselves are full of eyes; moreover in Ezekiel the four living creatures are identified as cherubim (Ezk. 1:5ff.; 10:15, 20ff.).

If, on the basis of the similarities, the four living creatures described by St. John are understood to be cherubim, then their function as cherubim is that of attendants of the divine throne and executants of the divine will, with particular reference to the fulfilment of the purposes of God in and through the various orders of creatures that belong to the animate realm. In this perspective, the whole impulse of the animate creation, whose origin, continuance, and destiny are in God's hands, is God-ward, and the joy and harmony and also the expectation of the sentient world find their focus and their concentrated expression in the adoration around the throne of these four living beings. In the new heaven and earth the whole creation, delivered from the bondage of corruption caused by man's sin, participates in the glorious liberty of the children of God (Rom. 8:19–22). This explains the worship which is offered *without ceasing* to *the Lord God Almighty* by the four living creatures. It is the unification of the worship of creation in unremitting adoration of the Lord who is the omnipotent Creator and the gracious Redeemer of the world. The trisagion, *Holy, holy, holy*, is addressed to the blessed Trinity, Father, Son, and Holy Spirit, Three in One and One in Three (*cf.* Is. 6:3), *who was and who is and who is to come*, and who therefore alone is eternally sovereign over all (*cf.* 1:8). He it is who is to be praised by all. This adoration is memorably expressed in Psalm 148, which is a call to the whole of creation in all its ordered diversity to praise the Lord.

> *And when the living creatures give glory and honour and thanks to him who is seated on the throne, who lives for ever and ever, the twenty-four elders fall down before him who is seated on the throne and worship him who lives for ever and ever, and cast their crowns before the throne, saying, Worthy art thou, our Lord and God, to receive the glory and the honour and the power; for thou didst create all things, and by thy will they existed and were created* (4:9–11).

The ceaseless worship of the four living creatures (verse 8) does not imply that this worship is their sole activity, but rather that it is their constant disposition; their every action is an expression of adoration; praise is ever on their lips. The temporal qualification here, *when* they *give glory and honour and thanks*, is not a contradiction of the preceding assertion that they do this 'without ceasing'. It is just a case, once more, of human language being inadequate to describe fully the sequences that are not of this world which St. John saw in his vision. The richness of the vision of the all-transcending joyfulness of the world to come is such that its realities can be communicated only in a variety of manifestations and symbolisms. Thus, though the adoration of the four living creatures represents the adoration of the animate creation in its completeness, including man, it is important to remember that man, formed in the image of God, is above and apart from all the other creatures. In his divinely assigned position of eminence and responsibility, man in his fallenness drags down the other creatures with himself; and the restoration of man by the grace of redemption effects also the restoring of creation to its proper harmony and wholeness. That is why the twenty-four elders, by whom the company of redeemed mankind is signified (see on verse 4), are seen as distinct from the four living creatures. There is a unity of the worship of the four and of the twenty-four, but this worship is rightly perceived under different aspects that are doctrinally significant. In the heavenly scene to which St. John has been introduced, mankind is fully conformed to the divine image and destiny of his creation. The wonderful potentiality of man's nature is made actual as he enjoys complete unanimity with the Creator and his will. His dominion, in Christ, over the earth, freed from the devastating disorder induced by his sinfulness, is now in accord with the perfect order of the mind of God.

The twenty-four elders not only *fall down before him who is seated on the throne*, prostrating themselves in total adoration as they *worship him who lives for ever and ever*, but they also *cast their crowns before the throne*. Crowned as overcomers who have faithfully finished the course (2:10; 4:4; 2 Tim. 4:8; Jas. 1:12; 1 Pet. 5:4), they nevertheless ascribe all the glory of their victory to the Redeemer and his grace, acknowledging by their action that their crowns are really his, and that they have nothing which they have not received (1 Cor. 4:7). And so all worthiness is attributed by them to God, and to God alone, as they offer their praise and gratitude, saying: *Worthy art thou, our Lord and God, to receive the glory and the honour and the power* (the use of the definite article with each of the three nouns indicates totality), *for*, they proclaim, *thou didst create all things, and by thy will they existed and were created*. God, they are saying, in bringing all things into existence did so *by his will*, and providentially sustains all things *by his will*, and also brings all things to their predestined consummation *by his will*. Because it is *God's* will, which cannot fail of fulfilment, the divine purpose of creation is, and always has been, assured of attainment. Redemption connects the beginning to the completion. St. John was granted a preview of the glory which is to be revealed to all who are one in and with Christ Jesus.

The scroll with seven seals, 5:1 – 8:1

1. THE LAMB ALONE WORTHY, 5:1–14

And I saw in the right hand of him who was seated on the throne a scroll written within and on the back, sealed fast with seven seals (5:1).

The **scroll** now seen by the Apostle had the familiar appearance of a papyrus sheet covered with writing and wound around a central rod. The scroll in the vision had writing on both sides: **within**, that is, when rolled up, on the inside face, **and on the back**, that is, on the outer face. Any one wishing to read it would have to unroll it; but unrolling it presented a problem because it was **sealed fast with seven seals** which appeared to make it virtually unopenable and therefore unable to be read. That the seals were seven in number indicates that the scroll was sealed by God. We are reminded of Isaiah's vision which became 'like the words of a book that is sealed', with the consequence that when it was handed to one who could read with the request, 'Read this,' he replied, 'I cannot, for it is sealed' (Is. 29:11). Ezekiel, on the other hand, had a vision in which 'a written scroll' was spread out before him. It was written, like the scroll seen by St. John, 'on the front and on the back', but, unlike St. John's scroll, was unsealed and unrolled, and seen to be filled with 'words of lamentation and mourning and woe' (Ezk. 2:9f.). The contents of the scroll in the passage before us would prove to be not dissimilar. Placed **in the right hand** of the enthroned Lord God, it is being held forth for someone to take and to open and to read what it says (*cf.* the hand stretched out, Ezk. 2:9).

And I saw a mighty angel proclaiming with a loud voice, Who is worthy to open the scroll and to loose its seals? And no one in heaven or on earth or under the earth was able to open the scroll or to look into it. And I wept much because no one was found worthy to open the scroll or to look into it (5:2–4).

This particular **angel** is perceived to be **mighty** here because he makes a proclamation *with a loud voice* to the world at large (for other manifest-ations of strength in angels see 10:1–3 and 18:21) as he offers the invitation, *Who is worthy to open the scroll and to loose its seals?* But there is no response to the invitation because *no one* in the whole of creation, *in heaven or on earth or under the earth*, not a single person *was able* to unseal and *look into* the scroll. This tragic inability was attributable not to lack of physical strength but to moral incompetence. No one was able to open the scroll because no one was *worthy* to do so; and this unworthiness is the evil consequence of sinfulness. The univer-sality of human sinfulness, which is a pervasive theme of Scripture, is forcefully set forth by St. Paul in Romans 3:9ff., where he insists that 'there is none righteous, no not one' and that 'all have sinned and fall short of the glory of God'. It is no wonder that St. John *wept much*, for there is nothing more deplorable and more calamitous in the story of mankind than our total unworthiness as sinful creatures in the presence of our Maker. Nothing is more lamentable than the fact that by our own ungodliness we have deprived ourselves of all worthiness.

> *And one of the elders said to me, Do not weep; behold, the Lion of the tribe of Judah, the Root of David, has overcome, and so is able to open the scroll and its seven seals* (5:5).

The weeping Apostle is addressed by *one of the elders*, who as such is representative of the redeemed of mankind (see on 4:4 above), and who is presumably the same elder that speaks to him in 7:13 below. Bidding St. John to cease weeping, he points him to the incarnate Son, now enthroned in glory, who *has overcome* the enemy and, being alone without sin, is alone worthy to unseal the scroll. In him the human tragedy has been turned to triumph. All weeping ceases when we look away from our defeated and unworthy selves and put our trust in him through whom all tears are wiped away (7:17; 21:4; Heb. 2:14; 4:15).

The dignity of the victorious Lord is defined in a double title. Firstly his designation as *the Lion of the tribe of Judah* denotes his oneness with our human nature by virtue of the incarnation. It defines a human lineage (*cf.* Heb. 7:14). The tribe of Judah was the tribe of David from whom the kingly line proceeded and to whom the promise was given of a son the throne of whose kingdom would last for ever (2 Sa. 7:13, 16). Subsequently, Isaiah had prophesied concerning the Son who was to be given, who would occupy the throne of David, and whose kingdom would be established everlastingly (Is. 9:6f.). And when the time of his birth arrived there arrived also the fulfilment of the ancient promise. Thus the archangel assured Mary the mother of Jesus: 'He will be great, and will be called the Son of the Most High; and the Lord God will give to him the throne of his father David, . . . and of his kingdom there will be no end' (Lk. 1:32f.). Likewise John the Baptist's father Zechariah

praised God for having 'raised up a horn of salvation for us in the
of his servant David, as he spoke by the mouth of his holy pro~ .~~
from of old' (Lk. 1:68–70). Jacob, when blessing his sons, spoke of Judah
as 'a lion's whelp' (Gn. 49:9). As 'the Lion of Judah', Jesus Christ is the
concentration and the consummation of all that this appellation implies.
As The Lion in an absolute sense he is the true King who is paramount
over all.

But, secondly, there is also his designation as **the Root of David**,
which implies that he who came after David was also *before* him; and this
is a pointer to his pre-existence as the eternal Son of God. To the same
effect the prophet Isaiah had proclaimed the advent of him who is 'the
root of Jesse', David's father (Is. 11:10), and who yet was to 'come forth a
shoot from the stump of Jesse' (Is. 11:1). In short, the incarnation is the
event whereby the Root of David becomes the Lion of Judah, or the Root
of Jesse becomes the Shoot of Jesse. The two truths of this double title
are strikingly juxtaposed in the interchange between Jesus and his
critics, to whom, when they asked, 'You are not yet fifty years old and
have you seen Abraham?', he responded, 'Truly, truly, I say to you,
before Abraham was, I am' (Jn. 8:57f.). He who came forth from Bethlehem to rule is he 'whose origin is from of old' (Mi.5:2; *cf.* Rom. 1:3f.;
Heb. 7:14). Truly God and truly man, the incarnate Son is uniquely able
to say of himself, 'I am the root and the offspring of David' (see 22:16
below), and he alone is worthy and *able to open the scroll and its seven
seals.*

> *And in the midst of the throne and of the four living creatures and
> in the midst of the elders I saw a Lamb standing as though it had
> been slain, with seven horns and seven eyes, which are the seven
> Spirits of God sent forth into all the earth (5:6).*

The description of the Lamb as being *in the midst* means that he is the
central figure on whom the attention of all is focused. The glorified
Redeemer is frequently spoken of as the *Lamb* in this book. It is a
designation that is grounded in the sacrificial typology of the Old Testament, with particular reference to the passover lamb of Exodus 12 (*cf.*
1 Cor. 5:7, 'Christ our passover [lamb] has been sacrificed') and the
sacrificial lamb in the Aaronic system symbolizing the innocent and
unblemished victim offered up for sinners. This significance is classically
expressed in Isaiah 53 – a passage that informs the redemptive teaching
of the New Testament – in which it is said of the Lord's Servant that 'the
Lord has laid on him the iniquity of us all' and that he is 'like a lamb that
is led to the slaughter' (Is. 53:6f.). It explains the mind of John the Baptist
when, on the appearance of Jesus to commence his ministry, he proclaimed: 'Behold, the Lamb of God who takes away the sin of the world'
(Jn. 1:29). It is also behind St. Peter's assurance to dispersed Christians

that they were ransomed 'with the precious blood of Christ, like that of a lamb without blemish and without spot' (1 Pet. 1:18f.). As perceived, the Lamb was *as though slain*, that is, bearing the marks of a violent death, in token that the cross of Calvary is the place and the moment of atonement and reconciliation between God and man. Yet the Lamb is *standing*, that is, no longer dead but alive, no longer entombed but risen and glorified, in accordance with the self-attestation of 1:18: 'I am . . . the Living One; and I was dead, and behold, I am alive for evermore'.

The Lamb, moreover, has *seven horns.* In the Old Testament horns are a symbol of strength (*cf.* for example, Dt. 33:17; Ps. 18:2; 1 Ki. 22:11). The seven horns here denote divine power, in other words, omnipotence. Thus the risen Jesus announced to his apostles: 'All authority in heaven and on earth has been given to me' (Mt. 28:18). And the *seven eyes* which the Lamb has signify his divine omniscience: nothing is hid from him, for he sees and knows all (*cf.* the repeated 'I know . . .' in the seven letters of chapters 2 and 3), with the penetrating gaze of him whose eyes are like a flame of fire (1:14; 2:18; 19:12). But there is, further, the identification of the seven eyes of the Lamb as *the seven Spirits of God*, that is, the divine Spirit who is the Holy Spirit (as in 1:4 above). For it is the Holy Spirit, who is also the Spirit of Jesus Christ (Acts 16:7; Rom. 8:9), the Son of God (Gal. 4:6), that knows the deep things of God and reveals them to us, thus conforming the regenerate mind to the mind of Christ (1 Cor. 2:10–16).

The explanation that the seven eyes are the seven Spirits *sent forth into all the earth* recalls the mention by the prophet Zechariah of the seven eyes of the Lord 'which range through the whole earth' (Zc. 4:10). The reference in St. John's vision is not simply to the Holy Spirit's all-seeing omnipresence or ubiquity, but more specifically to the universal outpouring of the Holy Spirit at Pentecost in fulfilment of the Son's promise to send the Holy Spirit (Lk. 14:49; Jn. 15:26; 16:7), in whose power his disciples would be his witnesses 'to the uttermost part of the earth' (Acts 1:8).

It should not be thought incongruous for the Lord to be called both the Lion and the Lamb: the former title depicts the power and authority of the Son, the latter his humility and self-offering. Even a combination of similes can only begin to convey the profound truth of his person and his incarnation and his saving work on our behalf.

> *And he went and took the scroll from the right hand of him who was seated on the throne* (5:7).

The Lamb, incarnate, unstained by sin, slain, alive again, and glorified, alone is worthy and able to take the closely sealed scroll from the Father.

> *And when he had taken the scroll the four living creatures and the twenty-four elders fell down before the Lamb, each holding a harp*

and golden bowls full of fragrances, which are the prayers of the saints (5:8).

This scene indicates the prostration of all creation in adoration and gratitude before the Lamb. Each of the elders is **holding a harp**, the instrument whose music was associated with the offering of praise to God (*cf*. Ps. 33:2; 43:4; 150:3), **and golden bowls** (the plural should be understood as distributive, equivalent to 'each a golden bowl') **full of fragrances** such as are released by the burning of incense. These fragrances, St. John observes, are **the prayers of the saints.** In the ceremonial of the tabernacle, and later the temple, every morning and evening fragrant spice was burned on the altar of incense, which, located in the Holy Place, was overlaid with gold, to provide 'a perpetual incense before the Lord' (Ex. 30:1–8). In this way the prayer of God's people ascending like an acceptable fragrance was symbolized. The psalmist's petition, 'let my prayer be counted as incense before thee', expressed his desire to find acceptance with God (Ps. 141:2). So also for the people as a whole, the time of incense was the time of prayer (*cf*. Lk. 1:10, 'The whole multitude of the people were praying outside [the Holy Place] at the hour of incense'). That the prayers of the saints as they strive and suffer on this earthly pilgrimage are pleasing to their Heavenly Father, who lovingly cares for them, is not to be doubted; but in this vision the golden bowls are filled with the fragrant prayers of the church of the redeemed in glory. It would be wrong, however, to insist on making a rigid distinction. The glory revealed to St. John is also a glory yet to be revealed, in that he is still a pilgrim on this earth (*cf*. Rom. 8:18; 1 Jn. 3:2). He witnesses the fulfilment without yet himself being fully part of it. What he sees is reality in the truest sense; yet for him the proleptic aspect of the revelation is, for the time being, unavoidable. So our prayers hereafter in the glory of the new creation are preceded by our prayers here and now in the creation which, in its present state, groans together with us for 'the liberty of the glory of the children of God' (Rom. 8:19–22).

And they sing a new song, saying, You are worthy to take the scroll and to open its seals, for you were slain and with your blood you purchased men for God from every tribe and tongue and people and nation, and you made them a kingdom and priests to our God, and they shall reign on earth (5:9–10).

The **new song** is a eulogy of the Lamb whose worthiness to **take the scroll and open its seals** has been established through his blood-shedding for the redemption of mankind. Exhortations to sing a new song to the Lord, whether for his unfailing goodness or at times of marvellous deliverance and joyful celebration, are familiar to us in the

Old Testament (see, for example, Ps. 33:3, 40:3; 96:1; 98:1; 144:9; 149:1; Is. 42:10). The praise of the Lamb is new not just at the beginning (so to speak) of eternity, but throughout eternity. It is a song that will never grow old, because the wonder and joy of this salvation will never pall, because, indeed, in the new heaven and earth no one and nothing becomes old. Newness is the hallmark of the renewed creation in which there is no staleness, no slowing down, and no wearing out. The Lord's redeemed people are evermore new creatures for whom the new has come (2 Cor. 5:17). As citizens of the new Jerusalem they hear the Lord's new name (2:17; 21:1f.), and they rejoice for ever in the realization of the Creator's proclamation, 'Behold, I make all things new!' (21:5). This newness is both the restoration of the newness of creation as it first came from the hand of God and, what is more, the enhancement of that newness with the transcendental glory for which it was designed and predestined.

The purpose of the Son's incarnation was that he might be *slain* as a lamb. Bethlehem leads to and is the means to Calvary, just as the Christian year proceeds from Christmas to Good Friday. It was at the cost of his own blood, vicariously shed for us on the cross, that the Lord *purchased* our redemption. It is a worldwide redemption embracing men, women, and children *from every tribe and tongue and people and nation* (as is not only plain from the comprehensive 'every' but is also implicit in the fourfold classification; see also 7:9, 10:11, 11:9, 13:7, 14:6, 17:15, and the comment of 4:6 above). This redemptive purchasing is indeed for us – as the Nicene Creed says, 'for us men and our salvation'; and it is purchasing by God. But it is also *for God*, since it is the means whereby God brings us back to himself and effects the fulfilment of all his purposes as the Creator of the universe. Bought with this price, then, the redeemed are not their own; their true self-fulfilment is to glorify God (1 Cor. 6:19f.). In accord with what St. John records here, St. Peter affirms that the price of our redemption was 'precious blood, as of a lamb without blemish and without spot' (1 Pet. 1:18f.). Moreover, rescued from their sinful fallenness, the Lord's redeemed people are exalted to the height of honour that is their true destiny in Christ, the dominion, namely, of *a kingdom* and the service of *priests* (see comments on 1:6 above; *cf.* 20:6). In the new creation there will be no falling short of the glory of God (*cf.* Rom. 3:23) and no idleness or aimlessness or lack of vocation.

The assurance is given, further, regarding the redeemed, that *they shall reign on earth.* Though the life and the glory of the world to come are not seldom described as being 'in heaven' and 'heavenly' (*cf.*, for example, 'our citizenship is in heaven', Phil. 3:20; the 'heavenly kingdom', 2 Tim. 4:18; a 'heavenly country', Heb. 11:16), the future of redeemed mankind is not one in which the earth is discarded or eliminated. As the earth is an integral part of God's creation, the renewal of creation includes the new earth as well as the new heaven (21:1). In the world to come man, who was created in the image of God to have dominion on earth (Gn. 1:26ff.), will at last attain to the realization of his true and destined potential as, responsibly reigning on the earth, he joyfully exercises the faculties bestowed on him to the glory of the Creator and in perfect harmony with the divine will.

> *And as I looked I heard the voice of many angels around the throne and the living creatures and the elders, and their number was myriads of myriads and thousands of thousands, saying with a loud voice, Worthy is the Lamb who was slain to receive power and wealth and wisdom and might and honour and glory and blessing (5:11–12).*

Added to the praise of the created order and of redeemed mankind is the loud music of the angelic host, whose number, as the language implies, is beyond calculation. Thus in Hebrews 12:22 the beneficiaries of the new covenant are said to have come 'to the city of the living God, the heavenly Jerusalem, and to myriads of angels'. The Lamb, already hymned as worthy to unseal the scroll, is now acclaimed by the choir of angels as worthy to receive all the majestic attributes that belong to God alone. The sevenfold form of these attributes, **power and wealth and wisdom and might and honour and glory and blessing**, is itself a pointer to the deity of the Lamb (as also in 7:12 below).

> *And I heard every creature in the heaven and on the earth and under the earth and in the sea, saying, To him who is seated on the throne and to the Lamb be the blessing and the honour and the glory and the might for ever and ever. And the four living creatures said, Amen, and the elders fell down and worshipped (5:13–14).*

The homage of praise and worship is offered by every created being, each with its ordered place and function in the harmony of the whole, **to him who is seated on the throne**, that is, to God the Creator of all, **and to the Lamb**, that is, to the incarnate Son in whom God is the Redeemer. The fourfold structure of the homage serves to emphasize its universality: **blessing** and **honour** and **glory** and **might**. The concluding **Amen** is the confirming utterance of all creation under the representation of the four living creatures (*cf.* 3:14 and comment there), while the elders prostrated in worship represent the redeemed of mankind, who, formed in the divine image, are the creatures uniquely equipped to approach God in a personal, spiritual, and rational relationship (see comments on 4:4ff. above, regarding the significance of the elders and living creatures).

2. THE FIRST SEAL OPENED, 6:1–2

> *And I saw when the Lamb opened the first of the seven seals, and I heard one of the four living creatures say, as with a voice of thunder, Come!* (6:1).

The Lamb, who alone is worthy to do so (5:5, 9), now begins to unseal the scroll, and each seal is undone in turn. Presumably there is a progressive disclosure of the contents as the successive openings take place; that is, a disclosure that corresponds to the particular vision that accompanies each act of unsealing. The first four unsealings are followed by a summons uttered, in turn, by each of the four living creatures, *'Come!'*, and each summons is followed by the appearance of a horseman. To whom the summons is addressed is not stated, but it seems most suitable as an address to each of the riders, who thereupon enter the scene, one for each of the first four sealings. This interpretation is confirmed, if anything, by the information that the first living creatures spoke *as with a voice of thunder* (as, it may be assumed, the other three did also, though this is said only of the first); for such a voice, ominous, alarming, impossible to disregard, befits the calamitous nature of each consecutive vision. This makes sense of the numerical correspondence between the four horsemen and the four living creatures who each thunder out, 'Come!'

> *And I saw, and behold, a white horse, and he who was seated on it had a bow, and a crown was given to him, and he went out conquering and to conquer* (6:2).

Each of the four horses associated with the opening of the first four seals has its own distinctive colour. The prophet Zechariah describes a vision of four chariots, each drawn by horses of a different colour, which were sent out to the north, south, east, and west to patrol the earth (Zc. 6:1ff.); but, apart from the respective colours of the horses, there is no close parallel between that vision and this. Upon the opening of the first seal the first horseman comes forward, and he is seated on *a white horse.* Many commentators have wished to identify this horseman with Christ, who in 19:11ff. appears as the all-conquering Lord seated on a white horse. This connection is at first sight attractive, but it is inappropriate to the context of the passage before us. The horseman here is one of a sequence of four, all bearing weapons or powers of death and destruction as enemies of the Creator, and all unnamed except for the fourth who is a personification of death. There the horseman is alone and unique and so amply described that his identity is not in doubt. Here each successive horseman is linked to developments that are catastrophic for the earth's inhabitants: tyranny, bloodshed, famine, death (verses 2, 4, 6, 8). The **bow** which the first horseman carries is a symbol of violence, the **crown** he is given signifies despotic rule, and the **white** colour of his horse betokens conquest, while his going forth **conquering and to conquer** expresses his lust for power and world domination.

3. THE SECOND SEAL OPENED, 6:3–4

And when he opened the second seal I heard the second living creature say, Come! And another horse, bright red, came forth; and it was given to him who was seated on it to take away peace from the earth, so that people should slay one another; and a great sword was given to him (6:3–4).

With the opening of the second seal and the issuing of the second summons, 'Come!', the second horseman appears, riding on a **bright red** horse, a colour that is suggestive of bloodshed. This rider wields **a great sword**, a weapon that typifies lethal violence and his ability **to take away peace from the earth.** But it is important to notice that it is only because it is given or permitted to him that he is able to do so – given, that is, by God. The blood-thirsty terrorist or warmonger may seem to be all-powerful as he robs people of peace and security and causes them to engage in killing and destruction; but the control of human affairs remains in God's hands. The agent of disorder and anarchy is, as it were, on a tether which sets limits to his activity, and it is God, the righteous Judge, who at last will destroy the destroyers of the earth (11:18).

4. THE THIRD SEAL OPENED, 6:5–6

And when he opened the third seal I heard the third living creature say, Come! And I saw, and behold, a black horse, and he who was seated on it had a balance in his hand. And I heard what sounded like a voice in the midst of the four living creatures, saying, A measure of wheat for a denarius and three measures of barley for a denarius, and do not harm the oil and the wine (6:5–6).

In response to the summons that accompanies the opening of the third seal the third horseman enters on the scene. The colour of his horse is **black**, a colour that symbolizes famine and dearth. In his hand he carries **a balance** or pair of scales, which, in the Old Testament, is most commonly mentioned in connection with injunctions to weigh out just measures of food (*cf.* Lev. 19:36; Pr. 16:11; Ezk. 45:10; Ho. 12:7; Am. 8:5; Mi. 6:11). When St. John says that he heard *what sounded like a voice*, the note of uncertainty relates to the identity of the speaker, not to the words that were spoken, which, it is evident, were readily discernible. The Apostle is able only to declare that the source of what he heard was *in the midst of the four living creatures.* It is probably reading too much into the text to interpret this information as denoting 'the protest of Nature against the horrors of famine' (Swete); yet there is the possibility that the relating of the voice to the four living creatures, though only in their midst, not directly as the speakers, may carry this overtone.

The *measure* weighed out in the balance here was approximately the equivalent of a dry quart, corresponding to a labourer's daily ration; the *denarius* was the labourer's daily wage. Because it was a grain superior to barley, wheat cost three times as much. The situation in view is one of dearth and scarcity, and the prices mentioned are famine prices. As with the previous horseman, however, there are limits beyond which this rider is not allowed to go. Grain will not become unobtainable, and he is forbidden to *harm the oil and the wine*; for grain, oil, and wine constituted the staple diet of the population and as such were necessities for survival. Times like this of scarcity should have the beneficial effect of inducing people to turn away from themselves and to put their trust in the Lord, thus bringing good out of this horseman's malign influence. The limitations placed on his operations are an indication that while the day of grace continues it is not too late to repent and believe in the gospel.

5. THE FOURTH SEAL OPENED, 6:7–8

> *And when he opened the fourth seal I heard the voice of the fourth living creature say, Come! And I saw, and behold, a pale horse, and the name of him who was seated on it was Death, and Hades followed with him. And power was given to them over the fourth part of the earth, to kill with sword and with famine and with pestilence and by the wild beasts of the earth* (6:7–8).

With the opening by the Lamb of the scroll's fourth seal and the utterance of the summons, 'Come!', by the fourth living creature the fourth horse appears. Its *pale* colour is descriptive of the ashen grey pallor of a dead body or of a person in a state of extreme fear. Appropriately, the name of its rider is *Death*, and this rider is closely followed by *Hades.* The two have already been spoken of as companions in 1:18, where the Lord who had experienced death and is alive for evermore has the keys, that is, is the master of Death and Hades. They hold no terror for him who by his own death and resurrection has 'destroyed death and brought life and immortality to light through the gospel' (2 Tim. 1:10; *cf.* Heb. 2:14f.). There will, then, be no place for Death and Hades in the new heaven and earth. For, under the judgment of him who holds the keys, they will be consigned to 'the second death', which is none other than the death of Death and Hades (see 20:13f. below).

The lethal **power** exercised here by Death and Hades is power they have been **given**, that is to say, permitted to them by the One who wields supreme and absolute power. Ultimate power does not belong to Death and Hades, notwithstanding all appearances to the contrary. And once again, the power permitted is strictly limited. It extends only **over the fourth part of the earth**, and it is, in effect, a continuation and intensification of the calamitous powers of the preceding horsemen, the power **to kill** not only **with sword and with famine** but now also **with pestilence**[1] **and by the wild beasts of the earth.** The four afflictions mentioned here correspond to what the Lord God calls in Ezekiel his 'four sore acts of judgment' (Ezk. 14:12ff., 21; see also Ezk. 5:17; 33:27ff.; 34:25ff.; Lv. 26:25f.; Dt. 32:24f.; Je. 21:6f.). Catastrophic events of the kind mentioned here, which are restrained within certain limits, should be understood as sore acts of judgment which ungodly or apostate communities bring down upon themselves, and which at the same time are warnings to repent before it is too late and foretastes of total judgment yet to come.

6. THE FIFTH SEAL OPENED, 6:9–11

And when he opened the fifth seal I saw under the altar the souls of those who had been slain for the word of God and for the witness they had borne; and they cried out with a loud voice, saying, O Sovereign Lord, holy and true, how long before you judge and avenge our blood on those who dwell upon the earth? (6:9–10).

When the Lamb opens the fifth seal a quite different scene is disclosed. No horseman comes forward, nor is the spectacle again one of unrest and violence on earth. St. John is now given a vision of **the souls** of those who had suffered martyrdom **for the word of God and for the witness they had borne.** For the same reason he himself was an exile on the island of Patmos (1:2, 9); indeed, this is the only authentic ground

---

[1] Literally 'death' (*thanatos*) which should be understood as meaning 'pestilence' here, in line with a number of Old Testament passages where it is the rendering in the Septuagint (Greek version) of the Hebrew *deber*, 'pestilence'.

and motivation of all suffering that can be described as truly Christian (*cf.* 12:11, 17; 20:4). These martyrs had been *slain* by the enemies of the gospel, but their persons lived on. They were in themselves proof that men may kill the body but, as their Master had assured his disciples, cannot kill the soul; their persecutors, if unrepentant, would learn to their cost that God is able to kill both soul and body in hell (Mt. 10:28).

St. John's assertion that he *saw* these souls does not raise or answer the question about the visibility of disembodied souls. Such a question is entirely beside the point. The Apostle is simply granted an insight or perception that goes beyond the limits of what is ordinarily known to us. Presumably, for the purpose of this particular vision, these souls of the martyrs were made visible to him as persons.[1] Furthermore, when he says that he saw them *under the altar*, this should not be taken to mean that there is a literal altar in the heavenly realm. The altar of sacrifice in the Mosaic system, with its priesthood and offerings, pointed forward, typologically, to the altar of the cross, where Christ, both High Priest and Victim, offered himself up for us sinners. Because of the perfection and total sufficiency of that offering the cross is evermore the Christian altar, never to be superseded. It is, moreover, an altar on earth, not in heaven, though, as we have seen, the risen and glorified Son bears the scars of his self-offering. He is revealed to the seer as a lamb that had been slain (5:6). The saving effect of his atoning death is as permanent as he is himself. The altar under which the souls of the martyrs are seen is best understood as the symbol of their own self-offering. This is not in any sense a repetition of Christ's unique and unrepeatable self-sacrifice, but a response of gratitude and devotion to him who of his own will and from pure love shed his blood for their redemption. Thus the Apostle Paul, who had written to the believers in Rome that to offer their bodies 'a living sacrifice, holy, acceptable to God', was their 'logical service' (Rom. 12:1), affirmed his readiness to be sacrificed when the hour of his martyrdom was at hand (2 Tim. 4:6). For the souls of St. John's vision, then, the altar under which they are placed is the emblem of their martyrdom. A literalistic interpretation is incompatible with St. John's declaration concerning the heavenly city of the new Jerusalem: 'I saw no temple in it, for its temple is the Lord God the Almighty and the Lamb' (21:22).

The souls of those who have been martyred for their faithful witness to Christ and his gospel cry out to their *Sovereign Lord* for the execution of judgment not merely on those by whom they were slain but, more widely, *on those who dwell upon the earth* – that is to say, on the ungodly in general whose opposition to the truth and rejection of grace fuel the flames of persecution and give strength to the hands of those

---

[1] The Greek noun (*psychai*) of which 'souls' is a translation is also used in the New Testament in the sense of 'persons' (*cf.*, for example, Acts 2:41; 27:37; 1 Pet. 3:20)

who actually do the slaying. The shedding of innocent blood always cries out for justice, and the blood of the martyrs, no less than the blood of Abel, cries out to the Lord for vindication (Gn. 4:10). But at the same time the martyrs are secure in the knowledge that the blood of Jesus, shed for their eternal redemption, speaks something better than the blood of Abel (Heb. 12:24). They, or their souls, are not vengeful or frustrated or turned in upon themselves, as though concerned for their own persons. How could they be, who have gladly given themselves up to death for the sake of their Lord; who, like St. Stephen, the first Christian martyr, prayed, after the example of Christ himself, for his murderers (Acts 7:60); and, like the aged Polycarp and countless others, blessed God for the honour of being brought to the day and hour when they could seal their witness with their blood? Nor are they unhappy and insecure. How could they be, who are at home with the Lord (2 Cor. 5:8; Phil. 1:21, 23) and whose state is one of blessedness (Rev. 14:13)? Since unholiness and falsehood are a rebellious affront to their Lord, who is *holy and true*, they desire that he should purge the earth of the ungodliness and violence by which it is defiled. They also long for the final judgment, which will be in absolute accordance with holiness and truth; and they look forward eagerly to being clothed with their resurrection bodies which will be conformed to the body of Christ's glory (Phil. 3:21) and to serving him in the renewed creation that will be free from all evil and injustice (Rev. 21:1ff.; 22:1ff.; 1 Pet. 1:18f.; 2 Pet. 3:13).

> *And a white robe was given to each of them, and they were told to rest a little longer, until the number of their fellow servants and their brethren, who were to be killed as they themselves had been, should be complete (6:11).*

The *white robe* given to each of these souls of the martyrs is a symbol of purity, and particularly of the absolute purity and righteousness of Christ with which his saints are invested (*cf.* 3:4f., 18; 4:4; 7:9, 13; 19:8, 14). It signifies also the martyr's wholeness in Christ and conformity to his likeness whose garments of glory are 'white as light' (Mt. 17:2; Mk. 9:3; Lk. 9:29; 2 Cor. 3:18).

The hour for the consummation of their salvation anticipated by these souls has not yet struck, however, and they are enjoined *to rest a little longer.* This is an injunction that indicates that theirs is the blessedness of those who, having died in the Lord, now rest from their labours (14:13; see comments on preceding verse). Their present rest must continue for a while longer, it is explained, because *the number* of their fellow believers who are also to suffer martyrdom is not yet *complete.* This implies not only that more of Christ's faithful witnesses will be killed, but also, that in the case of martyrdoms as of all things else, God is in control. The determination as to when their number is complete is in his hands. According to human suppositions and outward appearances the deaths of the martyrs are in the hands of those who persecute them; but the true reality is the purpose of God and his sovereign overruling. The book of Revelation shows that martyrs have a special importance in the mind and the plan of God (*cf.* 1:9; 2:13; 3:8; 7:14; 11:3ff.; 12:11; 14:12f.; 20:4). A martyrdom, whereby one of the Lord's faithful witnesses is silenced in death, looks like a defeat for God and a damaging setback for the church; but it leads, over and over again, to the progress of the gospel and to an increase of power and blessing for the Lord's people. Hence Tertullian's famous dictum, that 'the blood of the martyrs is the seed of the church'. So also, Nicholas Ridley wrote to John Bradford, as they both awaited their own martyrdom: 'Where the martyrs for Christ's sake shed their blood and lost their lives, oh what wondrous things hath Christ afterward wrought to his glory and confirmation of their doctrine!'[1]

7. THE SIXTH SEAL OPENED, 6:12–17

And I saw when he opened the sixth seal, and there was a great earthquake; and the sun became black as sackcloth, and the full moon became like blood, and the stars of the heaven fell to the earth as a fig tree sheds its unripe fruit when shaken by a strong wind; and the heaven was withdrawn like a scroll being rolled up, and every mountain and island was removed from its place (6:12–14).

The opening of the sixth seal sets in motion the stupendous events that accompany the close of the age. The symbolical language is characteristic of apocalyptic literature which graphically depicts the terror of God's wrath and judgment. Thus in 2 Samuel 22:8 we read that 'the earth reeled and rocked; the foundations of the heavens trembled and quaked, because he was angry. . . .'; and in the prophecy of Joel the Lord declares: 'I will give portents in the heavens and on the earth, blood and fire and columns of smoke. The sun shall be turned to darkness, and the moon to blood, before the great and terrible day of the Lord comes' (Joel 2:30–31). Through Haggai the ultimate shaking of the world was foretold: 'For thus says the Lord of hosts: Once again, in a little while, I will shake the heavens and the earth and the sea and the dry land; and I will shake all nations' (Hg. 2:6f). This is a passage which relates the cosmic shaking to the shaking of human society, so that only what is genuine and true will be left standing. Accordingly, it is cited in

---

[1] *The Works of Nicholas Ridley* (Cambridge, 1841), p. 378.

Hebrews 12:26 with this comment: 'This phrase, "Yet once more", signifies the removal of the things that are shaken, ... in order that those things which are not shaken may remain.'

The cataclysmic shaking is likened to that of *a great earthquake* which reduces human structures to rubble. Only what is of God stands firm. The sun becoming *black as sackcloth* (literally 'sackcloth made of hair', which is 'black' because the hair is that of black goats) indicates the total lostness of the impenitent in the darkness of their unbelief as this day of grace comes to an end. The blood-red appearance of the moon portends the horror of carnage and the falling of the stars the dislocation of all that has been regarded as stable. The *unripe fruit* of the *fig tree* denotes the winter figs which have no prospect of maturing and are easily shaken loose when *a strong wind* blows, a simile of the sterile futility of all effort that is unblessed by God and exposed to his judgment. The concept of *the heaven* withdrawing *like a scroll* that is being *rolled up* conveys the sense of the most chilling catastrophe, as also does the imagery of mountains and islands being removed from what have always seemed to be their positions of permanence.

This perspective is precisely that not only of the ancient prophetic warnings concerning the Day of the Lord (*cf.* Is. 34:4: 'All the host of heaven shall rot away, and the skies roll up like a scroll. All their host shall fall, as leaves fall from the vine, like leaves falling from the fig tree'; also Je. 4:23ff., Na. 1:5, *etc.*) but also that of Christ himself. For he declared: 'The sun will be darkened and the moon will not give its light, and the stars will be falling from heaven and the powers in the heavens will be shaken; and then they will see the Son of Man coming in clouds with great power and glory' (Mk. 13:24ff.; also Mt. 24:29ff.; Lk. 21:25ff.). The language depicts the terror that will be experienced by the ungodly when the hour of final judgment strikes, as the verses that follow dramatically confirm.

> *And the kings of the earth and the great men and the generals and the rich and the strong, and every one, bond and free, hid themselves in the caves and rocks of the mountains; and they say to the mountains and rocks, Fall on us and hide us from the face of him who is seated on the throne and from the wrath of the Lamb; for the great day of their wrath has come, and who is able to stand?* (6:15–17).

The judgment of God is absolutely just. There is no respect of persons with him (Rom. 2:11; Acts 10:34; Eph. 6:9; Col. 3:25). To be wealthy or powerful confers no right to claim special favour. Divine judgment overtakes all, great and small. There is no escaping it or hiding from it. All the desperate attempts to do so will prove utterly futile. To be crushed by the mountains and rocks will seem far preferable to meeting with the Creator and his judgment which none can withstand. The judgment of *him who is seated on the throne* coincides with *the wrath of the Lamb*, for the Father and the Son are one both in Deity and in will (*cf*. Jn. 1:1; 10:30; 4:34; 6:38). Ungodliness and unbelief are compounded of rebellion against the Creator (Rom. 1:18ff.) and rejection of the grace of the gospel that flows to us from the cross where the Lamb offered himself up as the propitiation for our sins (1 Jn. 2:1f.). This day of final judgment is *the great day*, the last day of these last days, the day of reckoning which is the prelude to the establishment of the new heaven and earth in which, purged from all sin and defilement, peace and perfection and righteousness will prevail everlastingly (ch. 21:1ff.; 2 Pet. 3:13; Is. 65:17ff.).

The utter hopelessness in that dread day of those who have rejected the grace of the gospel is expressed in the despairing question: '*and who is able to stand?*' This is the damning question-mark that robs every ungodly life of ultimate meaning. The dark horror of the death of the unregenerate is not simply the dying but the awareness of coming judgment (Heb. 9:27; 10:27, 31). As Ezra prayed: 'Behold, we are before thee in our guilt, for none can stand before thee because of this' (Ezr. 9:15; *cf*. Jb. 41:10; Pss. 1:5; 76:7; 130:3). The same question was uttered by the prophets as they warned the people of impending judgment: 'Who can stand before his indignation? Who can endure the heat of his anger?' (Na. 1:6), and 'Who can endure the day of his coming and who can stand when he appears?' (Mal. 3:2). But, as Jeremiah declared, the Lord promises mercy and salvation to those who repent and believe: 'If you return, I will restore you, and you shall stand before me' (Je. 15:19). The appalling tragedy of the unrepentant multitude of persons, great and small, seen by St. John in this vision, is that the day of grace has come to an end; the great day of divine judgment has overtaken them; and it is now too late to turn and believe.

8. INTERVENING VISION, 7:1-17

A. *The 144,000 sealed, 7:1-8*

> *After this I saw four angels standing at the four corners of the earth, holding the four winds of the earth, so that no wind should blow on the earth or on the sea or against any tree (7:1).*

The first six seals have now been opened. Before the loosing of the seventh and last seal (8:1) the visions described in this chapter intervene. Later on there is a comparable interruption between the blowing of the sixth and seventh trumpets (10:1 – 11:14). Far from being haphazard or out of order, however, the placing of this seventh chapter fulfils a purpose, namely, to demonstrate that in the day of judgment God's people, whose righteousness is in Christ, are kept secure and unscathed, in accordance with the Lord's promise that those who believe have eternal life and will not come into judgment because they have passed from death to life (Jn. 5:24).

As usual in this book, the number four signifies universality; and so **the four corners of the earth** denote the earth as a whole with its four compass directions. At the four corners St. John sees **four angels** with **the four winds** in their control. The ministry of angels seems to have associations with or to be in some way comparable to that of the elements. Hebrews 1:7 quotes Psalm 104:4 to the effect that God makes his angels winds and his servants a flame of fire, apparently with reference to the swiftness and ardour of their service; and later on in Revelation mention is made of 'the angel who has power over fire' (14:18) and of 'the angel of water' (16:5). Here it is angels who have control of the winds, restraining them from blowing destructively on the earth or sea or uprooting trees. The devastating potency of high winds is suggestive of the gale force of divine judgment.

> *And I saw another angel ascending from the rising of the sun, with the seal of the living God; and he called with a loud voice to the four angels to whom it was given to harm the earth and the sea, saying, Do not harm the earth or the sea or the trees until we have sealed the servants of our God on their foreheads* (7:2–3).

From the east another angelic figure now appears holding **the seal of the living God**. This seal, different from the seven seals of chapters 5 and 6 with which the scroll was fastened, is a seal of identification for marking **the servants of our God**; and until this is done the four angels at the four corners of the earth who control the four winds are instructed not to harm earth, sea, and trees by releasing the winds. The ministry of angels has a special concern for those who are the heirs of salvation (Heb. 1:14). The seal stamped **on their foreheads** is plain to see. Ezekiel, in the account of his vision, described 'a man clothed in linen' who was sent by the Lord to 'put a mark upon the foreheads of the men who sigh and groan over all the abominations that are committed' (Ezk. 9:2–4).

The seal, however, is more than a stamp of identification. It is a mark of ownership designating those who are sealed as *God's* servants; a mark of security because being God's they are constantly guarded by him (*cf.* 1 Pet. 1:5); and also a mark of their preciousness to God (just as a treasure used to be sealed). Thus the prophet Malachi wrote of those who fear the Lord: 'They shall be mine, says the Lord of hosts, my special possession on the day when I act, and I will spare them as a man spares his son who serves him' (Mal. 3:16f.). The fact that they have been *sealed* ensures that the servants of God will not be harmed by the gales of his judgment. It is the equivalent of the writing of God's name on those who overcome (3:12; see comments there).

The reality that is symbolized in this vision is the sealing of those who belong to the Lord with the Holy Spirit. The seal of the Spirit is an indelible seal which gives the assurance of total security now and for ever. Accordingly, St. Paul teaches that God 'has sealed us and given us the guarantee of his Spirit in our hearts' (2 Cor. 1:22), and that Christian believers have been 'sealed with the promised Holy Spirit who is the guarantee of our inheritance' (Eph. 1:13f.). He warns the members of the Ephesian church: 'Do not grieve the Holy Spirit of God in whom you were sealed for the day of redemption' (Eph. 4:30); and, in a statement that summarizes the whole significance of this sealing, he encouraged Timothy: 'God's firm foundation stands, bearing this seal: The Lord knows those who are his' (2 Tim. 2:19).

> *And I heard the number of those who were sealed, a hundred and forty-four thousand, sealed out of every tribe of the sons of Israel: twelve thousand sealed from the tribe of Judah, twelve thousand from the tribe of Reuben, twelve thousand from the tribe of Gad, twelve thousand from the tribe of Asher, twelve thousand from the tribe of Naphtali, twelve thousand from the tribe of Manasseh, twelve thousand from the tribe of Simeon, twelve thousand from the tribe of Levi, twelve thousand from the tribe of Issachar, twelve thousand from the tribe of Zebulun, twelve thousand from the tribe of Joseph, twelve thousand sealed from the tribe of Benjamin (7:4–8).*

The number 144,000 stands here for the complete company of the redeemed. As with the numbers elsewhere in this book, it is a symbolical figure, and therefore should not be taken literally. Compounded of twelve times twelve times 1,000, the number twelve represents the twelve patriarchs of Israel (as named in these verses) and also the twelve apostles. The number 1,000 conveys the notion of magnitude and of completeness. Moreover, the number twelve, which is three times four, may be taken as signifying the grace and salvation of the Triune God extended to all the nations in the four quarters of the earth – not just the saints of Old Testament days, but the believers of the periods of both Old and New Testaments, who together constitute 'the Israel of God' (Gal. 6:16; Heb. 11:39f.; 12:22; Gal. 3:29; and see the comment on the twenty-four elders in 4:4 above). This interpretation is confirmed by the later vision in which St. John sees the 144,000 standing with the Lamb on Mount Zion. They have his name and the name of his Father written on their foreheads (which corresponds with the sealing of verses 3ff. here); and they sing a new song which no one can learn 'except the one hundred and forty-four thousand', namely, those who have been 'redeemed from the earth' (14:1, 3). This makes their identity very clear.

B. The white-robed multitude, 7:9–17

After this I looked, and behold, a great multitude which no one could number, from every nation and from all tribes and peoples and tongues, standing before the throne and before the Lamb, clothed in white robes and with palms in their hands (7:9).

The **great multitude** is the vast company of the redeemed, a truly international assemblage (note the fourfold specification: nations, tribes, peoples, tongues, that is, from the four quarters of the earth). This host, symbolically numbered in the preceding verses as 144,000, is, humanly speaking innumerable (**which no one could number**). It is, in fact, the authentic seed of Abraham which, according to God's promise, would be innumerable as the stars of heaven and as the sand of the seashore (Gn. 15:5; 22:17; 26:4; 32:12). They are authentic, though, only by virtue of their being 'one in Christ Jesus' who in a uniquely particular sense is the true seed of Abraham (Gal. 3:6–9, 16, 28f.). They have been brought into the immediate presence of God their Creator and Redeemer, for they are **before the throne**. That is, they are before the Lord God enthroned as sovereign over all, and **before the Lamb**, who is distinct as the incarnate Son now glorified at the right hand of the Majesty on high (Heb. 1:3, 8:1; 10:12; Eph. 1:20ff.), not isolated from but conjoined to the throne.

Moreover, this great concourse is **standing** before the Lord God Almighty, not, however, like that other multitude of the ungodly (in 20:12 below), who receive the Judge's condemnation. Against that there is no standing, and they, as we have seen, will plead with the mountains and rocks to fall on them and hide them 'from the face of him who is seated on the throne and from the wrath of the Lamb', for when 'the great day of their wrath' comes 'who', they ask, 'is able to stand?' (6:16f.). On the contrary, the multitude of the redeemed stand with confidence before their God as those who, justified by divine grace 'through the redemption that is in Christ Jesus' (Rom. 3:24) and sealed with the Holy Spirit (Eph. 1:13; *cf.* verse 3 above), have the assurance that 'there is therefore now no condemnation to those who are in Christ Jesus' (Rom. 8:1). They are also the proof that God 'is able to keep you from falling and to cause you to stand without blemish before the presence of his glory with exceeding joy' (Jude 24). This is the significance of the **white robes** with which they are adorned in token of the spotless purity and righteousness of their Redeemer that covers them (see on verse 14 below), and also of the **palms** which they hold aloft as a symbol of victory and rejoicing. Palm branches were associated with the annual feast of booths under the old covenant which was the occasion for the thanksgiving of the community at the ingathering of the harvest (Lv. 23:39ff.). The presence of the innumerable company of the redeemed before the throne of God is the great ingathering of the eternal harvest (*cf.* Mt. 13:30). As we have seen (3:4f. above), it is the over-comers who will be clad in white garments; and this is the apparel of Christ's bride, the church triumphant, sanctified by him and cleansed from all defilement (19:7-9, Eph. 5:25-27).

> *And they cry out with a loud voice, saying, Salvation belongs to our God who is seated on the throne and to the Lamb (7:10).*

There is no confusion of tongues here, for Babel is a thing of the past and this is a shout of unanimity which is heard as a single voice. Single-mindedly the vast multitude ascribe their salvation to God and the Lamb. They claim no merit or righteousness of their own. The initiative belongs entirely to the God of grace, for, as St. Paul says, 'God shows his love for us in that while we were yet sinners Christ died for us' and in that 'while we were enemies we were reconciled to God by the death of his Son' (Rom. 5:8, 10). From beginning to end *salvation belongs to our God*; it is all from God (2 Cor. 5:18, 21). This is a constantly recurring theme in Scripture. Moses and the people of Israel sang after their crossing of the Red Sea: 'The Lord is my strength and my song, and he has become my salvation' (Ex. 15:2). The psalmist declared that 'the salvation of the righteous is from the Lord' (Ps. 37:39; *cf.* 3:8; 62:7); and through his prophet Isaiah God proclaims: 'I am the Lord, and besides me there is no saviour' (Is. 43:11; *cf.* 12:2; 45:21; Ho. 13:4; Jon. 2:9). Hence also the apostolic insistence that 'there is salvation in no one else' than Jesus Christ who, as the incarnate Son, is the Lamb of God (Acts 4:12) and 'our great God and Saviour' (Tit. 2:13; *cf.* 3:4-7).

> *And all the angels were standing round the throne and round the elders and the four living creatures; and they fell on their faces before the throne and worshipped God, saying, Amen! Blessing and glory and wisdom and thanksgiving and honour and power and might be to our God for ever and ever! Amen (7:11-12).*

The angelic host together with the elders, representative of the redeemed of mankind, and the four living creatures, representative of the renewed creation (see comments above on 4:4ff.), prostrate them-selves in total submission and adoration before God (*cf.* 4:9-11). The sevenfold ascription of their worship signifies that their worship is offered solely to God. That the multitude of the redeemed and the twenty-four elders who represent or symbolize them appear together in the same vision should not be regarded as incongruous. Throughout the book the picture is a composite one, and it is usual for these elders to be associated with the living creatures (the exceptions in 6:1, 6 and 15:7 are explained by the particular circumstances in which they occur). Now St. John sees not only the elders but also the reality that is signified by them.

> *And one of the elders answered, saying to me, Who are these clothed in white robes, and whence have they come?* (7:13)

As though addressing a question in the Apostle's mind, **one of the elders answered**. He answered, indeed, with a question which was precisely the question in St. John's mind concerning the identity and provenance of this white-robed multitude; not that the elder was ignorant of the answer, for he gives it in the next verse; it is his way of preparing the seer to receive the important information he is seeking.

> *And I said to him, Sir, you know. And he said to me, These are they who come out of the great tribulation, and who have washed their robes and made them white in the blood of the Lamb* (7:14).

St. John politely turns the question back to the elder to answer. Despite the brevity of this exchange, the implication is that the Apostle is anxious to receive instruction and is aware that the elder is there to give it. The identity of the great multitude is then communicated: **These are they who come** ('come' being a timeless present indicating the totality of those who come from every generation) **out of the great tribulation**, by which is signified not some particular period of tribulation, as some commentators have supposed, but the awesome totality of tribulation which from century to century has been the experience of the people of God. The perennial hatred of the gospel and the brutal attempts to extinguish its light are unparalleled in history. One has only to recall the sufferings of the saints and prophets of the Old Testament and of the apostles and fathers and reformers and uncounted others in our era, including those who even now are enduring affliction because of the witness they bear to Jesus as their Redeemer and Lord. Such is the company of those who have been 'tortured, refusing to accept deliverance, that they might obtain a better resurrection', who have been 'tested by mockings and scourgings, and chains and imprisonment', who have been 'stoned, sawn in two, put to the sword', and who 'went in sheepskins and goatskins, destitute, afflicted, ill-treated – of whom the world was not worthy – wandering over deserts and mountains and in dens and caves of the earth' (Heb. 11:35–38).

To his followers Jesus has said:

> If the world hates you, you know that it has hated me before hating you. If you were of the world, the world would love its

own, but because you are not of the world, but I chose you out of the world, therefore the world hates you. . . . But they will do all these things to you for my name's sake, because they do not know him who sent me (*Jn. 15:18–21*).

It is in this perspective that the great tribulation of Christ's servants throughout the course of history is to be understood. Nor do such sufferers regard their afflictions as a cause of sorrow and regret. On the contrary, they rejoice that they are counted worthy to suffer dishonour for his name (Acts 5:41), and they know that their brief sufferings are infinitely transcended by the eternal glory that awaits them hereafter (Rom. 8:18, 2 Cor. 4:17; Mt. 5;12).

This great company of the redeemed, St. John is told, had **washed their robes**, indicating that previously their lives had been clothed with defilement and unrighteousness. Just as the prophet lamented: 'We have all become like one who is unclean, and all our righteous deeds are like a polluted garment' (Is. 64:6), and as the psalmist wrote: 'They have all gone astray, they are all alike corrupt' (Ps. 14:3, Rom. 3:9ff.), all without exception are in need of cleansing. And that cleansing is effected by blood – not their own blood, shed, actually or symbolically, in the suffering they endure, for that would be self-righteousness and self-salvation, but the blood of Christ shed vicariously for them on the cross as he bore their sins and died the death due to them. Their robes have been **made white in the blood of the Lamb**. That is the blood by which God reconciles us to himself, 'the blood of Jesus' which 'cleanses us from all sin' (1 Jn. 1:7). This is the foundation of all blessedness and of our standing and acceptance in the presence of God: 'Blessed are those who wash their robes', we read in 22:14, for 'theirs is the right to the tree of life'.

> *Therefore are they before the throne of God, and serve him day and night in his temple; and he who is seated on the throne will shelter them with his presence (7:15).*

As the conjunction **therefore** denotes, it is because they have been cleansed and are clothed with Christ's perfect righteousness, and also have remained steadfast and faithful through all trials and afflictions, that they are **before the throne of God**, that is, in God's immediate presence. Now that at last they are completely pure in heart they see God and behold his face (Mt. 5:8; Rev. 22:4). The expectation of the psalmist, 'As for me, I shall behold thy face in righteousness', is fulfilled (Ps. 17:15); and this expectation should radically affect our conduct in the meantime. 'We know that when he appears we shall be like him, for we shall see him as he is', St. John wrote elsewhere, 'and every one who thus hopes in him purifies himself as he is pure' (1 Jn. 3:2f.; *cf.* 1 Cor. 13:12).

When it is said that this great throng of the redeemed **serve him day** *and night*, the expression 'day and night' is a manner of speaking that means simply 'without ceasing' (as in 4:8 above). Consequently, there is no conflict with the assertion in 22:5 that 'night shall be no more' and that there will be no need of lamp or sun because 'the Lord God will be their light'. The scene is one of perpetual light. With the break of the eternal day all shadows flee, for in God, who is Light, there is no darkness at all (1 Jn. 1:5).

It is *in his temple* that the members of this multitude unceasingly serve God – all of them, without exception, for this temple-service is the full fruition of the priesthood of all believers (see comments on 1:6 above). Again, there is no conflict here with St. John's statement in 21:22 below that he saw no temple in the heavenly city and his explanation that 'the Lord God the Almighty and the Lamb are its temple'. This explanation, rather, actually helps us to interpret this constant service in God's temple as service in his glorious presence. The Greek noun *naos* which is used here and throughout the book of Revelation for 'temple' means the inner shrine or sanctuary, corresponding to the holy of holies, or the holiest place of all, in the wilderness tabernacle and Jerusalem temple of the Old Testament period. By his triumphant ascension our great High Priest, the incarnate Son who is both our sacrificial Lamb and our risen Lord, not only himself entered into the heavenly sanctuary but also opened the way for us into that true holy of holies, which is the glorious presence of God (see Heb. 4:14–16; 10:11–22). This priestly service is already being exercised, though as yet imperfectly, by all believers as they daily offer themselves in gratitude to God and with prayer and praise, as those who are 'created in Christ Jesus', perform those good works that he has prepared for them to walk in (Rom. 12:1; Eph. 2:10; Heb. 13:15).

The presence of the Lord God as he dwells with his people is the guarantee of their complete security, as it is also the attainment of that perfect relationship of personal harmony which binds the Creator to those who are created, and in Christ re-created, in his image. In this dwelling together in reconciliation the age-old promise, 'I will make my abode among you . . . And I will walk among you, . . . and you shall be my people' (Lv. 26:11f.) finds its fulfilment; for it is reaffirmed in the terms of the new covenant of which Christ is the Mediator: 'I will make a covenant of peace with them; . . . and will set my sanctuary in the midst of them for evermore. My dwelling place shall be with them, and I will be their God, and they shall be my people' (Ezk. 37:26f.). Because of this holy and pervasive presence the name of the eternal city of God will be *The Lord is there* (Ezk. 48:35; see 21:2–4 below, where St. John returns to this theme). Here, again, both the recovery of the blessedness of Eden is portrayed and also the realization of the glorious destiny always intended by God for man and the rest of his creation. As what follows makes plain, the renewed heaven and earth will be purged of all that mars and beclouds our world as we now know it.

> *They shall hunger no more, neither thirst any more, nor shall the*
> *sun strike them, nor any scorching heat; for the Lamb who is in*
> *the midst of the throne will be their shepherd, and he will guide*
> *them to fountains of waters of life; and God will wipe away every*
> *tear from their eyes (7:16–17).*

The promises of the new covenant are further fulfilled in the scene of renewal and bliss in these verses. Hence the continuing use of the language of the new covenant. In Isaiah 49:10, accordingly, the promise is given concerning the Lord's people: 'They shall not hunger or thirst, neither scorching wind nor sun shall smite them, for he who has pity on them will lead them, and by springs of water will guide them'. It is not surprising, then, that Jesus, the Mediator of the new covenant (Heb. 9:15) should proclaim: 'I am the bread of life: he who comes to me shall not hunger, and he who believes in me shall never thirst' (Jn. 6:35), and should give the assurance: 'Whoever drinks of the water that I shall give him will never thirst; for the water that I shall give him will become in him a spring of water welling up to eternal life' (Jn. 4:14). That is why he, uniquely, issues the invitation: 'If any one thirst, let him come to me and drink' (Jn. 7:37; *cf.* 22:17 below). **Hunger** and **thirst** and **scorching heat** are among the trials that belong to the great tribulation of God's people. They will be unknown in the regeneration of all things.

The Lamb is seen **in the midst of the throne** because he is the central figure in the glorious reveval of all things. Far from being egocentric or introspective, the attention of all who constitute the multitude of the redeemed will be concentrated, gratefully and worshipfully, on him through whom they have been reconciled to God. To say that the Lamb **will be their shepherd** must seem strangely incongruous to those who do not understand, as must also the concepts of Christ as the High Priest who at the same time is the victim he offers up (Heb. 7:26f.) and God who through the incarnation becomes also our fellow man (Jn. 1:1, 14). The incarnation is, indeed, the key to the comprehension of what to our limited minds seems like a paradox. Christ is truly the Shepherd who is the leader of his sheep. But he is more than that, for he is the Good Shepherd who laid down his life for the sheep, and who, precisely by doing so, became at the same time the Lamb of God who takes away the sin of the world (Jn. 10:11; 1:29). As the Shepherd he is our God tenderly caring for his people, and as the Lamb he is our fellow human being, who offered up himself to death on the cross in our place (1 Pet. 1:18; Is. 40:11; 53:6f.). In the eternal glory of the new heaven and earth he is still the Lamb who was slain for us and is alive for evermore (1:18; 5:6). In the eternal perspective, therefore, he is seen by the redeemed as both the Shepherd and the Lamb.

The *fountains of waters of life* to which the Shepherd *will guide* the white-robed throng are one and the same as 'the fountain of the water of life' from which he promises to 'give water without price to the thirsty' (21:6) and 'the river of the water of life flowing from the throne of God and of the Lamb' (22:1; 22:17). The further and complementary promise is added that *God will wipe away every tear from their eyes*, and this again echoes the terms of the new covenant with its assurance that the Lord 'will swallow up death for ever, and . . . will wipe away tears from all faces' (Is. 25:8). Implicit in all these promises is the undoing of the curse that man in his fallenness brought upon himself and upon the earth (Gn. 3:17ff.).

9. THE SEVENTH SEAL OPENED, 8:1

And when he opened the seventh seal there was silence in heaven for about half an hour (8:1).

The clause *when he opened the seventh seal* is in sequence with the clauses that introduce the opening of the six previous seals (6:1, 3, 5, 7, 9, 12). The unsealing is done by the Lamb (5:1ff.; 6:1), and the account is now resumed after the intervening vision described in chapter 7. The loosing of this final seal is followed by *silence in heaven* which contrasts dramatically with the massive music of praise and adoration which St. John has been hearing from the concourse of redeemed mankind and the hosts of angels (7:10–12). The length of the duration of this absolute silence, *about half an hour,* indicates the passage of time as St. John experienced it. There is a long and ominous silence as he awaits what this final unsealing will disclose. It feels to him like half an hour; there is no need to seek some symbolical significance from the calculation. There is a close connection with the scenes revealed by the opening of the sixth seal, for now the terrors of that last day, the day of judgment, will be more graphically unveiled. The silence is the silence of awesome expectation. It is explained by the prophecy of Zephaniah:

> Be silent before the Lord God! For the day of the Lord is at hand . . . A day of wrath is that day, a day of distress and anguish, a day of ruin and devastation, a day of darkness and gloom, a day of clouds and thick darkness . . . I will bring distress on men, so that they shall walk like the blind, because they have sinned against the Lord . . . Neither their silver nor their gold shall be able to deliver them on the day of the wrath of the Lord *(Zp. 1:7, 15, 17, 18).*

On the day of judgment there will also be silence on earth, at least in this respect that all who have rejected the grace of God will, because of the absolute justice of God's judgment, be speechless as those who are entirely without excuse (*cf.* Rom. 1:20; 2:1; Jn. 15:22).

The seven trumpet blasts, 8:2 – 11:19

1. THE SEVEN ANGELS AND THE ANGEL WITH THE GOLDEN CENSER, 8:2–6

And I saw the seven angels who stand before God, and seven trumpets were given to them (8:2).

These **seven angels who stand before God** are perhaps the seven archangels. Archangels, however, are not prominent in Scripture, though they are doubtless included when the angel hosts are mentioned. In the New Testament 'the archangel Michael' is mentioned in Jude 9 and is also named, without being designated an archangel, in 12:7 below (in Dn. 12:1 he is called 'the great prince'). In Luke 1:19 and 26 'the angel Gabriel' who appears in turn to Zechariah and Mary and speaks with them is traditionally known as one of the archangels, and in 1 Thessalonians 4:16 the manifestation of the Lord at the end of the age is accompanied by 'the archangel's call and the sound of the trumpet of God'. This association of the archangel and the trumpet of God suggests a definite link with the association of angels and trumpets here, as also does Gabriel's description of himself in Luke 1:19: 'I am Gabriel, who stand in the presence of God', since the seven angels here are those who stand before God or in God's presence. The seven angels will sound their trumpets in turn and each sounding will be followed by cataclysmic events of eschatological significance. But first there is an intervention by another angel.

And another angel came and stood at the altar with a golden censer, and much incense was given to him to mingle with the prayers of all the saints on the golden altar before the throne. And the smoke of the incense rose with the prayers of the saints from the hand of the angel before God (8:3–4).

The altar and the **golden censer** seen by St. John correspond to the altar of incense and the censer of the earthly tabernacle which was 'a copy and shadow' of the heavenly reality (Heb. 8:5; 9:1ff.). Here again, as previously in 5:8, the aromatic *smoke of the incense* is identified with *the prayers of all the saints.* If the *much incense* which was given to this angel is distinct from the prayers of the saints, as the language may suggest, then this added incense may represent the prayer of Christ for those who are his, since 'he ever lives to make intercession for them' in the heavenly sanctuary as their great High Priest (Heb. 7:25; 9:24; Rom. 8:34; Jn. 17:9f., 20ff.). This incense of prayer ascends to *the throne,* that is to the immediate presence of God, before whom this angel is standing, thus confirming not only that the prayers of the saints do indeed reach God but also that they are well-pleasing to him like a delightful aroma.

> *And the angel took the censer and filled it with fire from the altar and threw it on the earth; and there were thunders and voices and lightnings and an earthquake (8:5).*

Now that the sweet-smelling prayers of the saints have ascended to God, the angel fills the censer with burning coals from the altar of incense and hurls the censer to the earth. This portends the arrival of the judgment for which the blood of the martyrs cries out (6:10f.). As forces of destruction, *fire* and *thunders and voices and lightnings* and *earthquake* are symbols of judgment which have already been encountered in 4:5 and 6:12 (see also 11:19 and 16:18). The destruction of Sodom and Gomorrah is described in Jude 7 as 'a punishment of eternal fire'. The action of the angel here calls to mind the assertion of Christ: 'I came to cast fire upon the earth' (Lk. 12:49).

> *And the seven angels who had the seven trumpets made ready to blow them (8:6).*

The first six of the seven trumpet blasts now follow in sequence (8:7 – 9:21); then, as with the opening of the scroll's first six seals, there is an interruption before the sounding of the seventh trumpet (11:15). The first four of the seven trumpet blasts affect primarily the inanimate parts of creation, though inevitably with consequences for living creatures, while the last three relate more directly to mankind. This they do in a manner comparable to the opening of the seals, except that the judgments that follow the seven trumpet blasts are themselves the eventualities resulting from the unloosing of the scroll's seventh seal.

2. THE FIRST TRUMPET BLAST, 8:7

> *And the first angel blew his trumpet, and there followed hail and fire mixed with blood, and they were cast on the earth. And the third part*

of the earth was burnt up, and the third part of the trees was burnt up, and all green grass was burnt up (8:7).

Following the first trumpet blast, judgments symbolized by the elemental forces of *hail and fire* which are *mixed with blood* are *cast on the earth*. Hail and blood recall two of the plagues that were sent upon Egypt (Ex. 7:14ff.; 9:22ff.). The shattering effect of the hail on the trees in Egypt was compounded by the plague of locusts, as a result of which 'not a green thing remained, neither tree nor plant of the field' (Ex. 10:15). Hailstones and fire and bloodshed are components also of the retribution decreed against Gog in Ezekiel 38:22f. (*cf.* 11:19 and 16:21 below). The information that *the third part of the earth* and *of the trees* was *burnt up* indicates that what is now revealed is partial or provisional, not final, judgment. The seven trumpet blasts are in effect a recapitulation of the seven unsealings of the scroll, so that both sequences culminate in the day of final judgment; and this is again the case with the outpourings from the seven bowls (16:1ff.).

The statement that *all green grass was burnt up* has caused interpreters difficulty because it seems to be contradicted by the order in 9:4 prohibiting the locusts from harming the grass of the earth. As, however, the effects of the first four trumpet blasts are consistently limited to third parts (of earth and trees here, of the sea, verses 8f., of the waters, verses 10f., and of the heavenly bodies, verse 12), it is reasonable to infer that it is 'all green grass' on 'the third part of the earth' which was scorched that is intended by St. John here. That he should have contradicted himself, and within so short a space, is most improbable. There is a similar form of expression in verses 10 and 11, where the context shows that 'on the fountains of the waters' means 'on the third part of the fountains of the waters' (see comment there).

3. THE SECOND TRUMPET BLAST, 8:8–9

And the second angel blew his trumpet, and what looked like a great mountain, burning with fire, was thrown into the sea, and the third part of the sea became blood; and the third part of the creatures in the sea died, and the third part of the ships was destroyed (8:8–9).

A great flaming mass, apparently of mountainous proportions, is thrown into the sea following the sounding of the second trumpet. The imagery is of catastrophic significance. St. John sees the third part of the sea turned into blood, with disastrous consequences for the third part of its denizens and also for the third part of the ships traversing its surface.

Worthy of note, again, is the degree of affinity between this partial judgment and one of the Egyptian plagues, the one, namely, whereby the Nile and other waterways of Egypt were turned to blood, so that their fish suffered death and putrefaction (Ex. 7:20ff.).

4. THE THIRD TRUMPET BLAST, 8:10–11

And the third angel blew his trumpet, and a great star, burning like a torch, fell from heaven, and it fell on the third part of the rivers and on the fountains of the waters; and the name of the star is Wormwood; and the third part of the waters became wormwood; and many men died of the waters because they were made bitter (8:10–11).

With the sounding of the third trumpet there appears *a great star* which, falling from heaven like a blazing torch, has a devastating effect on *the third part of the rivers* and on *the fountains of the waters*, that is to say, on the sources of fresh water, in contrast to the waters of the sea which were in part affected after the second blast. Here, again, the judgment is limited to a portion of the whole. When it is said that the great star fell on the fountains of the waters as well as on the third part of the rivers, it is plain from what follows that a third part of the former is intended (since *the third part of the waters* is most naturally taken to mean that the fountains and the rivers belong together in this expression).

The flaming star bears the name *Wormwood*. Wormwood is known in particular for its bitterness, and the star is so named because it causes the waters to become bitter, with lethal consequences for those who drink them. Yet again the terminology has a close association with the concept of judgment. Thus in Jeremiah 9:12ff. the question is asked, 'Why is the land ruined and laid waste like a wilderness?', and the Lord gives this answer:

> Because they have forsaken my law which I set before them, and have not obeyed my voice, or walked in accord with it, but have stubbornly followed their own hearts and have gone after the Baals, as their fathers taught them. Therefore thus says the Lord of hosts, the God of Israel: Behold, I will feed this people with wormwood, and give them poisonous water to drink. *(See also Je. 23:15.)*

5. THE FOURTH TRUMPET BLAST, 8:12

And the fourth angel blew his trumpet, and the third part of the sun was smitten, also the third part of the moon and the third part of the stars, so that the third part of them was darkened, and the day did not show the third part of its light, and likewise the night (8:12).

The darkness that is heralded by this fourth trumpet blast is comparable to the Egyptian plague of darkness (Ex. 10:21ff.), except that the Egyptian darkness was total darkness, 'darkness to be felt', over the land, whereas what the Apostle perceives here is partial darkness afflicting sun, moon, and stars, and therefore depleting in the light of day and night. As in the case of Egypt, darkness is regarded by the prophets as an aspect of divine judgment. Joel, for instance, declares: 'The day of the Lord is near in the valley of decision. The sun and the moon are darkened, and the stars withdraw their shining'; and Amos announces: 'On that day, says the Lord God, I will make the sun go down at noon, and darken the earth in broad daylight' (Joel 3:14f.; Am. 8:9). The darkness of the Egyptian plague presages the total darkness of the whole earth when the day of the Lord in its ultimate fullness arrives. By turning away from God, who is the source of all light, the unregenerate of mankind wilfully choose for themselves darkness, and in the day of judgment they will receive the horror of their self-chosen darkness to the full. Their condemnation is this, 'that the light has come into the world, and they loved darkness rather than light, because their deeds were evil' (Jn. 3:19).

6. THREE WOES PRONOUNCED, 8:13

And I saw, and I heard an eagle saying with a loud voice as it flew in midheaven, Woe, woe, woe to those who dwell on the earth, because of the other trumpet blasts of the three angels who are about to blow (8:13).

This brief intervention in which St. John sees **an eagle** flying in **midheaven** indicates that the first four trumpet blasts, now completed, and the last three, still to be heard, form two related groups. The **eagle** is another symbol of judgment in the sense that where there is a scene of carnage it descends, like its cousin the vulture (which may be intended here), to pick off the flesh of the carcases. This is the point of the adage in Christ's eschatological discourse: 'Where the carcase is, there the eagles will be gathered together' (Mt. 24:28; Lk. 17:37; *cf.* Jb. 39:27–30; Ho. 8:1; Hab. 1:8; Ezk. 39:17ff.).

The three woes uttered by the eagle arise out of the three remaining trumpet blasts, as is indicated below in 9:12, 11:14, and 12:12. They are the woes leading up to the culmination of divine judgment, and they apply to **those who dwell on the earth** in a state of mounting rebellion against God. The intensification of ungodliness produces of itself an intensification of woe.

7. THE FIFTH TRUMPET BLAST, 9:1–12

> *And the fifth angel blew his trumpet, and I saw a star fallen from heaven to earth, and the key of the pit of the abyss was given to him (9:1).*

The events now introduced by the fifth trumpet blast are those of the first woe (see verse 12). The **star fallen from heaven to earth** evidently represents a spiritual being, who, however, is not identified by St. John. As such, the significance of this star is different from that of the star cast down from heaven in 8:10 above. To this being **the key of the pit of the abyss** had been given, and some commentators have wished to identify him with Satan, who, as we read in 12:9, was thrown down to the earth. But there is better reason for concluding that this being is one and the same with the angel mentioned in 20:1 who had the key of the abyss and with it the power to confine Satan in the abyss or to release him from it. Satan appears below, in verse 11, as Apollyon, 'the angel of the abyss' and the king of the hosts of evil, at the head of whom, presumably, he emerged from the abyss when it was opened. **The abyss** ('the pit of the abyss' means the pit that is the abyss, often called 'the bottomless pit') conveys the impression of a dark and chaotic and fathomless chasm that is the appropriate abode of Satan and his armies of fallen angels. Thus the demons cast out of the Gadarene demoniac begged Jesus 'not to command them to depart into the abyss', whence they had come (Lk. 8:31).

> *And he opened the pit of the abyss; and smoke arose from the pit like the smoke of a great furnace, and the sun and the air were darkened by the smoke from the pit (9:2).*

The opening of the abyss releases a volume of smoke which pollutes the air and darkens the sun. Such smoke is another symbol of the judgment of the ungodly. The smoke from the destruction of Sodom and Gomorrah, for example, went up, as does the smoke here in St. John's vision, 'like the smoke of a furnace' (Gn. 19:28). Smoke signified the awesome power of God's presence at Sinai, when the mountain 'was wrapped in smoke because the Lord descended upon it in fire, and the smoke of it went up like the smoke of a kiln' (Ex. 19:18). The smoke of divine judgment goes up for ever (Is. 34:10; ch. 14:11; 19:3).

The darkness caused by the smoke from the abyss, permeating the air and obscuring the sun (*cf.* Mk. 13:24; Mt. 24:29), typifies the darkness which he who is the Light of the world came to conquer and dispel (*cf.* Jn. 1:5; 3:19; 8:12; 12:46; 1 Jn. 1:5; 2:8, 9, 11; Mt. 4:16; Lk. 1:79). Exclusion in 'outer darkness' is the destiny of those who persist in unbelief (Mt. 8:12; 22:13; 25:30); for them 'the nether gloom of darkness has been reserved for ever' (Jude 13; 2 Pet. 2:17). The world darkened by this smoke from the abyss symbolizes the pervasive influence of Satan in human society.

> *And from the smoke locusts came on the earth, and power was given them as the scorpions of the earth have power; and they were told not to harm the grass of the earth or any green vegetation or any tree, but only those men who do not have the seal of God on their foreheads (9:3–4).*

One of the Egyptian plagues was a plague of locusts which stripped the land of all greenery (Ex. 10:12ff.); the locusts of this vision, however, are forbidden to damage grass and plants and trees. Endowed with the power of scorpions, it is human beings they are permitted to attack, and specifically those who have not been sealed by God (as recorded in 7:2ff. above), since those who bear this seal are protected from the judgment that overtakes the ungodly. As in the case of Egypt, *locusts* are yet another symbol of judgment (see also Joel 1:4; 2:25; Na. 3:15). Their multitudinous swarming resembled the invasion of a vast army (Jdg. 6:5; 7:12; Pr. 30:27). Moreover, the locusts seen by St. John have the deadly power of *scorpions.* Scorpions, indeed, together with serpents, feared because of the threat their poison posed to physical life, were a symbol of the hostile forces of evil with their lethal assault on spiritual life. At the end of their forty years of wandering in the wilderness the Israelites were reminded by Moses that the Lord God had led them 'through the great and terrible wilderness, with its fiery serpents and scorpions' (Dt. 8:15); and to the seventy whom he had sent out Jesus said: 'I have given you authority to tread upon serpents and scorpions, and over all the power of the enemy' (Lk. 10:19). The rejecters of the truth proclaimed by the prophet Ezekiel were likened to scorpions (Ezk. 2:6). So, too, here the locusts with the power of scorpions signify the forces that are intent on destroying mankind with their poison of falsehood and infidelity.

> *And they were allowed, not to kill them, but to torture them for five months; and their torture was like the torture of a scorpion when it stings a man (9:5).*

The attack on human society is permitted to go only so far. These forces, whose assault is likened to the painful and poisonous sting of the scorpion, are allowed (*they were allowed*, literally, 'it was given to them', that is, by God) to torture men but not to kill them, and to torture them only *for five months*, in other words, for a limited period of time. The point is that God is in control. The might of the enemy, formidable though it seems to us, is finite and his time is short, and God is not handing mankind over to him for destruction. On the contrary, the ultimate power of destruction rests in God's hands, and that final destruction will overwhelm Satan as well as those who have permitted him to poison their lives with his venom.

> *And in those days men will seek death and will not find it, and they will long to die, and death will fly from them* (9:6).

The harsh pain from which escape is sought results from the infecting of the lives of men and women with the venom of the inhumanity which is engendered by ungodliness, involving the corruption and brutalization of society, the terror of frustration and violence, and the senselessness of existence which has been robbed of meaning and purpose. Dying will seem preferable to living, in the false hope that it will be self-obliteration; but the godless will find no way of escape from the judgment they have brought upon themselves.

> *And in appearance the locusts were like horses prepared for war; and on their heads were what looked like crowns made of gold; and their faces were like the faces of men; and they had hair like the hair of women, and their teeth were like the teeth of lions; and they had chests like iron breastplates; and the sound of their wings was like the sound of chariots drawn by many horses rushing to war; and they have tails and stings like scorpions, and in their tails is their power to hurt men for five months* (9:7–10).

The complex imagery of this description rules out any literalistic understanding; nor is there any need to provide an interpretation for every detail of the locusts' appearance. The impression conveyed is one of frightening military strength, and the language is reminiscent, in part at least, of the opening section of Joel's prophecy, in which the land is invaded and devastated by a pestilence of locusts. This pestilence symbolizes a hostile nation whose 'teeth are lions' teeth', and the prophecy gives warning that 'the day of the Lord is coming'. The appearance of the locusts is that of 'war horses' and 'a powerful army drawn up for battle', before whom 'the earth quakes' and the 'heavens tremble' and sun, moon, and stars are darkened (Joel 1:4–7; 2:1f., 4ff.). As for the locusts of St. John's vision, *what looked like crowns made of gold* may be taken to indicate conquest and domination, the *faces like the faces of men* to mean that they are intelligent beings, not brute beasts, the long *hair like the hair of women* that they have the roughness of barbaric hordes, and the *teeth like the teeth of lions* their savage powers; while their seemingly ironclad bodies, with the mighty sound of their wings, arouses a feeling of their invincibility. Their having *tails and stings like scorpions* fits in with the assertion in verse 3 that they have the power of scorpions, and *their power to hurt men for five months* with their ability to torture men for five months in verse 5. Altogether, it is a most intimidating spectacle, humanly speaking. But the display of strength is more specious than real, for it is in no way intimidating to God, who alone is the Almighty One, and to whose supreme authority this vaunting army must in due course submit.

> *They have as king over them the angel of the abyss. His name in Hebrew is Abaddon, and in Greek he has the name Apollyon (9:11).*

The members of this fearsome army are not brute beasts (locusts or scorpions or any other of the lower creatures), as we have said; but neither are they 'flesh and blood', that is, human beings. They are 'the spiritual hosts of wickedness' (Eph. 6:12), the demonic forces of apostate angels, whose *king* is *the angel of the abyss*, that is to say, Satan. His Hebrew and Greek names mentioned here, *Abaddon* and *Apollyon*, mean respectively 'destruction' and 'destroyer' and are in effect synonymous, 'Abaddon' being the personification of destruction. His followers are 'the destroyers of the earth' who themselves are destroyed by God (11:18). In the Old Testament 'Abaddon' is the place of destruction, associated with Death and Sheol (see Jb. 26:8; 28:22; 31:12; Ps. 88:11; Pr. 15:11; 27:20). By introducing sin into the world, and with it death and destruction (Gn. 3:1ff.; Rom. 5:12), Satan arrogated to himself an inauthentic kingship, which, however, contrary to his intentions, is no real threat to the Lord God Almighty. That he will be overthrown is certain, but meanwhile, because of his apostate following of men as well as angels, he is described as 'the ruler of this world' (Jn. 12:31; 14:30; 16:11), 'the god of this world' (2 Cor. 4:4), and 'the ruler of the power of the air, of the spirit that is now at work in the sons of disobedience' (Eph. 2:2).

> *The first woe has passed; behold, after this there are still two woes to come (9:12).*

The first of the three woes (8:13) is fulfilled in the events that follow the sounding of the fifth trumpet blast (9:1ff.); the two woes yet to come are associated with the consequences introduced by the sixth and seventh blasts (9:13ff.; 11:14; 11:15ff.; 12:12).

8. THE SIXTH TRUMPET BLAST, 9:13-21

And the sixth angel blew his trumpet; and I heard a voice from the horns of the golden altar which is before God, saying to the sixth angel who had the trumpet, Let loose the four angels who are bound at the great river Euphrates (9:13-14).

The trumpet blast from the sixth angel is followed by the speaking of a voice emanating from *the horns*, that is, the horn-shaped protuberances at the four corners *of the golden altar.* This is the altar of incense, which is said to be *before God* because it is 'before the throne' (8:3) in the heavenly reality, as was foreshadowed in the earthly tabernacle where it was in line with the mercy-seat over which the glory of the Lord's presence was located. The speaker is not identified, but the command which is given must have come directly or indirectly from the Lord himself. That command is to *let loose* or set free *the four angels who are bound at the great river Euphrates.* Another group of four angels who stood 'at the four corners of the earth' and held 'the four winds of the earth' has already been seen, and it was the voice of an angel 'ascending from the rising of the sun with the seal of the living God' that restrained those four angels from harming earth and sea and trees until God's servants had been sealed (7:1-3). It may have been the same angel who issued the command here at the sounding of the sixth trumpet. This new group of four angels has also been under restraint, and the time has come for them to be loosed and, as the number four indicates, to execute a worldwide commission. That they are agents of judgment, wielding destructive powers, is evident from the next verse. Their activity is comparable to the declaration of Christ in Matthew 13:41: 'The Son of Man will send forth his angels, and they will gather out of his kingdom all that is offensive and all evildoers.'

The river Euphrates, where the four angels were bound, is one of the four branches of the river that flowed out of Eden in the account of the creation (Gn. 2:10ff.). Subsequently it appears as the eastern boundary of the promised land (Ex. 23:31, *etc.*). Because the book of Revelation as the end-piece of the Scriptures is closely related to the beginning at creation, especially in terms of the fulfilment and consummation of God's purpose by the renewal of creation, it may be that the Euphrates should be taken here as signifying the one great river that flowed out of Eden (being designated here as 'the great river'). Or it may stand for all four of the rivers into which the great river divided for the watering of the earth, that is, to bring worldwide blessing. Otherwise the Euphrates may be significant as the boundary line between the people of God and the hostile kings of the east (as it is, apparently, in 16:12 below). In any case, the unbinding of the four angels has the effect of unloosing the enemy forces of ungodliness.

And the four angels who had been prepared for the hour and day and month and year were let loose to kill the third part of mankind (9:15).

These angels, ministers of divine judgment, are set free and activated at the precise moment determined by the wisdom and purpose of God, who is the lord of time and history, and whose calendar sets not merely the *year*, *month*, and *day* but the very *hour* of the fulfilment of his will. The incarnate Son spoke similarly of 'times or seasons which the Father has fixed by his own authority' (Acts 1:7). Thus, also, St. Paul wrote that 'when the fullness of time came God sent forth his Son, born of a woman' (Gal. 4:4; *cf.* Mk. 1:15), and admiringly contemplated 'the mystery of his will, according to his good pleasure which he purposed in Christ, as a plan for the fullness of the times, to consummate all things in Christ' (Eph. 1:9f.).

As with the consequences of the previous trumpet blasts, the judgment here is partial and preliminary, affecting **the third part of mankind.**

And the number of the armies of horsemen was twice ten thousand times ten thousand; I heard their number (9:16).

This great host numbered not myriads of myriads but two times myriads of myriads, which, if taken literally would be two hundred million; but the 'two times' (*twice*) conveys rather the impression of the altogether exceptional magnitude of these fearsome armies, for 'ten thousand times ten thousand' would ordinarily suffice to describe a huge multitude. But, as we have seen, the Lord God also has his hosts of angels, 'myriads of myriads and thousands of thousands' (5:11), that is, of incalculable size; indeed, they are described in Psalm 68:17 as 'twice ten thousand, thousands upon thousands'. The unloosing of the four angels opens the way for the invasion of the demonic hordes who bring devastating judgment, the evil consequence of evil, on the unregenerate mass of mankind, though only to a partial degree (verses 15 and 18). The appalling carnage and brutality of human warfare, which in origin is fratricidal rebellion against the image of God in man, is demonic in impetus and intensity and is one manner in which these forces manifest their presence. When St. John says of these demonic armies that he **heard their number**, he is in effect making it clear that the number given was not arrived at by a calculation of his own. Indeed, it was beyond all computation. While such terrifying hosts are essentially hostile to God and the gospel, they are not envisaged at this juncture as directed against the people of God in particular but rather as destructive of fallen mankind in general. At all times, however, and in all temptations and afflictions, the people of God may apply to themselves the assurance given by Elisha to his servant concerning the presence of the Lord's invisible hosts: 'Fear not, for those who are with us are more than those who are with them' (2 Ki. 6:15-17).

> *And this was how I saw the horses in the vision and their riders, who had breastplates that were fiery red, smoky blue, and sulphurous yellow, and the heads of the horses were like lions' heads, and fire and smoke and sulphur issued from their mouths (9:17).*

Because they had heads *like lions' heads*, the appearance of the horses was all the more frightening. There are points of comparison with the 'locusts' of verses 7ff. above, which were 'like horses prepared for war' and had teeth 'like the teeth of lions'. The *fire and smoke and sulphur* have a direct correspondence with the colours of the riders' breastplates, showing the naturally close association between the riders and their horses. The combination of fire, smoke, and sulphur (brimstone), however, is symbolical of judgment, as in the case of Sodom and Gomorrah on which the Lord rained 'brimstone and fire . . . out of heaven' so that their smoke went up 'like the smoke of a furnace' (Gn. 19:24, 28; *cf.* Ps. 11:6; Ezk. 38:22; Lk. 17:29; ch. 14:10; 19:20; 20:10; 21:8 below).

> *The third part of mankind was killed by these three plagues, by the fire and the smoke and the sulphur that issued from their mouths; for the power of the horses is in their mouths and in their tails; for their tails are like serpents with heads, with which they do harm (9:18-19).*

The power of the horses is located in their leonine heads blasting forth fire and smoke and sulphur, described here as *three plagues*, and in the venomous bite of their serpentine tails, comparable in their deadliness to the scorpion-like tails of the 'locusts' in verse 10 above. The killing of *the third part of mankind* accomplishes the design announced in verse 15 above.

> *And the rest of mankind, who were not killed by these plagues, did not repent of the works of their hands to give up worshipping demons and idols of gold and silver and bronze and stone and wood, which can neither see nor hear nor walk; nor did they repent of their murders or their sorceries or their immorality or their thefts (9:20-21).*

The remaining two-thirds, described here as *the rest of mankind*, that is, rebellious mankind, who did not suffer death in the manner just narrated, continue to be unrepentant, though the partial character of the judgment provides them with an opportunity for a change of heart as well as being an unmistakable warning of the doom awaiting the impenitent. They are unwilling to give up the worship of **the works of their hands**, the powerless **idols** that **neither see nor hear nor walk**, and of the **demons** that are bent on their destruction. Greater folly and futility could not be imagined (*cf.* Dt. 4:28; 2 Ki. 19:18; Ps. 115:4; 135:15; Is. 2:8; 37:19; Je. 1:16; 10:3–5; 25:6f.; Acts 7:41; 19:26). The apostolic authors were well aware that idolatry is not limited to the worship of graven images; for, in essence, it is the worship of the creature rather than the Creator (Rom. 1:25). The much vaunted civilization of our day may be free from graven images, but it is certainly not free from idolatry. As St. Paul explained long since, the person who is covetous is an idolator (Eph. 5:5; Col. 3:5), and this means that virtually anything can become an idol: money, power, fame, pleasure, sex – in short, humanistic self-centredness in all its forms. Accordingly, the idolatry of which St. John speaks here is not remote from us and irrelevant to our situation. The worship of false gods, who in fact are no gods, is the expression of ungodliness which goes hand in hand with the breaking of all God's commandments. Hence the additional information that the worshippers of demons and idols failed also to repent of their **murders** and **sorceries** and **immorality** and **thefts.** Refusing to love the only true God, they fail also to love their fellow men as themselves. As always, ungodliness breeds inhumanity.

9. INTERVENING VISION, 10:1 – 11:14

A. *The angel with the little scroll, 10:1–11*

> *And I saw another mighty angel coming down from heaven, wrapped in a cloud, and a rainbow over his head, and his face like the sun, and his feet like pillars of fire* (10:1).

There is now an interlude before the sounding of the seventh trumpet (which comes at 11:15), much in the same way as chapter 7 intervened before the opening of the seventh seal. The **mighty angel** seems to be distinct from the 'mighty angels' encountered at 5:2 and 18:21. It may be that the designation of an angel as mighty denotes an archangel. Certainly the mighty angel described here has the appearance of a magnificent and powerful figure. Some commentators, indeed, because of the **cloud** in which he is enveloped, the **rainbow over his head,** and the brilliance of **his face like the sun** and **his feet like pillars of fire**, have wished to identify him with the glorified Redeemer who elsewhere in this book has been described in more or less similar terms – his feet 'like burnished brass, . . . refined in a furnace', his countenance 'like the sun shining in its strength' (1:15, 16), a rainbow around his throne (4:3), 'coming with the clouds' (1:7). But both the context (the Son, for example, would not swear by him who lives for ever and ever, verse 5) and the definition *another* angel are against this interpretation.

> *And he had a little scroll open in his hand; and he set his right foot on the sea and his left foot on the land (10:2).*

The impression is that of a colossal and dominating personage who, with his feet planted on land and sea, is an agent of destiny for the whole earth, the sphere, that is, occupied by mankind. He holds *a little scroll*, which, in contrast to the larger scroll sealed with seven seals (5:1), is *open* with its writing exposed.

> *And he called out with a loud voice, like a lion roaring; and when he called out the seven thunders uttered their voices (10:3).*

The angel's *loud voice* is a voice of authority which, being *like a lion roaring*, is also awe-inspiring. In the Old Testament the lion-like roaring of the Lord is linked with his execution of judgment (*cf.* Is. 31:4; Je. 25:30f.; Ho. 11:10; Joel 3:16; Am. 1:2). The greater roar of the mighty angel's voice is immediately followed by the sounding of *the seven thunders*. That these thunderings were not just atmospheric thunderclaps but were, or were the accompaniment of, intelligible communications is apparent from the next verse. Perhaps these communications conveyed what was written in the little scroll in the angel's hand. Thunder is significant in that it is frequently a concomitant of judgment, while the number seven may be taken as confirming that they announce divine judgment (*cf.* 4:5; 6:1; 8:5; 11:19; 16:18).

> *And when the seven thunders spoke I was about to write; and I heard a voice from heaven, saying, Seal up what the seven thunders have spoken, and do not write it down (10:4).*

The message spoken by the seven thunders is heard and understood by St. John, but he is forbidden to pass it on or to write it down. This means that it is also hidden from us, though it is probable that the words of the thunders are enacted in events subsequently recorded in this book. It would be vain, however, to speculate regarding the content of their utterance. St. Paul, too, had seen and heard things from the Lord which he was not at liberty to reveal to others (2 Cor. 12:2–4). In a quite different situation, when the voice of the Father was heard speaking to the incarnate Son, the bystanders considered that what they heard was the sound of thunder (Jn. 12:28f.).

When the Apostle is told, '*Do not write it down*', the implication is that he was about to set down in writing what he had just heard, and, further, that he was recording the visions and utterances, as they were disclosed to him, instead of waiting to do so later on. We have no certain information, however, about his customary practice in this respect.

And the angel whom I saw standing on the sea and on the land lifted up his right hand to heaven and swore by him who lives for ever and ever, who created the heaven and the things in it and the earth and the things in it and the sea and the things in it, that there should be no more delay (10:5–6).

The lifting up of the right hand when swearing an oath is a practice still traditionally observed in law courts when taking evidence and at ceremonies of installation to high office. Such swearing is, either implicitly or explicitly, before God who is the Creator and Judge of all, as is the case here in the oath affirmed by the angel (*cf.* Dn. 12:7; Dt. 32:40). The reason for this is that there is 'no one greater by whom to swear' (Heb. 6:13). What the oath asserted was *that there should be no more delay*, that is to say, the moment for final judgment was now at hand. The rendering of the older versions, 'that time should be no more', though it could be said to be literal (but the Greek noun *chronos* here means delay that is caused by the passing of time), lent itself to the misconception of time as a this-worldly entity opposed to the notion of a timeless eternity (a Greek philosophical concept). Time, however, far from being an entity in itself, is but a convention for understanding and recording the sequence of changes and happenings that belong to human experience and that constitute history as a whole. As depicted in this book of Revelation, eternity is certainly not an uneventful, static, and quasi-frozen state, for the new heaven and earth are full of activity. The angel's oath announces that delay, such, for example, as that indicated in 6:10f. above, is now at an end. At the same time, what in the human perspective seems to be delay must never be interpreted to mean that there is tardiness or unconcern or incompetence where God is concerned in the fulfilment of his promises and warnings (*cf.* 2 Pet. 3:3ff.). His word is always sure and his timetable firm (see comment on 9:15 above).

But that in the days of the voice of the seventh angel, when he is at the point of blowing his trumpet, then would the mystery of God be fulfilled, as he promised to his servants the prophets (10:7).

This verse is a continuation of the angel's oath proclaiming that there will be no further delay. The connection is now made with the sounding of the seventh angel's trumpet (see 11:15), which will be the signal for the arrival of the last day and the execution of final judgment. All this, moreover, is bound up with the fulfilment of **the mystery of God**, namely, the consummation of his constant purpose for purging the order of creation of all defilement and the restoration of all things, through the Son's mediation, by the establishment of the new heaven and earth. As in a number of other places in the New Testament, the term 'mystery' is used here of God's master-plan which is not clearly revealed until the first coming of Christ and not consummated until his second coming. This is what God **promised to his servants the prophets** for them to receive as good news (for the verb we have rendered as 'promised' means literally 'evangelized', 'proclaimed good news', in the same way as it is said by St. Paul that the gospel was 'preached beforehand' to Abraham, Gal. 3:8). Yet for them it had the character of mystery, for they received the promises without seeing their fulfilment and in faith could but peer as it were through the mists of the future (1 Pet. 1:10–12; Heb. 11:13–16). The coming of Christ, however, was the coming of light (Jn. 1:9); in him 'the mystery about which there was silence for long ages is now disclosed' (Rom. 16:25).

But while it is true that the mystery associated with the promises of the gospel has been disclosed by the saving events of Christ's first coming, there still remains the mystery regarding the consummation of all things which will be effected by Christ at his second coming at the end of the age, and this mystery will be disclosed only by the culminating events of that day. Or else it could be said that the mystery of God is unveiled in two stages, the first of which has made known all that is necessary to make us 'wise unto salvation through faith in Christ Jesus' (2 Tim. 3:15), and the second whose full disclosure will take place on that last day. It is with the latter that St. John's visions recorded in this book have mainly to do. As this book repeatedly shows, however, God's purposes of judgment are inseparable from his purposes of renewal and glorification. If there were no finality of judgment there would be no fullness of redemption. That is why St. Paul writes in the one place both of the day 'when the Lord Jesus is revealed from heaven, . . . inflicting vengeance on those who do not know God and who do not obey the gospel of our Lord Jesus', and also of that same day 'when he comes to be glorified in his saints and to be marvelled at in all who have believed' (2 Thes. 1:7–10; *cf.* Tit. 2:11–14), and can assert that 'our salvation is nearer to us now than when we first believed' (Rom. 13:11).

> *And the voice which I heard from heaven spoke to me again, saying, Go, take the scroll which is open in the hand of the angel who is standing on the sea and on the land. And I went to the angel and told him to give me the little scroll; and he said to me, Take and eat it: it will make your stomach bitter, but it will be sweet as honey in your mouth. And I took the little scroll from the*

*angel's hand and ate it; and it was sweet as honey in my mouth, but
when I had eaten it my stomach was made bitter (10:8–10).*

The voice already heard by St. John (verse 4) now instructs him to take
the scroll from the angel and to eat it, advising him that it will be sweet
as honey to the taste but bitter in his stomach; and so it proved to be
when he obeyed the command. All this takes place in the Apostle's
vision, and it illustrates the truth that God's word, which is received
with delight by his servants (*cf.* Ps. 119:103, 'How sweet are thy words to
my taste, sweeter than honey to my mouth!'), can be expected to have
harsh consequences for those who witness with faithfulness to its teaching, because of the hostility of ungodly persons. In similar manner,
Ezekiel, in his vision, was given a scroll to eat, which in his mouth was
'as sweet as honey', and commanded to speak God's words to the
people who were unwilling to listen to him (Ezk. 2:8 – 3:11).

Likewise, Jeremiah said to the Lord: 'Thy words were found, and I ate
them, and thy words became to me a joy and the delight of my heart' (Je.
15:16). Such was the sweetness of God's word to him; but there was also
a bitter after-effect: 'I have become a laughingstock all the day; every one
mocks me. . . . For the word of the Lord has become for me a reproach
and derision all day long.' But he found it impossible to be silent: 'If I
say, I will not mention him or speak any more in his name,' he continued, 'there is in my heart as it were a burning fire shut up in my
bones, and I am weary with holding it in, and I cannot' (Je. 20:7–9). And
so it is with all God's faithful witnesses, whose message of salvation has
no meaning if the judgment of God is not a reality.

*And they said to me, You must prophesy again concerning many
peoples and nations and tongues and kings (10:11).*

Who *they* are who said this to St. John is not stated. If, as is probable,
they said to me is a manner of expression equivalent to the impersonal
'it was said to me', then the voice he heard may be the 'voice from
heaven' of verses 4 and 8. He is told that his prophesying is not yet
completed, and the prophesying still to be fulfilled is set down in the
rest of this book, which is a book of prophecy (see 1:3; 22:7, 19).
Moreover, it is prophesying that is related to the worldwide scene;
hence the fourfold designation *concerning many peoples and nations
and tongues and kings*. Centuries earlier Jeremiah was a prophet to
whom the Lord said: 'I appointed you a prophet to the nations. . . . I
have set you this day over nations and over kingdoms' (Je. 1:5, 10). And
again we read that 'the word of the Lord came to Jeremiah the prophet
concerning the nations' (46:1). St. John's book is, because of its content,
the culmination of all prophecy, for the judgment it prophesies is final
judgment and the salvation it portrays is the fullness of salvation. This is

ultimate prophecy. There is no longer a place for prophecy of the penultimate kind.

B. *The Lord's two witnesses, 11:1–14*

> *And a measuring rod like a staff was given to me, and I was told, Rise and measure the temple of God and the altar and those who worship there (11:1).*

The events now to be described lead up to the sounding of the seventh trumpet (verse 15). Who it was that gave St. John the measuring rod and addressed him is not stated, but it was evidently Christ himself because the witnesses spoken of in verse 3 are described as 'my two witnesses'. He is instructed to **measure the temple**, or sanctuary, **of God**. As we read in Hebrews 8:1–5, Moses was 'instructed by God' to set up the tabernacle according to the pattern that was shown him on Mount Sinai; and that sanctuary, we are told, was 'a copy and shadow of the heavenly sanctuary'. The point is that in its dimensions and arrangements the earthly structure pointed to heavenly realities. As the heavenly realities can be set forth only in earthly language, we must be careful not to reduce them to the limitations of our present comprehension. Just as a shadow is not one with the substance by which it is cast, so the eternal reality absolutely transcends its earthly shadow and the language available to us for speaking of it. The temple of God, then, is not some kind of structure of this world erected in the heavenly realm. Nor did St. John think of it in this way. We have already discussed its significance in our comments on 3:12 above, according to the teaching given elsewhere in this book and in other books of the New Testament. The measuring commanded here is an indication to us of the ordered perfection of all that God purposes and performs, as the Creator and Restorer of the universe. That what he does is measurable in no way suggests that it is finite and restricted, but that it is proportionate to the ideal logic of the divine mind – that it is, in short, a *cosmos*, not a chaos.

The altar which is also to be measured corresponds to the altar of incense previously mentioned in 8.3 and 9:13 (not, as some have supposed, the altar of sacrifice, located outside the sanctuary in the courtyard, which was not to be measured, as we see in the next verse). Its measuring may be taken to mean that God is in control of all that happens to his servants and is attentive to all their prayers that ascend to him like a sweet aroma (*cf.* 8:3f.).

Also to be measured are **those who worship** in God's true sanctuary, that is to say, the redeemed of mankind, who are measurable in the sense that they are well known in number and by name to God. Their measurability testifies to the indefectible symmetry of the divine purpose, in accordance with which they are not only known, but indeed foreknown, and as such predestined and called and justified, and at last glorified by being conformed to the image of the Son (Rom. 8:29f.; Eph. 1:11).

In the Old Testament, there was a measuring of the temple together with its precincts which was seen by Ezekiel in his vision. That measuring, however, was not performed by the prophet, but by 'a man, whose appearance was like bronze, with a line of flax and a measuring reed in his hand' (Ezk. 40:1ff.; *cf.* also Zechariah's vision in which 'a man with a measuring line in his hand' went 'to measure Jerusalem', Zc. 2:1f.).

> *But leave out the court outside the temple, and do not measure it; for it is given to the nations, and they will trample the holy city under foot for forty-two months (11:2).*

It is surely mistaken to relate, as many commentators do, the distinction made here to the topography of the Jerusalem temple and its precincts, as though there were a precise correspondence. There is reason to conclude that *the court outside the temple* which is *given to the nations* (or Gentiles) as seen in this vision, should not be identified with the outer court of the Gentiles which, on the earthly scene, was separated from the inner areas of the temple courtyard from which the Gentiles were excluded. The advent of Christ radically changed this whole arrangement, as the old Mosaic covenant was superseded by the new (Heb. 8:6–13). Peace has been established by the blood of the cross (Col. 1:20), and the dividing wall of hostility separating Gentile from Jew has been broken down (Eph. 2:11–22). Moreover, the rending of the temple curtain has opened the way for all without distinction into the sanctuary of God's presence (Heb. 10:19–22). Those who are outside are now those who persist in their unbelief and ungodliness, designated here as 'the nations', who, St. John is told, *will trample the holy city under foot for forty-two months.*

In his prophetic discourse spoken within the precincts of the Jerusalem temple Christ foretold the destruction of both temple and city that took place in AD 70. This destruction, however, was but a foretaste or prototype of the final universal jugment that will mark the end of the age; hence the eschatological theme that is interwoven into the structure of this discourse (see Mt. 24, Mk. 13, and Lk. 21) and the apocalyptic imagery by which it is customarily accompanied (as, for example, in Lk. 21:10–19, 25–28). Not only did Christ declare that his disciples would be hated by all for his name's sake, but also that Jerusalem would be 'trampled under foot by the nations, until the times of the nations are fulfilled' (Lk. 21:17, 24). The 'nations' here stand for the generality of mankind in opposition to God, and it is they who are the haters of Christ's followers.

But in the New Testament 'Jerusalem' also has a double significance.

121

There is the earthly Jerusalem, which, in St. Paul's allegory, represents the bondage of those who are in unbelief; and there is 'the Jerusalem above', which 'is free' and the 'mother' of the Lord's people (Gal. 4:25f.). The latter is 'the holy city' of the Apocalypse (see ch. 3:12; 21:2, 10; 22:19) and its citizens are the community of the redeemed. 'Our citizenship is in heaven', St. Paul wrote, 'whence also we wait for a Saviour, the Lord Jesus Christ' (Phil. 3:30). The men and women of faith of old 'looked forward to the city whose builder and maker is God', and, the author of the Epistle to the Hebrews asserts, this is the city that God has prepared. Yet it is not only for them but for all the saints of both Old and New Testaments, for it is to 'the city of the living God, the heavenly Jerusalem', that we have all come, knowing that 'we have here no abiding city' (Heb. 11:10, 16; 12:22; 13:14)

It is thus the great multitude of the people of God who constitute the citizenry of this holy city which is the new Jerusalem; and the trampling under foot of the holy city by the nations (as revealed to St. John) depicts the hatred of Christ's disciples by the ungodly peoples and powers of this world. The persecution by which this hatred is expressed, however, has to be endured only for the time being. The 'trampling' lasts for *forty-two months*, that is, for a limited time. Once again we are taught that the forces of evil are, as it were, on a leash which is controlled by God's hand. As Christ indicated, the hour will strike when 'the times of the nations' will be fulfilled (Lk. 21:24). These 'times' are represented here by the 'forty-two months', the same period over which the worship of 'the beast' extends (see on 13:5 below), and also during which 'the woman' who is Christ's church is nourished and preserved by God (12:6, 14, where 'one thousand two hundred and sixty days' and 'a time, and times, and half a time', respectively, are other ways of stating the same period, a 'time' in the latter place being equivalent to a year, symbolically intended; see also verse 3 that follows here, and *cf*. Dn. 7:25; 12:7).[1] The enmity of the 'nations', by which they invite final judgment upon themselves, is overruled by God for the good of his suffering people. For, just as gold is tested and refined in the furnace, so also the genuineness of their faith is proved and their lives purified through the trials they endure (*cf.* 1 Pet. 1:6f.).

> *And I will enable my two witnesses, and they will prophesy for one thousand two hundred and sixty days, clothed in sackcloth (11:3).*

Numerous suggestions have been offered concerning the identity of the *two witnesses* referred to here, such as Moses and Elijah, or Enoch and

[1] The number three and a half (years) falls short by half, that is, hopelessly short, of the divine number seven, and is indicative of the futility of Satan's challenge to the supreme authority of God.

Elijah, or the Old Testament and the New Testament, or the law and the prophets, and so on. But, as their very number shows, such guesses are inconclusive and serve little purpose. The key to a proper understanding is present, rather, in the number two itself, for two is the number of witness. Thus Christ said to the Pharisees: 'In your law it is written that the witness of two persons is true; I am one bearing witness to myself, and the Father who sent me bears witness to me' (Jn. 8:17f.; Dt. 19:15). Christ also sent his disciples out two by two as his witnesses (Mk. 6:7; Lk. 10:1). Here, then, we take the Lord's two witnesses to symbolize the witness of his servants in a hostile world throughout the period specified, namely, **one thousand two hundred and sixty days** (the equivalent of the forty-two months of the preceding verse). This signifies the duration of Christian witness, which, prolonged though it may seem to us, is a period limited and overruled by God in accordance with his sovereign purpose. The interval between the two comings of Christ is in an essential respect the period of the church's witness to him. This is made perfectly plain in the commission given by the Lord to his disciples at the time of his ascension: 'You will receive power when the Holy Spirit has come upon you, and you shall be my witnesses in Jerusalem and in all Judea and Samaria and to the end of the earth' (Acts 1:8).

That the two witnesses are **clothed in sackcloth** signifies that they stand for those who have repented and believe, who are no longer proud but humble, who have denied self to affirm Christ, and who, regarded by this world as poor, yet make many rich, and as having nothing, yet possess all things (*cf.* 1 Ki. 20:31f.; Ne. 9:1; Ps. 69:10f.; Is. 32:11; Je. 4:8; 6:26; Joel 1:13; Jon. 3:5ff.; Mt. 11:21; Lk. 10:13; 2 Cor. 6:10).

These are the two olive trees and the two lampstands that stand before the Lord of the earth (11:4).

The imagery is similar to that of Zechariah's vision in which the prophet saw a golden lampstand with seven lamps and two olive trees, one on either side of the lampstand, which, he was told, are 'the two anointed [ones] who stand by the Lord of the whole earth' (Zc. 4:2f., 14). Oil from the two olive trees kept the lamps of the lampstand burning. Here, in St. John's vision, the Lord's two witnesses are doubly described as **olive trees** and **lampstands**, the former being in closest association with and supplying the fuel for the latter: filled with the oil of the Holy Spirit, these witnesses shine as lights in this world's darkness. Thus Christ described his disciples as 'the light of the world' (Mt. 5:14–16), not, however, because they are that light of themselves, but because the light of him who is uniquely the Light of the world (Jn. 8:12; 9:5) shines forth from them (Jn. 1:4f., 9). In much the same way, as we have seen, lampstands with their light are a symbol of the churches and their

123

witness (ch. 1:20). As for the olive tree, it had long been regarded as a symbol of the person who enjoys the Lord's favour. The psalmist, for example, likened himself to 'a green olive tree in the house of God' (Ps. 52:8). Because of their evil ways the house of Israel and the house of Judah, whom the Lord had once called 'a green olive tree, fair with goodly fruit', were threatened with destruction (Je. 11:16). St. John's fellow apostle St. Paul depicted Christian believers as the branches of God's olive tree (Rom. 11:13ff.).

The number *two*, as we pointed out in our comments on the preceding verse, is the number connected with the concept of witness, and the Lord's two witnesses indicate the witness of God's faithful servants in these last days between the two comings of Christ. The two olive trees and the two lampstands, which these witnesses are said to be, serve by their imagery to confirm the importance of the faithful and constant witness of God's people. It is as Spirit-filled witnesses, like oil-fed lampstands, that they **stand before the Lord of the earth**, upright because of the grace of their justification in Christ, unbowed by affliction and persecution suffered for his sake, and secure in the immutability of his promises, since their destiny is in him with whom they are eternally united.

And if any one wishes to harm them, fire comes forth from their mouth and consumes their enemies; and if any one wishes to harm them he must be killed in this way (11:5).

The Lord's witnesses may be hated and ill-treated, and even done to death, but they cannot be harmed. Though they may appear to be overcome by enemies, yet it is they who are the overcomers (2:7, *etc.*). Fragile earthen vessels, they are afflicted, perplexed, persecuted, struck down, but not crushed or in despair or forsaken or destroyed (2 Cor. 4:7–9). The **fire** that **comes forth from their mouth and consumes their enemies** is the word of their witness, for that word is the word given them by the Lord, whose word either saves or destroys (Jn. 12:47f.; *cf*. Is. 11:4). In this respect the witness of the persecuted prophet Jeremiah is of particular interest. 'The Lord put forth his hand and touched my mouth,' he wrote, and then he set down the assurance by which he was sustained: 'and the Lord said to me, Behold, I have put my words in your mouth. . . . I am watching over my word to perform it. . . . They will fight against you; but they shall not prevail against you, for I am with you, says the Lord, to deliver you' (Je. 1:9, 12, 19). And again, concerning those who have been 'utterly faithless', we read: 'Therefore thus says the Lord, the God of hosts: "Because they have spoken this word, behold, I am making my words in your mouth a fire, and this people wood, and the fire shall devour them"' (Je. 5:11, 14). We are to understand in the same way the consuming fire that issues from the mouth of the Lord's two witnesses.

They have power to shut the sky, so that no rain falls during the days of their prophecy, and they have power over the waters to turn them into blood and to smite the earth with every plague as often as they wish (11:6).

The *power* exercised by the Lord's witnesses, whether *to shut the sky* or *over the waters to turn them into blood* or *to smite the earth with every plague*, illustrates, like the fire proceeding from their mouth in the preceding verse, the judgment that is effected through *their prophecy*, that is to say, by their faithful proclamation of God's word. 'The days of Elijah', to which Christ referred, are called to mind, 'when the heaven was shut up for three years and six months so that a great famine came over all the land' (Lk. 4:25; 1 Ki. 17:1; *cf.* Jas. 5:17), as a judgment on the people because of their apostasy under Ahab and Jezebel. One is reminded, also, of the power exercised by Moses to turn the waters to blood and to smite the land of Egypt with various other plagues (*cf.* 1 Sa. 4:8, where the Philistines exclaim, 'Who will deliver us from the power of these mighty gods? These are the gods who smote the Egyptians with every sort of plague!'), for these, too, were manifestations of the judgment of God against those who opposed his will. Those who heed the witness of God's servants find that God opens the windows of heaven to pour down abundant blessing upon them (Mal. 3:10); whereas those who continue in impenitence are shut off from divine blessing and perish from aridity and barrenness of soul. So also the society of the ungodly is plagued in different ways at the very heart of its being. To walk in darkness and chaos is the inescapable consequence of rejecting the light that shines forth from the Lord's witnesses (*cf.* Jn. 3:19). Men and demons constantly attempt to extinguish this light of witness which they hate, but God keeps it burning brightly from generation to generation. By it the distinction is made between those who walk in the light and those who walk in darkness.

And when they have finished their witness the beast that ascends from the abyss will make war against them and overcome them and kill them (11:7).

It is from *the abyss*, as we have seen (9:1ff.), that the hosts of evil ascend with 'the angel of the abyss', Satan, as their king (9:11). *The beast* that comes from the same place *to make war against* the Lord's witnesses is the antichrist, that is, the concentration of animosity to Christ and his gospel, the agent of Satan's agent who later in St. John's vision (13:1) is seen emerging from the sea. This warfare has every appearance of being successful when the witnesses are *overcome* and killed; but it is important to notice that this happens only *when they have finished their witness*. The beast here is comparable to, and perhaps meant to be identical with, Daniel's fourth beast, one of whose horns 'made war with the saints, and prevailed over them' – but only 'until the Ancient of Days came, and judgment was given for the saints of the Most High, and the time came when the saints received the kingdom' (Dn. 7:21f.). This means that in fact the victory belongs not to the beast but to the Most High, and that, despite all appearances to the contrary, all is well with the Lord's witnesses. Indeed, the absolute power of God and the radical impotence of the beast who seems so powerful are displayed in the fact that the witnesses cannot be killed before their witness has been completed. The Lord's witnesses have a course to finish, namely, 'the ministry received from the Lord Jesus to testify to the gospel of the grace of God' (Acts 20:24). They have good works to perform 'which God prepared beforehand that we should walk in them' (Eph. 2:10). That course may seem to be soon finished, as in the case of St. Stephen, or to be prolonged, as in the case of St. John; but God sovereignly preserves his servants and fulfils his purpose through them until the moment when their witness is complete. Hence the confident assertion of St. Paul, when the time was at hand for him to be killed by the violence of antichrist: 'I have fought the good fight; I have finished the course; I have kept the faith. Henceforth there is laid up for me the crown of righteousness, which the Lord, the righteous Judge, will give me at that day; and not only to me, but also to all who have loved his appearing' (2 Tim. 4:7f.). The killing is followed by the crown!

> *And their dead bodies will lie in the street of the great city which is called, allegorically, Sodom and Egypt, where also their Lord was crucified. And for three and a half days members of the peoples and tribes and tongues and nations look at their dead bodies, and do not permit them to be placed in a tomb. And those who dwell on the earth rejoice over them and make merry and will send gifts to each other, because these two prophets tormented those who dwell on the earth (11:8–10).*

The Lord forewarned his witnesses that the world by which he was hated and killed would hate and kill them also (Jn. 15:18), and, instructed by him, they have learned not to fear those who kill the body but cannot kill the soul (Mt. 10:28). That is why the triumph of the beast is an empty triumph. So great, however, is the animosity of the beast and his followers that the two witnesses whom they have killed are not even accorded the dignity of burial; their corpses are contemptuously exposed as a warning to all of the shocking end awaiting those who bear witness to the grace of the gospel. Left to *lie in the street*, that is, in the central thoroughfare, *their dead bodies* are on public display to become a focus of popular celebration and merry-making. This, with the exchanging of *gifts*, gives expression not only to jubilation over this imagined victory but also to relief that *these two prophets*, whose witness had *tormented* their guilty consciences, are now silenced.

The great city, where the corpses of the witnesses are exposed to the public gaze, should not be taken to mean some particular geographical location or metropolis. It denotes, rather, the worldwide structure of unbelief and defiance against God – as is confirmed by the fourfold designation of the inhabitants as belonging to *peoples and tribes and tongues and nations*. This applies equally to 'the great city' with the name 'Babylon' which has a prominent place later in this book (14:8; 16:19, 18:10, *etc.*) and the mystical significance of which is identical with that of the great city here called *allegorically* (literally, 'spiritually', that is, not in a literal but in a mystical sense) *Sodom and Egypt*. The prototype of the worldly city is Babel (of which Babylon is a variant), which was built as 'a city, and a tower with its top in the heavens' to challenge the supremacy of the Creator (Gn. 11:1ff.). Thus Babylon became the symbol of the world-city of mankind puffed up with self-assertive pride against God. As such, 'the great city' of which St. John speaks is not found in the atlas, but is the mounting structure of human arrogance which defies the authority of Almighty God. It is the aggregation of humanistic strongholds constructed of vaunting pretensions and rationalistic speculations. The Christian warfare, as St. Paul says, is waged with weapons that are not fleshly, but which through God are powerful to demolish these strongholds of human sophistry and every proud structure that is raised high against the knowledge of God (2 Cor. 10:3–5).

That 'the great city' is not a place pin-pointed on a map is confirmed by the name 'Sodom and Egypt' it is given here; for Sodom, though a city, was not a great city, and Egypt is not a city but a country, and a country, moreover, in which Sodom was not located. Therefore it is for us to seek to understand what is signified by this double name. *Sodom* has typified throughout history the lowest depth of human depravity which can only meet with God's judgment of total destruction (Gn. 19:13, 24f.; Je. 23:14; *cf.* Is. 1:9f.; 3:9); while *Egypt* denotes stiff-necked opposition to the will of God and the degrading idolatry of the unregenerate. In combination, then, Sodom and Egypt symbolize the ungodly corruption of human society in general and the spirit of anti-christianity in the world.

There is no need to conclude that the designation of 'the great city' as the place *where also their Lord was crucified* indicates that the city of Jerusalem is intended by 'Sodom and Egypt'. Jerusalem is involved, indeed, to the extent that its inhabitants belong to the unholy world-city. In any case, it should be remembered that the witnesses' Lord was not crucified in Jerusalem but *outside the city*, where he was put to death on the supposedly unholy ground appropriate for the execution of unholy persons. The soil of Calvary, in fact, should not be regarded as soil associated narrowly with Jerusalem but as the soil of our whole world in its fallenness. The dying of the Holy One on that world-soil, moreover, has reclaimed it as holy ground which is destined to share in the glory of the new heaven and earth (21:1). In the meantime, however, the holy city which is the new Jerusalem (3:12; 21:2), and whose citizens are the Lord's faithful witnesses, is being trampled under foot by 'the nations' (verse 3 above). We see, then, that there is a relationship between the shameful death of the two witnesses and the shameful death of their Lord, in that both take place in the great world-city. The Lord's witnesses suffer where he suffered: in this world which he came to save and which continues to reject his witnesses as it rejected him (cf. Jn. 15:18ff.). The present world-city is not their city, for 'they are not of the world', just as their Lord is not of the world; yet 'they are in the world', and, just as their Lord was sent into the world, so he has sent them 'into the world' (Jn. 17:11, 14, 16, 18). The great world-city is the sphere of their witness, and as they face affliction for their Lord's sake they are reminded that 'Jesus suffered outside the gate [of the city] in order to sanctify the people through his blood', and accordingly are urged to 'go forth to him outside the camp', knowing this, that 'here we have no lasting city, but we seek the city which is to come' (Heb. 13:12–14).

The exultation over the silencing of the two witnesses whose dead bodies are openly exposed in the street of the great city lasts *for three and a half days* – that is, for a period of time on which a limit has been placed by God. As what follows shows, the celebrations of the inhabitants of the world-city are misjudged and short-lived because theirs is a hollow victory. As elsewhere, the number three and a half, whether used of days or of years, signifies a restricted or abbreviated duration.

> *And after the three and a half days the breath of life from God entered into them, and they stood up on their feet; and great fear fell on those who beheld them. And they heard a loud voice from heaven saying to them, Come up hither! And they went up into heaven in the cloud; and their enemies beheld them (11:11–12).*

The three and a half days refer to the time specified in verse 9 during which the witnesses' corpses are left lying in the street of 'Sodom and Egypt'. Now the jubilation over their death is brought to a sudden end as *the breath of life from God* revitalizes and raises up the witnesses. Though it is not Christ but his servants of whom St. John is writing here, the foundational paradigm is the killing of Jesus and his rising from the dead on the third day.[1] The Lord himself is pre-eminently the faithful

---

[1]The number three and a half in this passage is purely symbolical and is not to be connected with the number three denoting the day of Jesus' resurrection.

and true witness (3:14), and his rising from the dead is both the power and the guarantee of the rising from the dead in turn of his own faithful witnesses (1 Cor. 15:20ff.; *cf.* 2 Cor. 4:14, 'knowing that he who raised the Lord Jesus will raise us also with Jesus'). This resurrection power is not solely a phenomenon to be disclosed on the last day; it is already active in the course of this eschatological age of the last days. Even now the Lord's suffering witnesses are able to say with St. Paul: 'While we live we are always being given up to death for Jesus' sake, so that the life of Jesus may be manifested in our mortal flesh', and, 'though our outer man is wasting away, yet our inner man is being renewed day by day' (2 Cor. 4:11, 16). The power of Christ's resurrection is at this present time a hidden but vitalizing reality for his witnesses in their suffering for his sake.

It may be said, too, that this vision in which God raises up his witnesses draws attention to the futility of all the enemy's attempts to silence the witness of his people. The oil of the Holy Spirit does not cease to feed the flame of the lampstands (verse 4). The light is not extinguished by imprisonment and killing. Thus, for example, the stoning of Stephen, the first Christian martyr, who with his bold witness had tormented the opponents of the gospel, was followed by the raising up of Saul of Tarsus, as though from the dead, to become Paul the Apostle. The death-throes of the saints are at the same time the birth-pangs of the church as it is reborn from generation to generation.

Far from being dead when they are killed, the Lord's faithful witnesses are alive in the power of their Risen Redeemer. St. Stephen, about to die, saw the heavens opened and the glory of God and Jesus standing to welcome him to that glory (Acts 7:54–56). That spectacle would have been an empty delusion if Stephen was about to become no more than the dead flesh of a corpse. And so here, revivified and upstanding, the two witnesses, by whom the great multitude of the redeemed is signified, correspond to the dry bones of Ezekiel's vision, which, when the breath of God came into them, 'lived, and stood upon their feet, an exceedingly great host' (Ezk. 37:10).

Were the witnesses slain by the armies of the beast dead and done for, there would be no possibility of their hearing and responding to the **voice from heaven**, however **loud** it might be, summoning them to **come up hither**. But this is what they did, as, with their enemies watching, **they went up into heaven in the cloud**, for the voice is the all-powerful voice of their Creator and Redeemer, which unfailingly effects what it speaks. The cloud enveloping them as they ascend is not any cloud, but *the* cloud, that is, the resplendent cloud of the Lord's shekinah glory, which is the cloud of his own ascension (Acts 1:9) and of his transfiguration (Mt. 17:5). Thus it is that the Lord's witnesses who have suffered and died will be at no disadvantage when he comes for his own at the end of the age. For, as St. Paul teaches, 'the dead in Christ will rise first', and then those 'who are alive, who are left, will be caught up together with them in the clouds to meet the Lord in the air'; and so all his witnesses 'will ever be with the Lord' (1 Thes. 4:16f.). It is no wonder that *great fear* fills *their enemies* as they behold the rising and the ascending of those they have struck down, for it now remains for them to suffer the righteous judgment of Almighty God whose grace they have treated with contempt.

> *And at that hour there was a great earthquake, and the tenth part of the city fell; and seven thousand persons were killed in the earthquake, and the rest were terrified and gave glory to the God of heaven. The second woe has passed. Behold, the third woe is coming quickly (11:13–14).*

As in 6:12, with the opening of the penultimate seal, so here, prior to the sounding of the last of the seven trumpets, there is *a great earthquake*, which is an apocalyptic symbol for the catastrophic shaking of human society and its structures (see comments above on 6:12). Thus, for example, 'a great shaking' was one of the ways in which, speaking through his prophet Ezekiel, the Lord God declared he would show his greatness and his holiness and make himself known in the eyes of many nations (Ezk. 38:19, 23). The earthquake seen by St. John causes the destruction of *the tenth part of the city*, that is, the world-city known as 'Sodom and Egypt' (verse 8), with the death of *seven thousand persons*[1] – figures which indicate judgment that is partial, but which are also a portent of the final and total judgment that is impending. As a visitation of divine displeasure it leaves those who are still alive in a *terrified* state and constrains them to give *glory to the God of heaven*. Not only what follows with the sounding of the seventh trumpet, but the whole context plainly shows that the great world-city of Sodom and Egypt (also known as 'Babylon') continues in existence and that the intensity of its ungodliness increases until the moment of final judgment. If the giving of glory to the God of heaven by its inhabitants meant that they had repented and renounced their wickedness, there would then be no 'great city' left; but there is no indication here of any such change of heart, and it is appropriate to conclude that the giving of glory to God was a reaction of panic by which the beast's followers hoped to save their own skins, and that their concern was only for themselves, not really for God and his glory.

Notice is given that *the second woe* is now over and that *the third woe* is at hand. The three woes are connected with the fifth, sixth, and

---

[1]As with the seven thousand who had not bowed their knees to Baal in 1 Ki. 19:18, the seven thousand who lost their lives in this earthquake suggest a not inconsiderable number, though not a majority.

seventh trumpet blasts respectively and the calamitous events that follow the sounding of these blasts. The last of the seven trumpet blasts, now about to be heard, heralds the arrival of the last of the three woes. As with the opening of the seven seals, the movement as the trumpets sound forth and the woes occur in succession is towards the great final day of judgment.

10. THE SEVENTH TRUMPET BLAST, 11:15–19

And the seventh angel blew his trumpet; and there were loud voices in heaven, saying, The kingdom of the world has become the kingdom of our Lord and of his Christ, and he shall reign for ever and ever (11:15).

The last of the trumpet blasts presages the clearing of the way for final judgment and the Lord's everlasting rule in the new heaven and earth. The *loud voices in heaven* herald the momentous consummation of all God's purposes for mankind and the world, as the *eschaton*, the Day of the Lord, the last day of the last days, is reached and the true king and lord of all is conclusively shown to be the *Lord and his Christ* and not Satan, whose arrogant clutching at the kingship of the world is revealed as totally futile and worthless. Though the absolute sovereignty of Almighty God was never insecure, the world went after a false god and a false king (*cf.* Mt. 4:8–10; Jn. 12:31; 14:30; 16:11; 2 Cor. 4:4); but now, redeemed by the incarnate Son, the world is brought back to its true allegiance. It is in this sense that the kingdom of the world *has become* the kingdom of the true God.

To speak of his kingdom as *the kingdom of our Lord and his Christ* does not imply that the eternal kingdom has two kings. There is but one God and one kingship. This is made plain by the singular subject and verb of the immediately following sentence: *and he* (not 'they') *shall reign for ever and ever*. Christ is the incarnate Son, anointed by the Father with the Holy Spirit for the fulfilment of his redemptive mission to our world. This mission is fulfilled by his death on the cross for the sins of the world, and its fulfilment is attested by his resurrection from the dead and his ascension to the glory he had left for our sakes. As God, the Son's rule is inseparably one with that of the Father (who is designated 'our Lord' here) and of the Holy Spirit. As Man, the Son is inseparably one with us. There is, accordingly, a distinction to be made between his own divine glory as the eternal Son (*cf.* Jn. 17:5) and his glorification as the incarnate Son, who, his mission to earth completed, is exalted to the place of honour at the Father's right hand (Heb. 1:3; 12:2; Acts 2:32f.). Having come to do the Father's will, with which his own will as incarnate is altogether one (Jn. 4:34; 5:30; 6:38), and having been obedient even to the death of the cross, 'therefore God has highly exalted him and bestowed on him the name which is above every name' (Phil. 2:8f.). Conceptually, then, there is this distinction between the Son as incarnate and the Son as pre-incarnate. In that The Son is himself the Image of God in which man was created (Col. 1:15ff.; Gn. 1:27) there was from the first a deep bond linking man to the Second Person of the Holy Trinity, a theanthropic 'potentiality' which was redemptively actualized in the incarnation. It is as the God-Man, our divine-human Lord, that by his death, resurrection, and ascension he has opened the way into the Father's presence for us (Heb. 10:19ff.).

The incarnation of the Son as the Father's missionary to our fallen world (Jn. 17:18; 20:21) does not interrupt or diminish the sovereign rule of the Trinitarian God. All along the Son has been sustaining the universe by his word of power (Heb. 1:3); but the exaltation of the incarnate Son is at the same time – and this is the new factor of central importance for us – the exaltation to his glory of our humanity which he took to himself at Bethlehem, redeemed on the cross, and raised from the grave to newness of life on the third day. It is as the incarnate Son that Christ now reigns at the Father's right hand, and will do so until, in fulfilment of the psalmist's prophecy, he has made 'your enemies your footstool' (Ps. 110:1). When, at the final judgment, every enemy has been subdued, 'then comes the end', and then, having triumphantly fulfilled the purpose of the incarnation, namely, the bringing of many sons to glory (Heb. 2:10), he will hand over the kingdom to God the Father, 'that God may be all in all' (1 Cor. 15:24-28). The God who is all in all is the Trinitarian God. And it is then that redeemed humanity will exercise dominion over the renewed creation, in and through Christ, in accordance with the constitution of man in the divine image for this purpose.

> *And the twenty-four elders who were seated before God on their thrones fell on their faces and worshipped God, saying, We give thanks to thee, Lord God Almighty, who art and who wast, because thou hast taken thy great power and reigned (11:16-17).*

It is in Christ that *the twenty-four elders*, representative of the totality of redeemed mankind (see on 4:4 above), are enthroned before God (*cf.* 3:21); but their status in Christ does not alter the fact that they are creatures who through all eternity owe God their worship and their gratitude (*cf.* 4:10). The terminal moment of the history of the world in its present condition has arrived, and the elders *give thanks* to God for taking his *great power* and reigning. This thanksgiving does not imply that God had not been all-powerful in his sovereignty throughout the course of history, accomplishing all things according to the counsel of his will (Eph. 1:11). Any such notion is ruled out by the manner in which they address God as the **Lord** who is **Almighty**, and unceasingly so (**who art and who wast**; *cf.* 1:4, 8; 16:5). But now the great consummating moment has come for which not only the redeemed but also the whole created order has been expectantly waiting and longing, 'the glorious liberty of the children of God' (Rom. 8:19–23) – the moment which gives the clinching proof of God's sovereign authority.

> *And the nations raged, and thy wrath came and the time for the dead to be judged and to reward thy servants the prophets and saints and those who fear thy name, both small and great, and to destroy the destroyers of the earth (11:18).*

As they continue their thanksgiving the elders rejoice that the hour of reckoning has arrived, the moment when the infallible justice of God deals in a final manner with the injustice of apostate mankind. As graphically depicted in Psalm 2 (*cf.* Acts 4:25ff.), the defiant raging of the nations against God is utterly vain and leads to their destruction (*cf.* Ps. 46:6). God is not only the Creator but also the holy Judge of the world whose purposes are for ever established by his righteous judgment. When the last hour strikes, moreover, the judgment of God is not limited to those human beings who happen to be alive, for that would leave all the injustices of past generations unrequited. The time of final judgment is **the time for the dead to be judged**; it covers the whole sequence of human history from beginning to end. To die is not to escape or be deprived of judgment (Heb. 9:27). Though they have died and disappeared from the face of the earth, those who have inflicted injustice and those who have suffered injustice have not been cut off from the holy justice of God. The decisive dividing line is the line which separates the ungodly who persist in impenitence and unbelief from the **servants** of the Lord **who fear** his **name**, not one of whom is forgotten or overlooked – **the prophets and saints**, . . . **both small and great**, faithful in their witness and perseverance. The former meet with the divine **wrath**, the latter receive the divine **reward**.

The Lord's servants are rewarded for their faithfulness and per-severance, and yet this is not because of any intrinsic worth or merit in themselves, for everything, including the reward, is owed to the grace and power of God by which they have been enabled to endure and overcome (*cf.* 1 Cor. 15:10; 2 Cor. 12:9; Lk. 17:10). They have nothing that they did not receive (1 Cor. 4:7); they have been but faithful stewards of what was entrusted to them (*cf.* Mt. 5:12; 1 Cor. 3:8, 14; Col. 3:23f.; Heb. 10:35; 11:26). Indeed, the sum of it all is this, that Christ himself is their eternal reward (*cf.* Phil. 3:8; Gn. 15:1). For such, there is no terror of judgment to come, for their whole trust is in Christ who dealt with their judgment once for all when he died for their sins, the righteous for the unrighteous (Jn. 5:24; 1 Pet. 3:18).

For the enemies of God and despisers of redeeming grace, however, the judgment to come holds terrors beyond description, as this record of St. John's visions makes very plain (*cf.*, for example, 6:15-17). It is they, with their ungodliness and hatred and impurity and violence and arrogance, whom God will justly *destroy*. In their hostility to the Creator they are the subverters of the order of creation, the agents of chaos, *the destroyers of the earth*. But it is they, not the earth, who are marked for destruction. The time has come, in this vision, for them to be destroyed, while the earth which they have been intent on destroying is restored and glorified in conformity with the indefectible purpose of Almighty God (*cf.* 21:1ff.).

> *And the temple of God in heaven was opened, and the ark of his covenant was seen in his temple; and there were lightnings and voices and thunders and an earthquake and violent hail (11:19).*

St. John is now enabled to look inside *the temple of God in heaven*, that is, the heavenly sanctuary (*cf.* on 3:12; 7:15; 11:1, 2 above), and there he sees *the ark of his covenant*, which in the earthly tabernacle or temple was located in the holy of holies. In Solomon's temple, as in the tabernacle in the wilderness, the ark was a chest of acacia wood covered with gold in which the two tablets of the law given to Moses at Sinai were placed. On it there rested the mercy-seat which intervened between the law of the covenant and the glory of God's presence between the cherubim above it, and on which the blood of atonement for the sins (the law-breaking) of the people was sprinkled. The ark and the mercy-seat were lost or destroyed probably at the time of the Babylonian capture of Jerusalem in the sixth century BC. Their disappearance, however, did not portend the abolition of God's law or the invalidation of his grace. To imagine, as some have done, that the ark from the earthly sanctuary was somehow transported to the heavenly sanctuary is certainly mistaken, for, as we have pointed out previously, the earthly temple with its contents was but a shadow of the heavenly reality, and not the reality itself (Heb. 8:5; 10:1). The appearance of the ark of the covenant in this vision indicates symbolically that God's law is the constant standard of his holiness and justice, and that, apart from the reconciling death of Jesus, whose blood is 'the blood of the everlasting covenant' (Heb. 13:20), the law-breaker, who is everyman, is under condemnation and subject to judgment. Hence the *lightnings*, the *voices*, the *thunders*, the *earthquake*, and the *violent hail*, which, as we have already observed, repeatedly appear as the apocalyptic accompaniments of judgment in these visions.

The woman, the male child, and the dragon, 12:1–17

1. THE BIRTH OF THE MALE CHILD, 12:1–6

And a great sign appeared in heaven, a woman clothed with the sun and the moon under her feet, and on her head a crown of twelve stars; and being with child she cried out in her birth pangs and in agony to be delivered (12:1–2).

This book of visions is to all intents and purposes a book of signs which by their symbolism point to realities of special importance. In calling what he now sees *a great sign* St. John is drawing attention to its exceptional significance. Though the spectacle is seen *in heaven*, events that take place on earth are involved. The identity of the *woman* who is the focal point of the vision is not immediately apparent, but she is obviously a personage of special distinction: her being *clothed with the sun* indicates her resplendent beauty, her having *the moon under her feet* betokens her authority, and her *crown of twelve stars* denotes her royal status. The number twelve provides a clue, for it is the number of the redeemed of mankind (see on 7:4–8 above), and what follows in this vision confirms that this woman symbolizes the church of God. The church, beloved of the Lord and purchased by his blood, will be presented by him cleansed and sanctified, 'without spot or wrinkle' and 'holy and without blemish', in a word 'resplendent' (Eph. 5:25–27;[1] Acts 20:28). The church, moreover, wields the authority of its Lord (Lk. 10:19; 24:49; Acts 1:8) and is destined to be crowned and to reign with him (1 Cor. 9:25; 1 Pet. 5:4; 2 Tim. 2:12; *cf.* ch. 2:10; 3:11; 22:5).

The woman's *birth pangs* have specific reference to the incarnation (as the birth of a son, verse 5, plainly shows). The connection with the prophecy of Isaiah 7:14, 'Therefore the Lord himself will give you a sign. Behold, a virgin [RSV margin] shall conceive and bear a son, and shall

[1]The Greek adjective *endoxos* in Eph. 5:27, 'that he might present the church to himself *endoxon*', means precisely 'resplendent', 'gloriously radiant'.

135

call his name Immanuel', should not be missed; for, as St. Matthew declares this prophecy was fulfilled when Jesus was born of the virgin Mary in Bethlehem (Mt. 1:20–23), so here, too, in St. John's vision, we have the sign and the childbearing. The transition in meaning from Mary to the church is not unnatural, since the church is also depicted in the New Testament as a woman, and in particular as the Bride of Christ (see 19:7; 21:2, 9; Je. 31:32). Mary, too, is essentially one with the church, of which she is a member.

> *And another sign appeared in heaven, and behold, a great red dragon with seven heads and ten horns and seven diadems on his heads; and his tail drew the third part of the stars of heaven and cast them to the earth; and the dragon stood before the woman who was about to give birth, so that he might devour her child when she gave birth (12:3–4).*

Now *another sign* is given as the drama of this vision develops before the seer's gaze: a *dragon* appears that is both *great* and *red*, literally 'fiery red', implying that he is fearsome and deadly. His aspect is all the more intimidating because he has *seven heads* that are crowned with *seven diadems*, which are the adornment of kingship (*cf.* Is. 62:3); the divine number seven indicating his crowning as god by apostate mankind (*cf.* 2 Cor. 4:4; and note 9:11, 'they have as king over them the angel of the abyss'). His appearance is also frightening because he has *ten horns*, which are a symbol of strength (*cf.* on 5:6 above); the number ten indicating the plenitude of power arrogantly claimed by him (*cf.* Mt. 4:9) and fanatically attributed to him by his followers in their futile defiance of the one true God who alone is all-powerful (*cf.* 1:8; 4:8; 11:17). Like the beast with ten horns in Daniel 7:7, this dragon is 'terrible and dreadful and exceedingly strong'; nor is this surprising, for in verse 9 below he is identified as 'the Devil and Satan, the deceiver of the whole world'.

The *stars* that are dragged down by the dragon's *tail*, that is, as his followers, represent the angels who joined Satan in his rebellion against God. The *third part* denotes a considerable proportion, but not a majority (*cf.* 8:7–12; 9:15, 18). The dragon positions himself to seize and destroy the woman's child. Nothing, indeed, is more urgent for him than to *devour* the Son who is coming into the world to destroy the devil and his works (*cf.* 11:18; 1 Jn. 3:8; Heb. 2:14). Herod's brutal slaughter of the innocents (Mt. 2:16ff.) was a satanic attempt to 'devour' the new-born Son who is the world's authentic King; but there was no way in which he or any other creature could frustrate and bring to nothing the gracious purpose of God in accordance with which the Son came into the world to procure our everlasting salvation.

And she gave birth to a son, a male child, who is to rule all the nations with a rod of iron; and her child was caught up to God and to his throne (12:5).

It is with the incarnation that the enmity between the serpent or dragon and the seed of the woman (see Gn. 3:15) reaches its greatest intensity. The **male child** to whom the Virgin Mary gives birth is preserved from the slaughter of the innocents, but the devil does not cease to attack him throughout his ministry and even during the hours of his dying.[1] The apparent defeat of his death and burial, however, is shown to be his complete victory by his rising from the grave and his ascension to the glory he had left behind for our sakes (Phil. 2:6–11). The power is seen to be his and not Satan's as the woman's child is **caught up to God and to his throne**, there **to rule all the nations with a rod of iron** which none can break. Thus is fulfilled the messianic prediction of the second psalm, in which the Lord says to his Anointed One: 'You are my son, today I have begotten you. Ask of me, and I will make the nations your heritage and the ends of the earth your possession. You shall break them with a rod of iron' (Ps. 2:7–9; *cf.* 19:15 below). Similarly, Isaiah prophesied that 'to us a child is born, to us a son is given', whose throne would be established in justice and righteousness for evermore (Is. 9:6f.). All his rule is directed towards the peace of the whole creation; for all along his rule is the rule of the Shepherd: the Greek verb translated to *rule* here (*poimainein*) means to act as a shepherd. His justice is in no way divorced from or contrary to his love!

And the woman fled into the wilderness, where she has a place prepared by God, there to be nourished for one thousand two hundred and sixty days (12:6).

Now that the incarnate Son has ascended to his throne on high, the dragon directs his hostility against **the woman**, who represents the true Church of God here on earth. The woman, however, flees **into the wilderness** and finds refuge in **a place prepared by God** for her. There, **nourished** by God, she is enabled to survive for **one thousand two hundred and sixty days**, otherwise defined, in verse 14 below, as 'a time and times and a half a time' and, in 13:5, as 'forty-two months', that is, for a peroid of limited duration which is short in comparison with the limitless eternity of peace and freedom that will follow in the new heaven and earth (see comments on 11:2 and 3 above). The woman's flight recalls the experience of the prophet Elijah whose life was sought by Jezebel and who was sustained by God in the wilderness (1 Ki. 17:2ff.; 19:4ff.). The symbolism in St. John's vision depicts the history of the

---

[1] See my *No Cross, No Crown* (Wilton, Connecticut, 1988), pp. 18ff.

people of God for whom the wilderness is the world in its fallenness and its hostility to the truth; consequently they acknowledge themselves to be 'strangers and exiles on the earth' whose true home is the heavenly country (Heb. 11:13–16). In the meantime they are nurtured by God who supplies their every need 'according to his riches in glory in Christ Jesus' (Phil. 4:19).

2. WAR IN HEAVEN. THE DRAGON CAST OUT, 12:7–12

And there was war in heaven, Michael and his angels fighting against the dragon; and the dragon and his angels fought and did not prevail, and there was no longer any place for them in heaven. And the great dragon was cast down, that ancient serpent, who is called the Devil and Satan, the deceiver of the whole world – he was cast down to the earth, and his angels were cast down with him (12:7–9).

The warfare against the forces of evil is not merely global, it is cosmic. Here the armies in conflict are the angelic hosts under the leadership of the great archangel **Michael** (*cf.* Jude 9) on the one side and the great archdemon, **the dragon**, on the other, and the engagement takes place **in heaven**, where the dragon has mobilized the great rebellion against God and his authority. The reference is to warfare that has long continued rather than to a particular battle, and the development of central importance here is that the climactic moment has arrived when the dragon and his angels are **cast down to the earth**. This does not mean that their evil influence had not previously been exercised on earth, for indeed it had, from Eden onwards. But now an event of literally crucial significance has taken place, namely, the death of the incarnate Son on the cross. The dragon's corrupting activity in the earthly sphere prior to this is perfectly clear from the way he is identified here as **that ancient serpent**, through whom sin was introduced into our world (Gn. 3), and as **the Devil and Satan**, who is **the deceiver of the whole world**. As such, he is the leader of 'the destroyers of the earth' (11:18). So he has long been active in our midst. But he and his followers now suffer a critical setback and a casting down. And this is but a stage on the way to their eternal downfall, for, as Christ said, their end is 'the eternal fire prepared for the devil and his angels' (Mt. 25:41; *cf.* 20:10 below).

The expulsion of Satan and his angels from heaven is directly associated with and follows after the completion of the Son's redemptive mission to earth, briefly indicated in verse 5 above by the catching up of the woman's male child to God and his throne. The fulfilment of the purpose of the incarnation is at the same time an assault on Satan's kingdom. Thus, as Christ perceived, the casting out of demons by himself and his disciples was symptomatic of Satan's fall from heaven (Lk. 10:17f.), and his offering of himself up to death on the cross portended the expulsion of the ruler of this world (Jn. 12:31; *cf.* 16:11, 33). The twofold purpose of his incarnation was, first, 'to destroy him who has the power of death, that is, the devil', and, second, 'to deliver all those who through fear of death were subject to lifelong bondage' (Heb. 2:14f.). And it was on the altar of the cross that the incarnate Son 'disarmed the principalities and powers' and triumphantly exposed their fraudulence to the world (Col. 2:14f.). This cosmic conquest was authenticated by his resurrection from the dead and his ascension to the throne on high. The momentous events that were realized through the incarnation were the earthly aspect of the warfare in heaven; indeed, they were the central and decisive thrust of that warfare.

> *And I heard a loud voice in heaven, saying, Now the salvation and the power and the kingdom of our God and the authority of his Christ have come, for the accuser of our brethren, who accuses them day and night before our God, has been cast down (12:10).*

The *loud voice in heaven* is the voice of jubilation, for the sovereign power of Almighty God and the unassailability of the salvation he has provided have been conclusively demonstrated, and the victorious authority of his Anointed One established, as at the same time the imposture of the devil who constantly brings false accusations against *our brethren* is exposed. Contrary to the ministry of the loyal angels, who 'serve for the sake of those who are to obtain salvation' (Heb. 1:14), the devil is unremittingly active, *day and night*, in his hostility to them. It is because of his slanders that he is called the *devil (diabolos)*, which means slanderer. Thus, for example, he slanderously accused God's servant Job: 'Does Job fear God for naught? . . . But put forth thy hand now, and touch all that he has, and he will curse thee to thy face' (Jb. 1:9–11; 2:5). Satan's doom is sealed, however, as this book clearly shows, and there is no way in which he can prevent the glorious consummation of all things in which the redeemed creation, of whom the four living creatures are the representation, never cease 'day and night' in their adoration and worship of God (4:8 above). The devil has but a short time (see verse 12 below).

> *And they overcame him through the blood of the Lamb and through the word of their testimony, and they did not love their life unto death (12:11).*

Instead of overcoming the brethren whom he slanders, the devil is

139

overcome by them. His accusations rebound against himself. Their victory, however, is not achieved by virtue of their own strength or goodness, but **through the blood of the Lamb**, that is to say through the Son's atoning sacrifice of himself in their place on the cross, which is the sole and the eternally secure basis of their justification before God (*cf.* comments above on 7:14), **and through the word of their testimony**, that is to say through their faithful witness to Christ in whose strength they stand firm (*cf.* Phil. 4:13; 2 Cor. 12:9f.). Their constancy is attested, moreover, by the fact that **they did not love their life unto death**, being willing and glad even to lay down their lives for the sake of him who first laid down his life for their eternal redemption (*cf.* the two witnesses of 11:3ff. above). This, then, is the prescription for all overcoming: in all circumstances and eventualities, in tribulation, distress, persecution, famine, nakedness, peril, sword, and in dying, 'we are more than conquerors through him who loved us' (Rom. 8:35–37). And so the very moment when the devil seems most to overcome and prevail, in the killing of the brethren, is the moment of their victory and his defeat.

> **Therefore rejoice, O heavens, and you who dwell in them! Woe to you, earth and sea, because the devil has come down to you in great wrath, knowing that he has but a short time** (12:12).

Defeated in the warfare above, the devil and his hosts have been cast down; but Satan is not yet immobilized, for **earth and sea** have now become the particular sphere of his activity (*cf.* verses 7–9 above). The **great wrath** with which he vainly seeks to destroy the church is explained by his awareness that **he has but a short time**, as already indicated by the symbolical figure of 1,260 days (verse 6). Hence St. Peter's warning to his fellow Christians: 'Your adversary the devil prowls around like a roaring lion, seeking someone to devour' (1 Pet. 5:8). The rejoicing over the victory above is balanced, so to speak, by the **woe** that Satan's raging brings to our world below. God's people below are not immune from the savage raging of the devil, but they remain eternally secure in Christ. This is the explanation of St. Paul's triumphant exultation in the face of persecution: 'If God is for us, who is against us? . . . Who shall bring any charge against God's elect? It is God who justifies! Who is the one to condemn? It is Christ Jesus who died, yes indeed, who was raised from the dead, who is at the right hand of God, who also intercedes for us!' (Rom. 8:31–34). If the devil's doom is sealed, so also is the salvation of God's elect against whom the satanic wrath is directed.

3. THE DRAGON PERSECUTES THE WOMAN AND HER OFFSPRING, 12:13–17

And when the dragon saw that he was cast down to the earth he persecuted the woman who had given birth to the male child. And the two wings of the great eagle were given to the woman so that she might fly into the wilderness, to her place where she is nourished for a time and times and half a time from the presence of the serpent (12:13–14).

Having failed to overthrow the woman's Son, the dragon, cast down to earth, turns his attention to the woman, intending her destruction. As we have said (see comments on verses 4–6 above), the identity of the woman now becomes one with that of the church whose members endure the dragon's persecution. The woman, however, is given **the two wings of the great eagle** – an allusion, perhaps, to the fourth living creature whose likeness is that of a flying eagle (4:7) – and is thus enabled to escape to **her place** in the wilderness where she is sustained by God for **a time and times and half a time** (see verse 6 above). This period denotes three and a half years and is the same as the 1,260 days in verse 6 and the forty-two months in 13:5. It symbolizes the time, limited by God, of the church's persecution by Satan on earth, the time, that is, between the comings of Christ. In the wilderness of this fallen world the church is unfailingly **nourished** by God, who brings his people safely through innumerable persecutions and afflictions to the glorious consummation of the purified and renewed creation. 'In the world you have tribulation', Christ told his disciples; 'but be of good cheer, I have overcome the world' (Jn. 16:33). In the course of all that they suffer they are borne aloft as though by eagle's wings, in accordance with the promise given through Isaiah, that 'they who wait for the Lord . . . shall mount up with wings like eagles' (Is. 40:31). The same metaphor is used of God's deliverance of the Israelites from the tyranny of the Egyptians: 'You have seen what I did to the Egyptians, and how I bore you on eagles' wings and brought you to myself' (Ex. 19:4). The church is not only preserved **from the presence of the serpent**, but is also brought to the presence of God himself.

And the serpent poured water like a river out of his mouth after the woman, to sweep her away with the flood; and the earth helped the woman, and the earth opened its mouth and swallowed the river which the dragon poured from his mouth (12:15–16).

The serpent spews forth a flood of hatred and violence which threatens to overwhelm the woman, but St. John sees the earth coming as it were to the woman's help by opening up and swallowing this river of malice.

141

Terrifying as the appearance of the dragon is, his attempts to dislodge the church from the Lord's protection are always futile. Moreover, God uses unexpected means for the preservation of his church when it is threatened with extinction by the flood of persecution – such, for example, as his keeping of the Israelites from destruction at the hands of the pursuing Egyptians by bringing them dryshod through the Red Sea. Deliverance from the floodwaters of affliction and persecution is a recurring theme in the Psalms, as the following passages show:

> The cords of death encompassed me. .... In my distress I called upon the Lord, to my God I cried for help. From his temple he heard my voice, and my cry to him reached his ears. ... Let every one who is godly offer prayer to thee; at a time of distress, in the rush of great waters, they shall not reach him. Thou art a hiding place for me; thou preservest me from trouble; thou dost encompass me with deliverance. .... If it had not been the Lord who was on our side, when men rose up against us, then they would have swallowed us up alive, ... then the flood would have swept us away, the torrent would have gone over us; then over us would have gone the raging waters (*Pss. 18:4, 6; 32:6f.; 124:2–5; cf. Is. 43:1f.*).

And so it has always been in the history of God's church.

> **And the dragon was enraged with the woman and went on to make war on the rest of her seed who keep the commandments of God and bear testimony to Jesus (12:17a).**

The developments depicted in the preceding verses apply, in our judgment, to the church throughout its history; but in the verse we are now considering a historical sequence seems to be discernible, to the effect that the dragon had at first hoped to overwhelm the church with the flood of persecution while its membership was still concentrated in Jerusalem and its neighbourhood. The earth, however, according to the imagery of this vision, had first 'opened its mouth' and swallowed the river of satanic wrath when Saul of Tarsus, the determined leader of the original fierce wave of persecution, was suddenly converted to become Paul the Apostle of Jesus Christ. This was an eventuality as startling as it was unlooked for. St. Paul's apostleship was directed in a special though not exclusive sense to the Gentiles, who may be seen here as constituting *the rest of* the woman's *seed*, and his warfare is now against the dragon (Eph. 6:10ff.). Consequently the dragon's rage extends to 'the rest of her seed' as the power of the gospel spreads from Jerusalem to the ends of the earth (*cf.* Acts 1:8), fulfilling the promise given to

Abraham that in his seed all the nations of the earth would be blessed (Gn. 22:18; *cf.* Gal. 3:6–9, 16, 27–29). This is the setting in which the age-old hostility of the serpent to the seed of the woman (Gn. 3:15) continues until the day of Christ's appearing. The authentic seed of the woman is specified here as comprising those **who keep the commandments of God and bear testimony to Jesus,** that is to say those who stand firm in their faith and witness in the face of all opposition (as in verse 11 above).

And he stood on the sand of the sea (12:17b).

The restless waters of the sea, a familiar sight to John on Patmos, provide a picture of the troubled society of mankind. 'The wicked', we read, 'are like the tossing sea; for it cannot rest, and its waters toss up mire and dirt. There is no peace, says my God, for the wicked' (Is. 57:20f.). What can the dragon bring up from the turbulent sea of human wickedness? The answer is in what follows.

The two beasts, 13:1–18

1. THE BEAST FROM THE SEA, 13:1–10

> *And I saw a beast coming up out of the sea with ten horns and seven heads, and ten diadems on its horns, and on its heads a name of blasphemy. And the beast that I saw was like a leopard, and its feet were like those of a bear, and its mouth was like the mouth of a lion; and to it the dragon gave his power and his throne and great authority (13:1–2).*

The *beast* that St. John now sees *coming up out of the sea* of humanity in its fallenness (see comment on preceding verse, 12:18) is a monster of terrifying aspect. Like the dragon, who is Satan, it has *seven heads* and *ten horns* (regarding which see comments on 12:3 above), and as such may be understood to be the dragon's agent or representative in human society, invested as it is with the dragon's *power and throne and great authority.* This beast should be taken as denoting the activity of the devil throughout the history of this age by the instrumentality of human movements and organizations rather than a single individual. While the dragon's seven heads were adorned with seven diadems, here it is the beast's ten horns on which *ten diadems* are placed. (The interpretation of this imagery is discussed below when we come to 17:9ff., together with the affinities between St. John's vision and that described in Dn. 7.) The *name of blasphemy* on the beast's heads is indicative of radical hostility to God. From early times this beast from the sea has been identified with antichrist, whose appearance was expected at the end of the present age. It is preferable, however, to see it as the spirit of antichristianity manifested, as we have said, through human agencies during the whole course of the Christian era, though perhaps achieving its final and fiercest force under the leadership of a malevolent personage in the ultimate climax of all history. St. John himself gives a lead in this respect in his first letter, where he writes: 'Little children, it is the last hour; and as you have heard that antichrist is coming, even now many antichrists have appeared; therefore we know that it is the last hour' (1 Jn. 2:18). This final age, however long it continues, is the last hour during which the Satan-inspired spirit of antichrist is present and active on earth. To quote St. John again: 'Every spirit which does not confess Jesus is not of God; and this is the spirit of the antichrist, of which you heard that it was coming, and now it is in the world already' (1 Jn. 4:3). If this was true in St. John's day, it is no less true in ours.

The beast described by the Apostle has characteristics associated with all four of the great beasts seen by Daniel coming up out of the sea in his vision: it was *like a leopard* (as also was Daniel's third beast); *its feet were like those of a bear* (Daniel's second beast was like a bear); *its mouth was like the mouth of a lion* (Daniel's first beast was like a lion); and (like Daniel's 'terrible and dreadful and exceedingly strong' fourth beast) it had *ten horns* (Dn. 7:3ff.). These features emphasize its fearsome aspect and also the concentration of the savage ungodliness of the successive empires of this fallen world.

> *And one of its heads seemed to have been mortally wounded; but its mortal wound was healed, and the whole earth wondered after the beast; and they worshipped the dragon because he had given his authority to the beast; and they worshipped the beast, saying, Who is like the beast and who is able to go to war with him?* (13:3-4).

Though favoured by many, the supposition is far from satisfactory that the apparently *mortal wound* sustained by one of the heads of the persecuting beast refers to the suicide, in AD 68, of the emperor Nero, who had treated the Christians with great brutality, and that the healing of the wound was effected by the dissemination of the rumour that he had returned to life (*Nero redivivus*) or by the revival of his persecution under Domitian in the latter part of the first century. It is more appropriate to understand this wounding of the beast as a reference to the phenomenal growth of the apostolic church in its earliest days, associated with which was the dramatic conversion of Saul of Tarsus, the leading agent of the first fierce wave of the beast's persecution, to become Paul the Apostle and a leading instrument in the Lord's hands of the spread of the gospel (*cf.* Acts 6:7; 9:1ff.). There was also the spectacular response to the preaching of Philip the Evangelist in Samaria. The apparent conversion of Simon Magus, who had been deceiving the populace with his sorcery, but who subsequently reverted to the teaching of error, so much so that he was known in the early church as the father of heresies, is also symptomatic of a blow to the beast from which it recovered (Acts 8:4ff.). In those early days 'the church throughout all Judea and Galilee and Samaria had peace and was built up, and walking in the fear of the Lord and in the comfort of the Holy Spirit was multiplied' (Acts 9:31), to such an extent that the apostles could be hostilely described as 'men who have turned the world upside down' (Acts 17:6).

The beast's *mortal wound was healed*, however, and the antichristian monster continues his savage persecution of the church for forty-two months (see verse 5 below), by which the period of the church's testing by affliction on earth, that is between the two comings of Christ, is signified. Yet the beast is in reality mortally wounded, for it, together with the dragon with whose authority it is empowered, is powerless against the victory of the incarnate Son on the cross and in his resurrection, and is unable to deprive the Lord's people of the eternal life which is theirs in him. Indeed, it is they who, even though the beast kill them, are the true overcomers (12:11, *etc.*). Its doom is all along decreed. In the meantime the vigour of the beast is regained and to the people on earth it is an impressive spectacle. We are told that *the whole earth wondered after the beast*; the deceit of the antichrist evokes the willing response of worldwide admiration. In this respect it is possible for St. John to assert that 'the whole world lies in the power of the evil one' (1 Jn. 5:19).

Not only did the people of the world wonder after the beast that appeared to be so invincible, but they also *worshipped* it and with it *the dragon* who had invested the beast with his authority, and in doing so they make him 'the god of this world' (2 Cor. 4:4), though he is in fact no god but a creature. Thus they show themselves to be ungodly persons who suppress the truth about God; as St. Paul says, 'they exchanged the truth about God for a lie and worshipped and served the creature rather than the Creator' (Rom. 1:18ff., 25). In a word, the world of fallen mankind has substituted the worship of Satan for the worship of God.

The beast, it may be said, convinces multitudes that if indeed Jesus received a mortal wound and yet was restored to life, the healing of its own mortal wound is no less wonderful and to all appearances demonstrates its superior power as it intensified its savage persecution of Christ's followers. Thus the beast that was slain fraudulently usurps the place of the Lamb that was slain (verse 8 below; also 5:6, 12), and the falsification of the truth has become the religion of the worldling. The genuine has been replaced by the counterfeit. The worship of the beast (antichrist) is actually the worship of the dragon (Satan), whose agent the beast is. Instead of declaring with David: 'Thou art great, O Lord God; for there is none like thee, and there is no God besides thee' (2 Sa. 7:22), and heeding the prophetic word spoken through Isaiah: 'To whom then will you liken God? . . . To whom then will you compare me, that I should be like him? says the Holy One' (Is. 40:18, 25), these false worshippers acclaim the beast as they cry, *Who is like the beast and who is able to go to war with him*? And so, instead of assigning all the glory to the true God and his Christ, they blasphemously glorify the devil and his antichrist.

And it was given a mouth uttering great and blasphemous words, and authority was given to it to be active for forty-two months; and

> *it opened its mouth to utter blasphemies against God, to blaspheme his name and his dwelling, even those who dwell in heaven (13:5–6).*

The beast is not as free and powerful as he appears to those on earth to be: both its **authority** and the **mouth to utter blasphemies** have been **given** to it by the dragon (*cf.* verses 1 and 2 above). But neither is the authority of the dragon endless and supreme: the time-limit of **forty-two months** within which the beast is active in human society applies also to the dragon. The moment when the activity of the dragon is brought to an end by God whose power alone is supreme and endless, is also the moment when the activity of its agent the beast is brought to an end (*cf.* 12:6). The devil knows 'that he has but a short time' (12:12). Rampant and raging though they are, the dragon and the beast are on God's leash throughout the course of this final age and can only go as far as God permits.

The blasphemous assault of Satan through his agent the antichristian beast is essentially rebellion **against God** and his supreme authority. It is all the more frantic and embittered because of the leash and the limitation of time. Moreover, to blaspheme against God is **to blaspheme his name** which is holy (*cf.* Ex. 20:7; Is. 57:15; Ps. 111:9; Dt. 28:58; Lk. 1:49) and also the company of the redeemed who are **his dwelling**, in accordance with God's covenant promise that he will dwell among them (*cf.* Ex. 29:45; Lv. 26:11f.; Ezk. 37:26f.). God's people are described as **those who dwell in heaven** because their true home and their true citizenship are not here and now, in this present pilgrimage, but in the glory that is to be revealed hereafter (*cf.* Phil. 3:20; Heb. 11:13, 16; 13:14; Rom. 8:18). The kingdom of total peace and righteousness awaits them; but in the meantime it is warfare (as the next verse shows).

> *And it was enabled to make war on the saints and to overcome them; and it was given authority over every tribe and people and tongue and nation. And all who dwell on earth will worship it, every one whose name has not been written from the foundation of the world in the book of life of the Lamb that was slain (13:7–8).*

All out warfare is what the devil is promoting, nothing less; and this is done through the agency of the beast whose power is that of antichrist derived from the devil himself. (**It was enabled**, literally 'it was given to it', that is, by the dragon who is Satan.) The beast, moreover, is empowered not only **to make war on the saints** but also **to overcome them.** That is to say, its warfare has every appearance of being successful as saints are arrested and imprisoned and put to death. Yet the beast's victory is more apparent than real; it is temporary, not permanent. To silence God's faithful witnesses by killing them may look like overcoming them, but, as we have seen, God's martyred saints are the true overcomers 'through the blood of the Lamb and through the word of their testimony' (12:11). The Lord's witnesses who are slain are raised up to life again (11:7, 11), as will happen, certainly, at the last day. But in the meantime the light of Christian witness is not snuffed out: in place of St. Stephen, who is stoned to death, God raises up Saul of Tarsus to become Paul the Apostle, who was called by God's grace to fulfil the ministry of witness for which he had been set apart before he was born (Gal. 1:15f.). Thus God is in control even when the beast is in the world's eyes gaining the victory. God, because he is God, is and cannot fail always to be the true and ultimate overcomer. Through his grace and power his saints are overcomers, no matter what may be done to them. Hence the great blessings promised by the Lord to those who overcome (in the letters to the seven churches, 2:7, *etc.*, also 15:2 and 21:7).

The *authority* which the beast is *given* by the dragon is worldwide in extent, as the fourfold designation *over every tribe and people and tongue and nation* both explicitly and symbolically discloses. By its subtle and deceitful propaganda the beast attracts the worship of *all who dwell on earth*, that is to say, inhabitants in every land. That the reference is not intended to be all-inclusive is clear from the explanation that 'all' here denotes *every one whose name has not been written . . . in the book of life of the Lamb.* Here we come face to face with the ultimate division of all mankind: those whose names are, and those whose names are not written in the Lamb's book, the regenerate and the unregenerate. The book of life has already been mentioned in 3:5 (see comments there). That the names of the Lord's elect have been written in it *from the foundation of the world*[1] testifies not only to God's transcendental sway over all, including the beast and the dragon, but also to the infallibility of his purposes in creation. These purposes are brought to fulfilment redemptively in Christ, *the Lamb that was slain* and by whose blood men, women, and children have been ransomed for God from every tribe and tongue and people and nation (5:9). This is a universality that prevails over that of the beast's power. It testifies also to the absolute security of those whose names, well known to God, and chosen before the foundation of the world (Eph. 1:4), are written in the Lamb's book of life.

The worship offered to the beast is the worship of all that is ungodly and unchristian: worldly wealth and power and lust and covetousness,

---

[1] The phrase 'from the foundation of the world' could be taken either with 'written' (written from the foundation of the world) or with 'slain' (slain from the foundation of the world). The former seems preferable, especially as in 17:8 we read of those 'whose names have not been written in the book of life from the foundation of the world', which is a repetition of what is said here.

the idols by which the worshippers of the beast are brought to perdition.

> *If any one has an ear, let him hear. If any one is for captivity, to captivity he goes; if any one is to be killed with the sword, with the sword he will be killed. Here is the endurance and faith of the saints (13:9–10).*

The admonition *If any one has an ear, let him hear* corresponds to the exhortation 'He who has an ear, let him hear' that is present in all of the letters to the seven churches of Asia (2:7, *etc.*). Here it introduces instruction concerning the persecution which *the saints* are called to endure. At first sight the assertion, *If any one is for captivity, to captivity he goes*, and, *if any one is to be killed with the sword, with the sword he will be killed*, looks like a pointless statement of the obvious; but in fact it conveys a message of profound significance for the Lord's people. The assertion is evidently based on the declaration of Jeremiah 15:2, 'Thus says the Lord: . . . those who are for the sword, to the sword; . . . and those who are for captivity, to captivity' (and Je. 43:11, where the order coincides with the order in the verse before us). In Jeremiah's prophecy the context is one of judgment for which an apostate people and a godless nation are destined and from which there will be no escape. Here, however, the reference is to God's faithful servants, giving them the assurance that in the suffering of imprisonment or death nothing happens to them that is not under God's control or contrary to his will. In all things the Lord rules and overrules. Those who face captivity or sword may be sure that it is in accord with his plan. It is in the acceptance of affliction that *the endurance and faith of the saints* are triumphantly demonstrated. Such testing gives proof of the genuineness of their faith and the unshakability of their hope in Christ. The suggestion of inevitability implies the supremacy of the divine will, which is always directed to the good and the blessing of the redeemed community.

2. THE BEAST FROM THE EARTH, 13:11–18

> *And I saw another beast coming up out of the earth, and it had two horns like a lamb and it spoke like a dragon. And it acts with all the authority of the first beast in its presence; and it causes the earth and its inhabitants to worship the first beast whose mortal wound was healed (13:11–12).*

St. John now sees *another beast*, this one *coming up out of the earth*, whereas the first beast had come up out of the sea (verse 1). This distinction may indicate a still closer association with human society, but too much should not be read into it.[1] The two beasts have a close relationship and they both have a malign influence in the course of human history. In appearance this second beast is thoroughly deceptive: *like a lamb* with *two horns*, it parades as a saviour similar to, but in reality quite other than, the Lamb that was slain for our redemption (verse 8). But it is a false saviour with a false message of salvation: *it spoke like a dragon* since its voice is no different from the voice of the dragon (verse 3) and its lying words are the lying words of the dragon. Because *it acts with all the authority of the first beast* and *in its presence*, which also implies that it does so under its control, it is the agent of the first beast as in turn the first beast is the agent of the dragon (verse 2). Thus both beasts are the instruments of Satan in his warfare against God. The primary function of the second beast is to promote the worship of the first beast by *the earth and its inhabitants*, that is, on a worldwide scale.

Later in this book the second beast is designated as the false prophet (16:13; 19:20; 20:10), and this indicates its activity as a voice or spirit of falsehood *within the church* – seductively lamb-like in mien but lethally dragon-like in teaching. The figure of the false prophet who is this beast is representative of all the false leaders who appear from generation to generation, just as Christ predicted. 'Beware of false prophets who come to you in sheep's clothing', he warned, 'but inwardly are ravening wolves' (Mt. 7:15). And again: 'False Christs and false prophets will arise and will show signs and wonders, to lead astray, if possible, the elect' (Mk. 13:22). St. Paul contended with false teachers who disguised themselves as apostles of Christ – 'and no wonder', he wrote, 'for even Satan disguises himself as an angel of light, so it is not strange if his ministers disguise themselves as ministers of righteousness' (2 Cor. 11:13–15). St. John likewise declared that many antichrists and many false prophets were active in his day (1 Jn. 2:18; 4:1), persons who rose up within the church (Jn. 1:19; as St. Paul also had given warning, Acts 20:30).

In Satan (the dragon), antichrist (the first beast), and the false prophet (the second beast) there is the manifestation of the unholy trinity of the Anti-God, the trinity of evil.

> *And it performs great signs, even making fire come down from heaven to earth in the presence of men; and it deceives the dwellers on earth by the signs which were given to it to perform in the presence of the beast, telling those who dwell on earth to make an image to the beast which had the wound from the sword and yet lives (13:13–14).*

[1] In Daniel's vision the four great beasts that come up out of the sea are explained as four kings who will arise out of the earth (Dn. 7:3, 17)

151

The second beast, who is the false prophet, **performs great signs** with the power it is **given** – power which comes to it from the dragon, who is Satan, by way of the first beast, who is antichrist (see verses 2 and 12). By its spectacular display it **deceives the dwellers on earth**, for the wonders it performs are the counterfeit of divine wonders. To make **fire come down from heaven to earth**, for example, is to counterfeit the calling down of divine fire by Elijah in his contest with the prophets of Baal (1 Ki. 18:38). So, too, the sorcerers of Egypt imitated the marvels performed by Aaron (Ex. 7:10f.). The ability of the beast to cause fire to come down from heaven, whether taken literally or not, signifies the diabolical ability with which it is invested for the purpose of persuading people that its power is divine power. In this respect the activity of this beast corresponds with St. Paul's admonition that the coming of 'the lawless one' would be 'in accordance with the working of Satan with all power and false signs and wonders, and with every deception of wickedness for those who are perishing because they rejected the love of the truth intended for their salvation' (2 Thes. 2:9f.).

Both beasts are energized by the malign power and authority of Satan, 'the deceiver of the whole world' (12:9). Their deceit is satanic deceit. The command issued by the second beast **to make an image to the beast which had the wound from the sword and yet lives** need not imply the setting up of a literal image or statue. There is a depth of evil here, for the intention is to obliterate the image of God in which man is created and to raise up in its place the image of antichrist – Christ himself being the Image of God in accordance with which man was formed and to which mankind is being redemptively restored (*cf.* Col. 1:15; 2 Cor. 3:18; 4:4; Rom. 8:29). In effect, the image of the first beast is the image of Satan, by whom it is energized. Its image portends the concentration of the world's religious impulses in a single humanistic worship that, being turned away from God, is self-worship, self-worship, however, that is induced by the devil, and is therefore the enthronement of the devil, the antigod, in God's place.

> *And it was given to it to give breath to the image of the beast, so that the image of the beast should even speak and cause as many as would not worship the image of the beast to be killed (13:15).*

The relationship of the two beasts denotes an unholy alliance of the antichristian state with the apostate church, in such a way that the latter becomes subservient to the former. The cult of the beast supplants the worship of the Lord God, who alone is to be worshipped (Mt. 4:10). Not only is this the worship of the creature rather than the Creator (Rom. 1:25), but it is also symptomatic of the frenetic attempt of the fallen creature *to be as God* (Gn. 3:5). The claim is made to the absolute power of life and death. **To give breath to the image of the beast** is to counterfeit the life-giving work of God in creation. To cause it to *speak* is to offer a spurious imitation of him who is the Word (Jn. 1:1), by uttering promises of satisfaction and fulfilment for all and of abundant life.

And together with the pretension to the power of life goes the pretension to the power of death, which is given verisimilitude by the killing of *as many as would not worship the image of the beast.* Typical of this deification of the state was the demand made by Nebuchadnezzar that all the populace should fall down and worship the great golden image that he had set up (Dn. 3:1ff.). Throughout the centuries worship has been diverted from God to kings and pharaohs and caesars, and hymns have been sung to tyrants, while those who have refused to participate in this idolatry have been put to death. The church has been secularized by bowing to the political and philosophical temper of the age, and in doing so has accepted the devil's mark of salvation which in reality is the mark of perdition; for the objective of the devil's fraudulent imitations is always the negation and the overturning of the divine order. The speaking of the counterfeit image is even in the very words of him who is the true Word, using the same transcendental terminology so as to deceive the unwary, but in such a way as to destroy its meaning and subvert the truth. Thus the devil darkens the senseless minds of all who 'exchange the glory of the immortal God for the likeness of an image . . . and the truth about God for a lie' (Rom. 1:21–23, 25).

> *And it causes all, both small and great, both rich and poor, both free and bond, to be marked on their right hand or on their forehead, so that no one can buy or sell unless he has the mark of the beast, that is, the name of the beast or the number of its name. Here is wisdom: let him who has understanding reckon the number of the beast, for it is the number of man; and its number is six hundred and sixty-six (13:16–18).*

We have already seen that the Lord's own people are sealed on their foreheads (7:3ff.), indicating that they are known to him and secure in him. Here we have another counterfeit, namely, the sealing of men and women of all sorts and conditions with **the mark of the beast** to give them a false sense of identity and security. Actually, it is a sign of perdition, for, though it bestows on them permission to **buy or sell** and the privileges of social respectability (the mark **on their right hand** perhaps denoting the licence to gain employment and conduct business and the mark **on their forehead** the granting of status and approval in the community of mankind), it stamps them as those who have allied themselves with Satan and thus who are doomed with him, and the benefits it confers are passing and insubstantial. This marking is a marking at the heart of a person's being rather than something merely external. The imagery no doubt comes from the practice of branding

153

slaves with the mark of their master – not, however, that this belongs to a supposedly less civilized past, for in our own day the Jews who were carried off to the concentration camps and gas-chambers of Hitler's holocaust had an indelible number stamped on their wrists.

The mark of the beast, we are told, is one with **the name of the beast**, which, while unspecified, is the equivalent of antichrist, **or the number of its name**, which is specified and is declared to be a mystical source of **wisdom** for the person **who has understanding.** That number is revealed as **six hundred and sixty-six.** Like the other numbers of this book, it has symbolical significance; its meaning is not exposed in a literal manner on the surface; it requires 'reckoning' to understand it.

The most popular device for the unlocking of this mystery has been the technique known as *gematria*[1] in which each letter of the alphabet has its own particular numerical equivalent.[2] The method was much favoured by the rabbinical sages, who used it for estimating the numerical value of words and phrases and thereby disclosing what were otherwise, supposedly, hidden significances. In the Christian church we find instances of the adoption of gematria as an interpretative technique as early as the sub-apostolic period. A survey of the marvellous results which this method is claimed to have disclosed when applied to this passage (not to mention others) gives abundant proof that it is readily amenable to the subjective presuppositions of each interpreter, and so can be manipulated to give quite different and even contradictory answers. Depending on each individual's ingenuity and credulity, the number 666 can be worked out to mean almost anything one wishes, and where the predetermined solution cannot be invented by the use of Greek letters there has been no scruple about resorting to Hebrew or Latin to unearth an acceptable significance. Thus, for example, it has been calculated that the mystic number 666 designates one or other of the Roman emperors, or of the popes, or of the protestant reformers, or Archbishop Laud, or Oliver Cromwell, or John Wesley.[3] The possibilities are legion!

The one clue that St. John gives is that the number of the beast, 666, is **the number of man.** The number six has understandably been regarded as a symbol of man, in that it falls short of seven, which is the divine number. On this basis the threefold six may be understood as indicative of a human or humanistic trinity, that is to say a counterfeit of the divine Trinity, with all the pretensions to supreme power and authority that

[1] The term *gematria* is a Hebrew adaptation of the Greek noun *geometria*.

[2] *Gematria* is also known as *isopsephism*, meaning numerical equivalence.

[3] David Brady, in his book *The Contribution of British Writers between 1560 and 1830 to the Interpretation of Revelation 13:16–18 (The Number of the Beast): A Study in the History of Exegesis* (Mohr: Siebeck, Tübingen, 1983), gives well over a hundred varying interpretations of the number 666, some based on Hebrew, some on Greek, some on Latin, which have been confidently proposed.

such a counterfeit implies. It may perhaps be inferred from the context that this pseudo-trinity is that of Satan (the dragon) plus antichrist (the first beast) plus the false prophet (the second beast), who are united in the one diabolical objective, namely, to dethrone the Creator and to enthrone the creature and to substitute the image of the beast for the image of God in man. An interpretation along these lines harmonizes well with the whole tenor of this book of Revelation and does justice to the warning elsewhere that in this final age the Christian's warfare is 'against the principalities, against the powers, against the world rulers of this present darkness, against the spiritual hosts of wickedness' (Eph. 6:12). That this is so becomes all the more apparent in the visions that now remain for St. John to recount.

Mount Zion and the vintage of the earth, *14:1–20*

1. THE 144,000 REDEEMED AND THE NEW SONG, 14:1–5

And I saw, and behold, the Lamb standing on Mount Zion, and with him a hundred and forty-four thousand who had his name and the name of his Father written on their foreheads (14:1).

Now once again St. John sees **the Lamb**, the true and authentic Lamb, as distinct from the false lamb who is empowered by the antichrist (13:11f.); moreover, the Lamb, once slain, is **standing** (as in 5:6), alive and strong, and he is standing on **Mount Zion**, the mountain of divine grace and reconciliation in contrast to Mount Sinai on which the law was given whereby all men stand condemned since all are law-breakers (Heb. 12:18–22; Rom. 3:20; 2 Cor. 3:7, 9). In prophetic expectation Zion was synonymous with the promised messianic kingdom of justice and peace. See, for example, Psalm 2:6, 'I have set my king on Zion, my holy hill'; Micah 4:7, 'The Lord will reign over them in Mount Zion'; and Isaiah 59:20, 'He will come to Zion as Redeemer'. Christian believers are given the assurance, accordingly, that they have come 'to Mount Zion and to the city of the living God, the heavenly Jerusalem, . . . and to the assembly of the firstborn who are enrolled in heaven' (Heb. 12:22f.).

The **hundred and forty-four thousand** whom the Apostle sees with the Lamb represent 'the assembly of the firstborn who are enrolled in heaven' now rejoicing in the glory of the promised kingdom. They are the same 144,000 we have encountered in 7:2ff. who have the seal of the living God on their foreheads, and who in turn are the great multitude of the redeemed which no man can number (7:9ff.) – the number 144,000 being symbolical of the great and complete company known and sealed by God in accordance with his creative and redemptive purposes. This immense concourse, whose robes have been washed and made white in the blood of the Lamb (7:14), have **his name and the name of his Father**, or, in other words, the seal of the living God, **written on their**

foreheads. There is a correspondence also with the Lord's promise in 3:12 above to write on those who overcome 'The name of my God and the name of the city of my God, the new Jerusalem, . . . and my own name', for 'the city of my God' is one with Mount Zion where the Lamb is seen standing with his redeemed as they enter into the blessing of their true and eternal citizenship – a destiny totally different from that of those whose foreheads are marked with the name of the beast (13:16f.) in the vain expectation that this is a guarantee of safety and security.

> *And I heard a sound from heaven like the sound of many waters and like the sound of loud thunder; and the sound I heard was like the sound of harpers playing on their harps; and they sing a new song before the throne and before the four living creatures and the elders; and no one was able to learn the song except the one hundred and forty-four thousand who had been redeemed from the earth (14:2–3).*

The **sound** St. John hears is the music of *a new song* being sung by the heavenly host. The likeness of the music to **the sound of many waters** and to **the sound of loud thunder** and also to **the sound of harpers playing on their harps** is descriptive of its cosmic profundity and melodious majesty. The voice of the Lamb was likened to the sound of many waters (1:15); one of the four living creatures has spoken 'as with a voice of thunder' (6:1); and all four living creatures together with the twenty-four elders have been seen holding harps and heard singing a new song in praise of the Lamb (5:8f.). The new song that is now heard is sung **before** or in the presence of the throne and the living creatures and elders who represent the redeemed creation. None but **the one hundred and forty-four thousand who had been redeemed from the earth** are **able to learn the song** – which confirms that 144,000 is the number that symbolizes the multitude of the redeemed (7:1ff., 9ff.). In 15:2ff, it is the redeemed, who having victoriously withstood the attack of antichrist, sing the song of Moses and the Lamb. Thus the new heaven and earth resound to the joyful strains of the purest music of praise and worship. Such hymnody is utterly alien to the lips of the unredeemed.

> *It is these who were not defiled with women, for they are virgins. They follow the Lamb wherever he goes; they were redeemed from mankind as firstfruits for God and the Lamb; and in their mouth no lie was found, for they are without blemish (14:4–5).*

The explanation that the 144,000 redeemed from the earth were **not defiled with women** and are **virgins** should not be understood literalistically as a condemnation of marriage or a demand for celibacy. The

negative attitude towards sexuality and marriage that is foun
of the patristic writings is not present in the New Testa
apostolic position in this respect is summarily expressed in Hᴇ_
13:4: 'Let marriage be held in honour among all and let the conjugal bed
be undefiled, for God will judge those who engage in immorality and
adultery.' It would certainly be strange to conclude that St. Peter and
others of the apostles who were married (see Mk. 1:30; 1 Cor. 9:5) are for
that reason excluded from the company of the redeemed. St. John's
meaning is made clear in the admonition given by the Apostle Paul to
the members of the church in Corinth, who were by no means all
unmarried and celibates: 'I betrothed you to one husband, that I might
present you a pure virgin to Christ' (2 Cor. 11:2). The purity in question
is that of spiritual faithfulness, which, of course, is not separable from
moral integrity; and the source of moral integrity is, as Christ taught, the
inward purity of the heart (Mt. 5:8), just as internal defilement is the root
of external transgression (Mk. 7:20–23).

The relationship of the church as the Bride to Christ who is the
Bridegroom has a place in the teaching both of Christ and of the
apostles. 'Husbands, love your wives', St. Paul wrote, 'even as Christ
loved the church and gave himself up for her, that he might sanctify her,
. . . that he might present the church to himself made glorious, without
spot or wrinkle or any such thing, but that she should be holy and
without blemish' (Eph. 5:25–27; cf. Jn. 3:29; Mt. 25:1; also 19:7; 21:2, 9
below). The purpose of Christ's coming was to make the defiled pure
and to sanctify the unholy. The virginity of which St. John is speaking is
the spotless purity of the incarnate Son. This is the white robe which
cleanses and covers the saints. It is because they 'have washed their
robes and made them white in the blood of the Lamb' that they stand
'before the throne of God and serve him day and night in his temple'
(7:14f.). Only by the cleansing power of the gospel can we be purified.
That is why, when admonishing the members of the Corinthian church
that 'neither immoral persons nor idolaters nor adulterers nor catamites
nor sodomites nor the greedy nor drunkards nor revilers nor extor-
tioners will inherit the kingdom of God', St. Paul reminded them not
only of their past uncleanness but also of the radical change the gospel
had effected in their lives, adding: 'And such were some of you; but you were
washed, you were sanctified, you were justified in the name of the Lord Jesus
Christ and in the Spirit of our God' (1 Cor. 6:9–11). It is in this way that the
redeemed who together form the church of God will be presented as a
pure virgin to their one Husband.

It is characteristic, further, of 'the redeemed from the earth' that **they
follow the Lamb wherever he goes.** Following the Lamb is, indeed, the
distinctive mark of the life of a Christian, for it is the focus of his calling,
which is to be like Christ. St. John himself had been summoned to leave
all and follow Christ, as had his brother James and the brothers Peter

and Andrew (Mt. 4:18ff.; *cf.* Mk. 2:14; Jn. 2:43); and to those who would be his disciples Jesus said: 'He who does not take his cross and follow me is not worthy of me' (Mt. 10:38). As the Good Shepherd he goes before his sheep and they follow him (Jn. 10:4). St. Peter, too, insists that it is in Christ's steps that we are to follow (1 Pet. 2:21), and in doing so we are following him who is both the Lamb and the Good Shepherd, for his coming as a lamb for the slaughter was his will and action as the Good Shepherd: paradoxical though this may seem, it simply means that by becoming man so that he might offer himself up in our place he did not cease to be simultaneously God in action reconciling the world to himself (2 Cor. 5:19–21).

The description of those who are **redeemed from mankind** as **firstfruits for God and the Lamb** does not here signify the first generation of Christian believers or a special group of disciples who are to be followed by a full harvest of the redeemed. It is true that the term 'firstfruits' is used in the New Testament in the sense of the first reaping of what is to be a much greater harvest (Rom. 8:23; 11:16; 16:5; 1 Cor. 15:20, 23). But here the redeemed from mankind are the 144,000 by which the totality of the redeemed is signified (verse 3), and the sense in which they are called firstfruits is that the firstfruits are holy to the Lord and belong to him as his own special possession, and that as such they are brought into the house of the Lord (*cf.* Ex. 23:19; Lv. 23:20f.; Dt. 26:2ff.; Ne. 10:35ff.; Je. 2:3). It is in this sense that the term is used of Christian believers in James 1:18: 'Of his own will God brought us forth by the word of truth that we should be a kind of firstfruits of his creatures'.

The observation that **in their mouth no lie was found, for they are without blemish** provides no ground or excuse for the teaching of perfectionism. As we have said, only the Lamb is without blemish (1 Pet. 1:19), for he alone is absolutely holy and true (3:7 above), and our standing is solely in him. Saved through him from sin, we have turned our backs on sinning. Thus St. John says elsewhere that no one who abides in Christ practises sin (1 Jn. 3:5f.); and yet, writing to the same persons he asserts that 'if we say we have no sin we deceive ourselves and the truth is not in us' (1 Jn. 1:8). The genuine believer does not love sin and should be growing in holiness which is likeness to Christ, and yet is not free from sin and fully conformed to the divine will; consequently, there is no one who does not need the assurance that the blood of Jesus, God's Son, cleanses us from all sin (1 Jn. 1:7).

2. THE HOUR OF DIVINE JUDGMENT, 14:6–13

And I saw another angel flying in midheaven with an eternal gospel to proclaim to those who dwell on earth, even to every nation and tribe and tongue and people, saying with a loud voice, Fear God and give him glory, for the hour of his judgment has come, and worship him who made the heaven and the earth and sea and fountains of water (14:6–7).

That the angel now seen by St. John is *flying in midheaven* may indicate that his mission is one of urgency, as indeed its content shows it to be. The *eternal gospel* he has been given to proclaim is a message of good news which has eternal consequences, and the proclamation is *to those who dwell on earth*, that is a worldwide proclamation, as is plain from the explanatory comment *even to every nation and tribe and tongue and people* (note also, once again, the universality implied by this fourfold designation). The announcement that *the hour of* God's *judgment has come* is bad news for all impenitent and ungodly earth-dwellers, but good news for the multitude of the redeemed since it will be the hour of their glorification and also of the renewal of the whole created order, which, having been subjected to futility by man's fallenness, will now attain the fulfilment that is its true destiny (*cf.* Rom. 8:19–23). At the same time the angel issues a last gospel call as he exhorts all to *fear God and give him glory* and to *worship him* who is the Creator of all, in other words, to stop worshipping the creature rather than the Creator (*cf.* Rom. 1:25).

And another, a second angel followed, saying, Fallen, fallen is Babylon the great, she who made all the nations drink the wine of the wrath of her fornication (14:8).

The *angel* that now appears is *second* in relation to the angel mentioned in verse 6, and he comes with the dramatic proclamation of the fall of Babylon. *Babylon the great* denotes not some particular earthly city or empire (such as Rome, which has been widely supposed) but the concentration of all ungodly arrogance and dissoluteness in all the world and throughout the course of history. Thus Babylon is personified as the whore who has corrupted *all the nations* with her whoredom (*cf.* 16:19; 17:5; 18:2), and is called *great* because of the pervasiveness of her presumptuous defiance of Almighty God. 'Babylon the great' here is synonymous with 'the great city which is called, allegorically, Sodom and Egypt' (11:8 above; see the comments there). Since the time of the Babylonian captivity the name 'Babylon' had stood for godless power and human degradation. The origin of the description of Babylon as 'great' is attributable to the unbridled boasting of Nebuchadnezzar: 'Is not this great Babylon, which I have built by my mighty power as a royal residence and for the glory of my majesty?' – which was immediately answered by God's sovereign announcement that his kingdom had departed from him (Dn. 4:29–31). This judgment foreshadowed the ultimate fall of the great Babylon of the world's apostate society whose doom was also foretold by the prophets (*cf.* Is. 21:9, 'Fallen, fallen is Babylon', which is echoed here, and Je.51:8, 'Suddenly Babylon has fallen and been broken').

The wine . . . of her fornication which the Babylonian whore has induced all the nations to drink is a symbol not only of sexual licentiousness but of every kind of excess which is the expression of unfaithfulness to God. It is in contrast to those who have abandoned themselves to her seductions that the redeemed, purified by Christ, are presented as undefiled virgins (verse 4).

The expression to **drink the wine of the wrath of her fornication** (which occurs again in 18:3) is best understood as a combination of two particular concepts, namely, that to drink the wine of the Babylonian whore's fornication is at the same time to drink the wine of the wrath of God. This interpretation is confirmed in verse 10 below where it is said that the worshippers of the beast and its image, who are precisely the ones in view here, 'will drink the wine of God's wrath' (see also 16:19 and 19:15). The imagery corresponds with that of Jeremiah 51:6f., where, speaking of the time of the Lord's wrath, Babylon is described as a 'cup in the Lord's hand, making all the earth drunken'. Thus the orgy of rebellion against God, far from incapacitating the divine power, activates the judgment of God which is as it were absorbed by the very defiance of those who in their unfaithfulness rebel against it.

> And another angel, a third, followed them, saying with a loud voice, If any one worships the beast and its image and receives a mark on his forehead or on his hand, he will also drink the wine of God's wrath poured unmixed into the cup of his anger, and he will be tormented with fire and brimstone in the presence of the holy angels and in the presence of the Lamb (14:9–10).

A **third** angel now appears to announce the punishment that awaits those who align themselves with the beast. As we have seen (13:15ff.), those who refuse to worship the beast and its image and to be stamped with its mark are persecuted and put to death in circumstances that are intended to convince the world that the power of life and death is sovereignly wielded by the beast; but here the falsity of this arrogant pretension to godlike power is exposed by the declaration that it is in fact the beast's followers who are under sentence of death. The total grace they have rejected becomes the total condemnation they have chosen for themselves. **The wine of God's wrath** that they drink from **the cup of his anger** will be **unmixed**,[1] for the day of grace will then be

---

[1] Literally wine that is 'mixed unmixed', that is, mixed with God's wrath and therefore strengthened, unmixed with water and therefore not weakened.

over. 'The harvest is past', they will lament, 'the summer is ended, and we are not saved' (Je. 8:20).

In contrast to the wine of God's wrath in the cup of his anger is the wine of his mercy in the cup of his salvation (Ps. 116:12f.), which is freely offered to us in this day of grace, and which Christ's bride, the church in glory, will drink with him at the marriage banquet of the Lamb (19:9 below). 'Truly I say to you', Jesus told his apostles as he passed the cup of wine to them at the last supper, 'I will not drink again of the fruit of the vine until that day when I drink it new in the kingdom of God' (Mk. 14:25).

To drink the wine of God's wrath and to be **tormented with fire and brimstone** are different ways of saying the same thing. The significance of the latter is derived from the destruction of Sodom and Gomorrah (Gn. 19:24f.) which ever thereafter was a portent of final judgment – as, for example, in Psalm 11:6, 'On the wicked he will rain coals of fire and brimstone' (*cf.* Is. 30:33; Ezk. 38:22; also 19:20; 20:10; 21:8 below).

It is **in the presence of the holy angels**, who minister on behalf of the inheritors of salvation (Heb. 1:14), and **in the presence of the Lamb**, who offered himself up for the world's salvation, that those who have chosen to follow and worship the beast stand condemned, their radical ungodliness 'laid bare to the eyes of him with whom we have to reckon' (Heb. 4:13). They do not continue in that holy presence, however, for the sentence passed upon them is one of *exclusion* from the endless bliss and glory of the divine presence (*cf.* 21:27; 22:14f.; Mt. 25:41; Mk. 9:43). As St. Paul asserts, 'when the Lord Jesus is revealed from heaven with the angels of his power in flaming fire', then 'those who do not know God and do not obey the gospel' will 'suffer the punishment of eternal destruction and exclusion from the presence of the Lord and from the glory of his might' (2 Thes. 1:7–9).

> And the smoke of their torment goes up for ever and ever, and they have no rest day and night, these worshippers of the beast and its image and whoever receives the mark of its name (14:11).

The background of this imagery of **smoke** which **goes up for ever and ever** from the torment of the idolatrous worshippers who bear the mark of the beast is still that of the destruction of Sodom and Gomorrah, the smoke of whose ruination was seen ascending by Abraham (Gn. 19:28), and whose devastation is described by St. Jude as 'a punishment of eternal fire' (Jude 7). The doom of the ancient kingdom of Babylon foretold by Isaiah has an ultimate fulfilment in the judgment of the worldwide Babylon of antichristianity: 'Babylon, the glory of the kingdoms . . . will be like Sodom and Gomorrah when God overthrew them' (Is. 13:19; *cf.* Je. 50:40); and the same prophet predicted a similar judgment for the state of Edom: 'The streams of Edom shall be turned into pitch, and her soil into brimstone; her land shall become burning pitch. Night and day it shall not be quenched; its smoke shall go up for ever' (Is. 34.9f.) – language that is echoed in the verse before us. Now the final judgment of which these and other earlier judgments gave warning is a reality in the vision seen by St. John. The earlier days of the Lord culminate in the final Day of the Lord. From this last judgment there is no reprieve; the sentence of death is irreversible; the destruction permits no recovery.

> *Here is the endurance of the saints, those who keep the command-*
> *ments of God and the faith of Jesus (14:12).*

This is virtually a repetition, somewhat expanded, of 13:10. The certainty of final judgment and of the triumph of justice is a strong encouragement to endure persecution and persevere in obedience to God's will and in the faith that is concentrated on Jesus (*cf.* Heb. 12:1–3).

> *And I heard a voice from heaven saying, Write: Blessed are the*
> *dead who die in the Lord. Yes indeed, says the Spirit, in that they*
> *may rest from their labours, for their works follow them (14:13).*

Death for the Christian does not mean the loss of blessing or separation from the grace and goodness of God; on the contrary, as the *voice from heaven* proclaims here, the state of *the dead who die in the Lord* is one of blessedness. Their trust is in the Lord and their security is in him, for they have the assurance that nothing, not even death, can possibly separate them from the love of God which is theirs in Christ Jesus their Lord (Rom. 8:38f.). Indeed, as St. Paul taught, to die is gain because it is 'to depart and be with Christ, which is far better' (Phil. 1:21, 23); it is actually to be 'at home with the Lord' (2 Cor. 5:8). The dead in Christ, then, are at no disadvantage; they are *blessed* now, and they will not miss participation in the glory still to be revealed, precisely because they are 'dead in Christ', the Living One, who died, and rose from the dead, and is alive for evermore (1 Thes. 4:13ff.; Rom. 8:18; 1:18 above). Moreover, their condition is one of *rest from their labours*, that is from the laborious toil and hardship of this present pilgrimage; and *their works follow them*, that is to say, the good they have done does not die with them but will continue to be fruitful to the glory of God. That this is so is confirmed by the emphatic *Yes indeed!* of the Holy Spirit. It is on the basis of this assurance and security in the Lord that his servants are exhorted: 'Therefore, my beloved brethren, be steadfast, immovable, always abounding in the work of the Lord, knowing that in the Lord your labour is not in vain' (1 Cor. 15:58).

3. THE WINEPRESS OF GOD'S WRATH, 14:14–20

And I saw, and behold, a white cloud, and seated on the cloud one like a son of man, with a golden crown on his head and a sharp sickle in his hand (14:14).

The personage *like a son of man* now seen by St. John is the incarnate Son in his exaltation and the *white cloud* on which he is seated is the luminous cloud of his glory, as witnessed on the mount of transfiguration (Mt. 17:5) and also at the time of his ascension (Acts 1:9). The title 'Son of Man' was frequently used by Christ of himself, and this vision is evidently closely linked with his declaration that all the tribes of the earth would see the Son of Man 'coming on the clouds of heaven with power and great glory' (Mt. 24:30; *cf.* 26:64). There is also a clear association with the vision of Daniel, who wrote:

I saw . . . , and behold, with the clouds of heaven there came one like a son of man. . . . And to him was given dominion and glory and kingdom, that all peoples, nations, and languages should serve him; his dominion is an everlasting dominion, which shall not pass away, and his kingdom one that shall not be destroyed *(Dn. 7:13f.)*.

Accordingly, the glorified Redeemer has *a golden crown on his head* to signify his royal supremacy, while the *sharp sickle in his hand* signifies that the moment for reaping the harvest of mankind has arrived (*cf.* Mt. 13:39, 'the harvest is the close of the age').

And another angel came out from the temple, calling with a loud voice to him who was seated on the cloud, Wield your sickle and reap, for the hour to reap has come, for the harvest of the earth is ripe. And he who was seated on the cloud wielded his sickle on the earth, and the earth was reaped (14:15–16).

In the unfolding drama of this passage three different angels have so far had parts to play (see verses 6, 8 and 9); and now a fourth angel appears, emerging from the sanctuary and calling on the crowned figure on the cloud to start reaping with his sickle, because *the harvest of the earth is ripe* – a call that brings to mind the cry in Joel's prophecy of the judgment of the nations: 'Put in the sickle, for the harvest is ripe' (Joel 3:13). In response to the angel's call the Lord of the harvest plies his sickle; and so *the earth was reaped.*

There are, however, two aspects or phases of this reaping of the earth. There is the reaping of the wheat and the reaping of the tares, the reaping of the redeemed and the reaping of the unregenerate, the

165

reaping to glory and the reaping to condemnation (*cf.* Mt. 13:36ff.). That the former reaping is in view at this point is indicated by the way in which in the immediately following verses the reaping of the wicked for judgment is specifically described. The distinction is plainly seen in Christ's teaching which depicts his faithful disciples as a field to be harvested (*cf.* Mt. 9:37; Lk. 10:2; Jn. 4:35–38). The kingdom of God, he declared, is like a man sowing seed on the earth; the seed sprouts and grows, producing 'first the blade, then the ear, then the full grain'; and then, finally, 'when the grain is ripe, at once he puts in the sickle, because the harvest has come' (Mk. 4:26–29). The compatibility of this parable with St. John's vision is unmistakable.

> *And another angel came out from the temple that is in heaven, who also had a sharp sickle. And another angel came from the altar who has power over fire, and he called with a loud voice to him who had the sharp sickle, saying, Wield your sharp sickle and gather in the clusters of the vine of the earth, for its grapes are ripe (14:17–18).*

A fifth angel is now seen, coming, like the last one, from the sanctuary, and, like the Lord of the harvest, carrying a sharp sickle. In Christ's parable the angels are the reapers sent by the Son of Man 'to gather out of his kingdom all causes of offence and all evildoers' (Mt. 13:30, 41). The Son, with his sickle, is pre-eminently in charge of the reaping; the angels are his agents, as exemplified by this angel with a sharp sickle. The reaping of the Son spoken of in the preceding verses related to the harvesting of the redeemed, who are like ripe wheat; but here the reaping relates to the harvesting of the ungodly, who are like grapes ready for the winepress of divine judgment.

The order to perform this reaping is given by a sixth angel, **who has power over fire** and comes **from the altar.** This may be the same angel who, in 8:5 above, after the opening of the seventh seal, filled the golden censer with fire from the altar of incense and threw it on the earth, to the accompaniment, significant of divine judgment, of 'thunders and voices and lightnings and an earthquake'. Whether or not this identification is correct, he gives the command to the angel with the sharp sickle to **gather in the clusters of the vine of the earth** which are now ripe for final judgment.

> *And the angel swung his sickle on the earth and gathered the vintage of the earth, and cast it into the great winepress of the wrath of God; and the winepress was trodden outside the city, and blood flowed from the winepress, as high as the horses' bridles, to a distance of sixteen hundred stadia (14:19–20).*

The reaping of this vintage harvest and the casting of the grapes into the winepress to be trodden under foot is an awesome picture of the righteous judgment of God executed upon those who defy his authority and spurn his gospel. What St. John sees flowing from *the great winepress of the wrath of God* is a deep tide of blood, reaching up to *the horses' bridles* (which we take to be a general observation without reference to any particular horses) and extending *to a distance of sixteen hundred stadia.*[1] The latter should certainly be regarded as a number of symbolical significance, four times four times a hundred, signifying judgment that is worldwide and thorough and complete. *The city* outside which the winepress is trodden is 'the holy city, New Jerusalem' (21:2; *cf.* Gal. 4:26; Heb. 12:22), into which 'nothing unclean, nor any one who practises abomination or falsehood, but only those who are written in the Lamb's book of life' can enter (21:27). It was *outside the city* (or, as in Heb. 13:12, 'outside the gate') that Jesus, unjustly condemned, was treated as unclean and abominable and was put to death, the Innocent for the guilty. It was there that he gave himself to be trodden in the great winepress of the wrath of God, bearing our sins and absorbing their punishment, so that we might be clothed with his pure and holy righteousness. And when the hour of final judgment strikes it is there, 'outside the city', that the rejecters of the grace that flows from the cross suffer the wrath of God that they have chosen for themselves by reason of their impenitence and ingratitude. The judgment Christ endured for them and despised by them is the judgment that now, by their own choice, rebounds against them.

The imagery of the treading of the winepress of divine wrath is present in Isaiah 63:1–6, a passage of graphic intensity in which the Lord whose will has been disregarded and mercy despised responds to the question, 'Why is thy apparel red, and thy garments like his that treads in the wine press?, by saying: 'I have trodden the wine press alone. . . . For the day of vengeance was in my heart, and my year of redemption has come. . . . I trod down the peoples in my anger, I made them drunk in my wrath, and I poured out their lifeblood on the earth.' To the same effect the Lord says in Joel 3:13: 'Go in, tread, for the wine press is full. The vats overflow, for their wickedness is great.' In his vision St. John sees the ultimate reality of what is presaged in these prophecies.

[1] 1,600 stadia, taken literally, would be some 200 miles.

The seven last plagues, 15:1 – 16:21

1. SEVEN ANGELS WITH SEVEN PLAGUES, 15:1

And I saw another sign in heaven, great and wonderful, seven angels with seven plagues, for in them the wrath of God is completed (15:1).

The Apostle has previously described two great signs that appeared in heaven, namely, the woman travailing in birth and the great red dragon waiting to destroy her child when he is born (12:1ff). Now *he sees another sign in heaven*, described as *great and wonderful*, namely *seven angels with seven plagues* which they will pour out on the earth in turn from the seven golden bowls that are full of the wrath of God (verse 7 below; 16:1ff.). The pouring out of these seven last plagues would seem to be associated with the third and last woe and the climactic events that follow the sounding of the seventh and last trumpet (11:14, 15ff., above), which conclude with the final judgment of the last day. The plagues are the consummation of the catastrophic effects of sin – effects which at last belong to the judgment of sin and those who commit it and their final elimination from God's creation. Moreover, the number seven, which stands for the being and the power of God, symbolically confirms the completeness of his work and the inevitability of his purpose, whether in judgment or in salvation. Thus in the pouring out of the seven plagues *the wrath of God is completed*: his justice is satisfied and all is ready for the new heaven and earth, the renewed creation that is free from sin and its consequences and therefore free from wrath.

2. THE SAINTS PRAISE GOD'S JUDGMENTS, 15:2–4

And I saw what was like a sea of glass mingled with fire, and those who had gained the victory over the beast and its image, and over the number of its name, standing on the sea of glass with harps of God (15:2).

The account of the seven angels with the seven plagues is interrupted briefly (verses 2–4) to give a preview, as it were, of the multitude of the redeemed rejoicing in the unclouded blessedness that is their destiny. They are described here as **those who had gained the victory over the beast** and over **its image** and **the number of its name** (13:11ff; *cf.* 7:14; 12:11). The likeness of **a sea of glass mingled with fire** where they stand corresponds to what appeared to be 'a sea of glass like crystal' described as before the throne in 4:6; the flashing of light reflected from the clear surface resembles flashes of fire. The scene is one of resplendent purity. The **harps of God** carried by the victorious saints are the instruments which accompany their praise; so also in 5:8f. the four living creatures, representing the whole animate creation, and the twenty-four elders, representing the company of the redeemed, join the music of the harps they hold with their singing of the new song, and in 14:2f. their singing of the new song is 'like the sound of harpers playing on their harps'.

> *And they sing the song of Moses, the servant of God, and the song of the Lamb, saying, Great and marvellous are thy works, O Lord God the Almighty! Just and true are thy ways, O King of the ages! Who shall not fear and glorify thy name, O Lord? For thou alone art holy, and all the nations shall come and worship before thee, for thy righteous acts have been revealed (15:3–4).*

Here, again, is the singing of a song (see comments above on the preceding verse) which is doubly designated **the song of Moses** and also **of the Lamb**. It is, firstly, the song sung by Moses,[1] who as the leader of God's people out of Egypt and its bondage is a type of the Redeemer (*cf.* Dt. 18:15, 18; Jn. 6:14; 7:40; Acts 3:22) and who himself belongs to the redeemed community (*cf.* Mt. 17:5), and, secondly, the song sung to the Lamb.[2] The song of Moses in Exodus 15:1ff. was a hymn of praise to the Lord following the destruction of the enemy in the waters of the Red Sea:

> I will sing to the Lord, for he has triumphed gloriously. . . . The Lord is my strength and my song, and he has become my salvation. . . . Thy right hand, O Lord, glorious in power, thy right hand, O Lord, shatters the enemy. . . . Who is like thee, majestic in holiness, terrible in glorious deeds, doing wonders? . . . The Lord will reign for ever and ever. *(See also the song sung by Moses at the end of his life, Dt. 32.)*

To the same purpose is the song of the white-robed multitude in glory, led, it may be, by Moses, **the servant of God**, whose honour is that of

---

[1] A subjective genitive; the singer is Moses.
[2] An objective genitive; the theme of the song is the Lamb.

faithful servanthood under the lordship of the Lamb, not that of worldly power and pride (*cf.* Heb. 3:5; Nu. 12:7). The sea is not now the Red Sea but 'the sea of glass' symbolizing the clear and translucent holiness of the divine presence and justice. Thus the wonderful works and the just ways of the Lord God Almighty are extolled, whose *righteous acts have been revealed; for*, it is acknowledged by all, *thou alone art holy.*

3. THE BOWLS OF DIVINE WRATH, 15:5–8

And after these things I saw, and the temple of the tent of witness in heaven was opened; and out of the temple came the seven angels with the seven plagues, clothed in pure bright linen and girded about their breasts with golden girdles (15:5–6).

St. John had already seen the heavenly sanctuary opened and the signs and sounds of divine judgment issuing from it (11:19; see comments there). *The tent of witness in heaven* denotes the reality of which the earthly tabernacle in the wilderness was but a shadow (Heb. 8:5; the wilderness structure had been known as 'the tent of witness', *cf.* Ex. 38:21; Nu. 1:50, *etc.*). *The temple* here, as elsewhere in this book, is properly the shrine or inner sanctuary of the tabernacle, formerly closed off from the people, but now, through the perfect sacrifice offered by Christ, opened up for all to enter (*cf.* Heb. 10:19f.).

In the tabernacle of old, the inner sanctuary of the holy of holies was entered on the Day of Atonement by the high priest who, for the forgiveness of the people's sins, sprinkled the blood of atonement on the mercy-seat there. But, as the present passage indicates, it is from the true sanctuary of God's presence that judgment and condemnation emanate, as well as grace and mercy. This perception is in line with St. John's teaching in his Gospel, which clearly warns that to reject the grace of salvation is to invite the judgment of condemnation upon oneself (see Jn. 3:17f., 36; 8:24; 12:47f.). The Lamb of God who bears away the sin of the world (Jn. 1:29) is also the Lamb from whose wrath the impenitent and unbelieving will seek in vain to flee (Rev. 6:16f). And so now it is out of the sanctuary that *the seven angels with the seven plagues* come. Their robes are white with the *pure bright* radiance of heaven and the *golden girdles* with which they are *girded about their breasts* are an emblem of the dignity and authority of the Lord whom they serve (*cf.* 1:13).

And one of the four living creatures gave the seven angels seven golden bowls full of the wrath of God who lives for ever and ever. And the temple was filled with smoke from the glory of God and

> *from his power; and no one was able to enter the temple until the*
> *seven plagues of the seven angels were completed (15:7–8).*

In an earlier vision St. John saw the living creatures and the elders holding 'golden bowls full of fragrances, which are the prayers of the saints' (5:8); now he sees the seven angels given seven golden bowls full of the wrath of God by one of the living creatures (*cf.* verse 1 above). From these bowls the plagues will be poured out on the earth, as described in the next chapter. The fragrant smoke of the prayers of the saints arose from the incense burning in the bowls of the earlier vision; now the smoke of judgment arising from the contents of the plague-filled bowls denotes God's glory and power. Indeed, the ascent of the sweet-smelling smoke of the prayers of the saints took place not only in 5:8 but also in 8:3f., preceding the opening of the seven seals and the sounding of the seven trumpets respectively; now the ascent of the smoke of divine wrath from the bowls held by the seven angels precedes the outpouring of the seven plagues.

The scene now described is reminiscent of the vision recorded by the prophet Isaiah, in which he saw 'the Lord sitting upon the throne, high and lifted up' and his temple filled with smoke, and then was given a prophecy of doom and judgment to proclaim to the faithless people (Is. 6:1ff.). The entry of the redeemed into the true sanctuary will not take place until the seven plagues are *completed*, that is, at the end of the age, when, the creation having been purged of all defilement, they are raised to life in the new heaven and earth (*cf.* Jn. 5:24, 29).

4. THE OUTPOURING OF THE SEVEN LAST PLAGUES, 16:1–21

> *And I heard a loud voice from the temple saying to the seven*
> *angels, Go and pour out on the earth the seven bowls of the wrath*
> *of God. And the first angel went and poured out his bowl on the*
> *earth; and there came a foul and evil sore on the men who had the*
> *mark of the beast and worshipped its image (16:1–2).*

The *loud voice* that is heard coming *from the temple*, that is, from the sanctuary of God's presence, commands the seven angels to pour out the plagues contained in the bowls they are holding. They do this, not all at once, but in an ordered sequence. The plagues differ from one another, but each in turn is a visitation of divine wrath. There are similarities between these seven plagues poured out on the earth and certain of the plagues with which Egypt was afflicted prior to the exodus of the Israelites under Moses, as was the case also with the

172

consequences of the trumpet blasts sounded by the seven angels in chapters 8 and 9. This reminds us that every visitation of divine judgment in the course of history is a foretaste and a forewarning of final judgment to come. By his sinful ungodliness man invites judgment upon himself. Hence the warning given to the Israelites: 'If you walk contrary to me and will not hearken to me, I will bring more plagues upon you, sevenfold as many as your sins' (Lv. 26:21). Accordingly here it is those *who had the mark of the beast and worshipped its image* who were afflicted with the plague poured out by the first of the seven angels, which was the plague of *a foul and evil sore* or ulcer. There is a correspondence with the sixth of the Egyptian plagues, but the literal sense need not be pressed here; the intention is, rather, to indicate the painful and incapacitating disorders that follow in the wake of persistent sinning. The consequences of evil are self-induced: 'If you will not obey the voice of the Lord your God. . . . The Lord will send upon you curses, confusion, and frustration' (Dt. 28:15, 20). Hence the acknowledgment of Ezra regarding the calamity of the Babylonian captivity: 'Thou hast been just in all that has come upon us, for thou hast dealt faithfully and we have acted wickedly' (Ne. 9:33). God is not a God of confusion (1 Cor. 14:33); to turn away from him is, therefore, to choose pain and frustration for oneself.

> *And the second angel poured out his bowl into the sea, and it became like the blood of a dead man; and every living creature died that was in the sea* (16:3).

There is a similarity between this plague and the first of the Egyptian plagues by which the water of the Nile and all other waters of the land were turned into blood (Ex. 7:14ff.). Here it is the sea that becomes like the stagnant blood of a dead person, bringing death to all marine creatures. The sounding of the second trumpet was followed by the turning of a third part of the sea into blood and the death of the same proportion of sea creatures and mariners (Rev. 8:8f.); now, however, the effect is total, for this is one of the seven *last* plagues through which the wrath of God is *completed* (15:1).

> *And the third poured out his bowl into the rivers and the fountains of waters, and they became blood* (16:4).

This third plague corresponds still more closely with the first Egyptian plague, and it has affinities also with the sounding of the third trumpet, following which a third of the rivers and sources of water were made bitter like wormwood, causing the death of many (8:10f.). But now, once more, the effect is total, not partial, for this is a plague of final judgment.

And I heard the angel of the waters saying, Thou, who art and wast, O Holy One, art righteous to judge in this way; for they have poured out the blood of saints and prophets, and thou hast given them blood to drink. They are worthy (16:5–6).

The angel of the waters apparently denotes the angel whose special responsibility is to superintend the waters of the earth – probably salt as well as fresh water in view of the nature of the two plagues so far described. Angels with comparable though different spheres of influence are the four angels with the control of the four winds (7:1) and the angel with power over fire (14:18). The association of angelic ministry with the elemental forces of nature is suggested elsewhere in Scripture (*cf.* Heb. 1:7; Pss. 104:4; 148:8).

As the Judge of all, God is absolutely righteous; he alone can be addressed as the **Holy One**. The acknowledgment here of God's holy justice matches and confirms the acclamation of those who overcame the beast: 'Just and true are thy ways, . . . for thou alone are holy' (15:4). The divine justice will be admitted by every sinner, whether penitent or not. David, for example, declared: 'Thou art justified in thy sentence and blameless in thy judgment' (Ps. 51:4), and Ezra confessed: 'O Lord the God of Israel, thou art just. . . . Behold, we are before thee in our guilt, for none can stand before thee because of this' (Ezr. 9:15). In the present vision, the angel declares it appropriate retribution that those who have shed the innocent **blood of saints and prophets** should themselves be given **blood to drink**. If the assertion, **They are worthy**, that follows refers to the persecutors of saints and prophets, it means 'This is what they deserve'. (The modern versions RSV, NEB, JB, NIV interpret it in this way.) But the reference may be to the worthiness of the saints and prophets, for the very same expression, 'they are worthy', has been used in 3:4 of those 'who have not soiled their garments' and will walk with the Lord in white. It is difficult to decide which meaning is intended. The unqualified use of the adjective 'worthy', as here, commonly is commendatory (see, for example, 4:11 and 5:12). Linked to a defining noun, however, its sense can be derogatory (as, for example, in Romans 1:32, where St. Paul writes of those who are 'worthy of death'). Either interpretation maintains the integrity of God's holy righteousness.

And I heard the altar saying, Yea, Lord God Almighty, true and righteous are thy judgments (16:7).

The praise of Almighty God's ways and judgments as **true and righteous** is a distinctive feature of the book of Revelation (*cf.* 15:3; 19:2). When St. John says that he heard **the altar** speaking he probably means, rather than a personification of the altar, the voice of the souls of the martyrs under the altar which he had previously heard crying out for justice (6:9f.), or possibly the prayers of the saints ascending, as it were, from the altar of incense (*cf.* 5:8; 8:3f.).

> *And the fourth angel poured out his bowl on the sun, and it was given to it to scorch men with fire; and men were scorched with great heat, and they blasphemed the name of God who has power over these plagues, and they did not repent to give him glory (16:8-9).*

At the sounding of the fourth trumpet there was a partial darkening of the sun (8:12); here, with the pouring out of the fourth plague, the effect on the sun is total, not, however, by the obstruction of its light but by the intensification of its heat, with the result that the followers of the beast are *scorched.* Since this is one of the *last* plagues, their impenitence is now incorrigible, and they show this by **blaspheming the name of God** and refusing to glorify him, just as the antichristian beast, to whom they have sold themselves, does (13:5f.). Their rebellious intransigence is the sin unto death (1 Jn. 5:16) by which they bring final judgment on themselves (see also verses 11 and 21).

> *And the fifth poured out his bowl on the throne of the beast; and his kingdom was darkened and they gnawed their tongues because of the pain; and they blasphemed the God of heaven because of their pains and sores and did not repent of their deeds (16:10-11).*

As declared in 13:2, **the throne of the beast** is the throne or dominion of the dragon, Satan, from whom the beast received it. Comparable to this, the fifth of the last plagues, was the ninth Egyptian plague by which the land was afflicted with darkness that could be felt (Ex. 10:21ff.). In comparison with the partial darkness associated with the fourth trumpet blast, the darkness of this fifth plague is total, indicating the total and final judgment which entirely befits those who have allied themselves with the beast and Satan whose rule is the rule of darkness (*cf.* Eph. 6:12; Lk. 22:53). It is in the darkness of ungodliness that the light of Christ has shined (Jn. 1:5; 1 Jn. 2:11) and from the dominion of darkness that his redeemed have been delivered (Col. 1:13) as he has called them 'out of darkness into his marvellous light' (1 Pet. 2:9; *cf.* Mt. 4:16; Acts 26:18; 2 Cor. 4:6; Eph. 5:8; 1 Thes. 5:4f.). The foundation of final judgment is this: 'that the light has come into the world, and men loved darkness rather than light, because their deeds were evil' (Jn. 3:19). Such are the ones who, immovable in their hostility to God and the gospel, are overwhelmed by the pain and terror of the last plagues.

> *And the sixth poured out his bowl on the great river, the Euphrates,*
> *and its water was dried up, to prepare the way for the kings from*
> *the east (16:12).*

We have already come across **the great river, the Euphrates**, in connection with the blast of the sixth trumpet, when the four angels who were bound at the river were loosed at the head of a great army to kill a third of mankind (9:13ff.). Here, with the outpouring of the sixth of the last plagues, the Euphrates is dried up, and thus the way is cleared for the kings from the east to advance with their hostile forces for the ultimate battle in the age-long warfare against God and his people. God's power to dry up waters had been shown on historic occasions in Israel's history at the Red Sea (Ex. 14:21f.) and at the river Jordan (Jos. 3:14ff.); accordingly, Almighty God is celebrated as the one 'who says to the deep, "Be dry, I will dry up your rivers"' (Is. 44:27).

Geographically, the Euphrates separated the Israelites from the heathen empires to the east, and formed a protective barrier. Here the drying up of the Euphrates symbolizes the setting of the stage for the climactic advance of the forces of antichrist in the attempt to destroy the dominion of God. Inevitably, however, it is an assault that leads to their own destruction.

> *And I saw three unclean spirits like frogs coming from the mouth*
> *of the dragon and from the mouth of the beast and from the mouth*
> *of the false prophet; for they are the spirits of demons, performing*
> *signs, which go forth to the kings of the whole world to gather*
> *them together for the warfare of the great day of Almighty God*
> *(16:13–14).*

Now **the dragon** (Satan, 12:3, 9), **the beast** (antichrist, 13:1), and **the false prophet** (the second beast, 13:11) are seen together, a trinity of evil, and from the mouth of each there comes an unclean spirit. These **unclean spirits** are **like frogs**, which were numbered among the unclean animals (Lv. 11:10f.), and **coming from the mouth** they represent every kind of blasphemy, false teaching, and filthy language. An oblique link with the Egyptian plague of frogs, when these loathsome creatures swarmed into the homes of the populace and on to their persons (Ex. 8:1ff.), may possibly be intended.

The widely ranging activity of these froglike spirits indicates the spread of falsehood and mutiny against God as world leaders are drawn into the culminating assault of creaturely defiance. Possessed of satanic power, they are enabled to perform signs (*cf.* 13:13), even as Christ had foretold: 'False christs and false prophets will arise and will show signs and wonders, to lead astray, if possible, the elect' (Mk. 13:22). St. Paul, too, had forewarned that the coming of 'the lawless one' would be 'according to the working of Satan with all power and signs and lying wonders, and with every deception of unrighteousness for those who are perishing because they refused to love the truth and so be saved' (2 Thes. 2:9f.). Likewise Timothy had been informed that 'the Spirit expressly says that in later times some will depart from the faith by giving heed to deceitful spirits and doctrines of demons' (1 Tim. 4:1).

These unclean spirits mobilize **the kings of the whole world**, that is to say, national, political, and intellectual leaders and their forces, for worldwide unification of power for the purpose of worldwide domination – in other words, for the dethroning of God. This is the great convulsion depicted in Psalm 2:1–3: kings, rulers, nations, and peoples setting themselves in battle array 'against the Lord and his anointed', namely Christ, and saying 'Let us burst their bonds asunder and cast their cords from us'. It is this frenzied animosity that accounts for the concerted attempt to destroy Christ by crucifying him (Acts 4:25–27) and will reach the summation of its fury on what is proposed to be the great day of Satan, but in actuality will prove to be **the great day of Almighty God** (*cf.* 6:16f.).

> (*Behold, I am coming like a thief! Blessed is he who is watchful and keeps his garments, lest he walk naked and his shame be seen!*) (16:15).

This verse is a brief parenthesis in the account of the vision relating to the outpouring of the sixth plague. The voice of the Lord intervenes with what is here a word of assurance and encouragement for his faithful servants rather than a warning, for the last of the last days is now at hand. It is a type of announcement frequently found in the teaching of Christ and his apostles, admonishing Christians to be faithful and to lead holy lives in expectation of their Lord's return (see on 3:3 above). Now, however, the message is one of reassurance to the Lord's people as they witness the formidable spectacle of the assembling of the world's antichristian forces in defiance of the sovereign authority of the Creator. Satan's host has every appearance of being invincible, while the servants of God are powerless in themselves to withstand the threatened onslaught. But the Lord is at hand and everything is under control. The outcome of all things is in his hands, and therefore victory is certain. His coming, however, will be sudden and unannounced, **like a thief**. Vile spirits are defiling the earth, but his saints, keeping their garments unspotted and watchfully looking for his coming, are in no danger of losing their blessedness. Just as the Lord appeared suddenly in the darkness of night when the disciples in their little boat seemed about to be overwhelmed by the elemental storm, and with his assuring words, 'Be of good courage, it is I, have no fear!', brought them the security of his presence and quelled the frightening tempest, so at the end of the age the same Lord promises his coming and his victory as the climactic storm of all history threatens to engulf his servants. This parenthesis, then, is of very special significance for God's struggling church.

> **And they gathered them together at the place which is called in Hebrew Armaggeddon (16:16).**

The account is now resumed from verse 14: the three unclean demonic spirits gathered the kings of the whole world together for warefare **at the place which is called in Hebrew Armageddon.** St. John tells his readers that 'Armageddon' is a Hebrew name, but he does not offer an interpretation, though Hebrew names commonly had specific meanings. Many have connected it with Megiddo, a site of battles from time to time in the history of Israel, but the admissibility of this identification is very questionable. It is not our purpose to investigate or discuss the various conjectures based on etymology and geography that have been proposed. This is the only place known where this name 'Armageddon' occurs, and because of the literary character of the Apocalypse it is almost certainly a term of symbolical significance, denoting worldwide revolt rather than a particular territorial locality.

> **And the seventh poured out his bowl on the air; and a loud voice came out of the temple, from the throne, saying, It is done! And there were lightnings and voices and thunders; and there was a great earthquake, such as had not been since men were on the earth, so great was that earthquake (16:17–18).**

The seventh angel pours out the last of the seven last plagues **on the air,** which like the other elements and components of creation is, so to speak, purged by judgment. Defiled and perverted by the sinfulness of man, the whole creation, as St. Paul says, groans to be 'set free from its bondage to decay' (Rom. 8:19–22). Now at last the moment of the final judgment of sinful humanity has arrived. The momentous pronouncement, **It is done!,** comes forth **from the throne** within the temple or sanctuary, which as the presence-chamber of the Lord God is also his throne-room. The throne is God's, not Satan's, as this pronouncement confirms. The proclamation 'It is done' or 'It has come to pass' heralds the completion of God's execution of judgment, by which Satan and his followers are destroyed and the cleansing of creation is effected. Just as the cry 'It is finished', uttered by the incarnate Son as he gave himself up to death on the cross, announced the completion, once and for all, of the saving work he had come to fulfil (Jn. 19:30), so also the judgment he executes against the despisers of divine grace is final for evermore (*cf.* Acts 17:31; Jn. 5:22, 27; Rom. 2:16).

The apocalyptic imagery of **a great earthquake** accompanied by *lightnings and voices and thunders* signifies the unprecedentedly terrible convulsion which is the final shaking of creation, 'in order that what cannot be shaken may remain' (Heb. 12:26f.; *cf.* Dn. 12:1; Joel 2:2; Mt. 24:21, 29; Hg. 2:6). The pouring out of these last seven plagues betokens the climactic concentration of all the disorder and distress occasioned by man's ungodliness from generation to generation which precedes the renewal of creation as it is brought to the resplendent destiny all along intended for it by God.

> *And the great city was split into three parts, and the cities of the nations fell; and Babylon the great was remembered in the presence of God, to give her the cup of the wine of the fury of his wrath (16:19).*

The great city is one and the same with 'the great city which is called, allegorically, Sodom and Egypt' in 11:8, and which denotes the worldwide organization of the forces opposed to God within human society in its fallenness. As the totality of *the cities of the nations* it stands in contra-distinction to the city of God (21:2ff.). Hence the assertion of Augustine: 'To this earthly city belong the enemies against whom I have to defend the city of God'.[1] And *Babylon the great* is likewise a designation of 'the great city' (see comments above on 11:8 and 14:8), all of whose injustice and shedding of innocent blood, far from being overlooked, however long-delayed final judgment may seem to be, is *remembered in the presence of God*. 'Babylon', as Augustine observed long since, 'means confusion' (Babel), and as such is a code-word here for the chaotic confusion and strife at the heart of human society in its alienation from God.[2] Now at last Babylon, 'who made all the nations drink the wine of the wrath of her fornication' (14:8), is given by God *the cup of the wine of the fury of his wrath* (*cf.* 14:19, 20; 17:2; 18:3, 13; 19:15). The splitting of the great city *into three parts* symbolizes the shattering of its power as it meets with the overmastering judgment of Almighty God whose supreme authority its citizens have presumed to defy. There is no place in the new heaven and earth for ungodly chaos.

> *And every island fled away, and no mountains were to be found. And great hailstones, about the weight of a talent, rained down on men from heaven; and men blasphemed God because of the plague of hail, for this plague was very great (16:20–21).*

As in 6:14, the removal of *islands* and *mountains*, which in appearance are so firm and strong, is symbolical of the final shaking of all things

[1] Augustine, *The City of God*, i, 1.
[2] Augustine, *op. cit.*, xviii, 41.

(Heb. 12:26f. again). The raining down of huge *hailstones* is also a sign of divine judgment (*cf.* Jos. 10:11; Jb. 38:22f.; Is. 28:2, 17; Ezk. 13:11–13; 38:22f.). There is a correspondence with the seventh Egyptian plague of hail and its destructiveness (Ex. 9:22ff.) and with the 'great hail' that followed the last of the seven trumpet blasts (11:19). As with the fourth and fifth of these last seven plagues, the ungodly rage in impotence and impenitence against the divine wrath and blaspheme the name of their Creator.

As always, however, God is the refuge and strength of his people, who therefore are without fear, 'though the earth should change and the mountains should shake in the heart of the sea' (Ps. 46:1; *cf.* Joel 3:16). They are assured, indeed, that they will receive 'a kingdom that cannot be shaken' (Heb. 12:28) – the kingdom that will break in pieces and bring to an end all enemy kingdoms, while it itself is indestructible and stands for ever (Dn. 2:44).

The fall of Babylon the great,
17:1–19:5

1. THE GREAT HARLOT JUDGED, 17:1 – 18:8

And one of the seven angels who had the seven bowls came and spoke with me, saying, Come, I will show you the judgment of the great harlot who is seated on many waters, with whom the kings of the earth have committed fornication; and those who dwell on earth have become drunk with the wine of her fornication (17:1–2).

In the course of this passage an explanation is given of the otherwise cryptic language that is used here, and in particular with regard to 'the great harlot' and the 'many waters' on which she is seated. It is plain from verse 5 that **the great harlot** is 'Babylon the great', who, as we have seen, denotes the ungodly civilization of the world in its fallenness (see on 11:8; 14:8; 16:19); and we are informed in verse 15 that the **many waters** on which the great harlot is **seated** are 'peoples and multitudes and nations and tongues' – terminology which both in its plain sense and also in its fourfold structure confirms the international extension of the influence of the great harlot who is great Babylon. The notion is developed from the manner in which Babylon was apostrophized by the prophet Jeremiah: 'O you who dwell by many waters, . . . your end has come' (Je. 51:12f.). If **the kings of the earth**, that is the leaders of men, **have committed fornication** with the great harlot, it is not surprising that mankind in general, **those who dwell on earth**, have followed their lead and **have become drunk with the wine of her fornication** (*cf.* 14:8, where 'Babylon the great' is described as 'she who made all the nations drink the wine of the wrath of her fornication'. In similar fashion Nineveh was denounced as doomed to destruction 'for the countless harlotries of the harlot, . . . who betrays nations with her harlotries, and peoples with her charms', Na. 3:4).

Even a great city that was once faithful can become a harlot (Is. 1:21); hence the symbolical distinction between the old Jerusalem which has become the city of this fallen world, in bondage to earthly passions, and the new Jerusalem, the city of God, which is free and pure (Gal. 4:25f.; Heb. 11:10, 16; 12:22; 13:14; Rev. 3:12; 21:2). The fornication or harlotry intended here is simply unfaithfulness to God, which comes to expression in the unholy pride and ambition of human self-centredness, in hatred and violence, in vice and immorality, and in every form of idolatry, which, whether it be the worship of images or of money or of wordly power, is the worship of the creature rather than the Creator (Rom. 1:25. In Jeremiah's prophecy the unfaithful people are accused of polluting the land with their harlotry, 'committing adultery with stone and tree', Je. 3:9; *cf.* Ezk. 16:15ff.; 23:1ff.; Ho. 4:1ff.).

> *And he carried me away in the Spirit into a wilderness, and I saw a woman seated on a scarlet beast that was full of names of blasphemy, with seven heads and ten horns (17:3).*

The angel spoken of in verse 1 above now carries the apostle away *in the Spirit*, that is to say, in a manner attributable to the operation of the Holy Spirit (*cf.* 1:10; 4:2), or 'in the spirit', that is, in an ecstatic state apart from or without consciousness of his body (*cf.* 2 Cor. 12:2f.), *into a wilderness*, which may be descriptive of human society in its state of fallenness and pollution. In this wilderness St. John sees *a woman*, that is, the great harlot whose judgment the angel had promised to show him (verse 1), as is plain from the verses that follow. *The beast . . . with seven heads and ten horns* is readily identifiable with the antichristian beast that rose from the sea (13:1). The interpretation of the heads and horns is given in verses 9ff. below and will be discussed there. The *scarlet* colour of the beast is the colour of sin (*cf.* Is. 1:18). The information that it was *full of names of blasphemy* also corresponds with 13:1, where the name of blasphemy is on the heads of the beast; and it is on this beast that the woman is *seated*, upheld in a position of prominence from which she deceives and seduces kings and nations.

> *And the woman was arrayed in purple and scarlet and adorned with gold and precious stones and pearls, holding in her hand a golden cup full of abominations, even the impurities of her fornication (17:4).*

The portrait is one of great opulence: *purple and scarlet* robes were the clothing of the rich (*cf.* Lk. 16:19) and the *gold and precious stones and pearls* with which her person was *adorned* represent the display of wealth that worldlings admire and worship. In striking contrast, Christian women are admonished to 'adorn themselves in seemly apparel, with modesty and sobriety, not with braided hair and gold or pearls or costly attire', knowing that good deeds are the proper adornment of women who profess godliness, and that 'a gentle and quiet spirit, which in God's sight is very precious', is 'an imperishable jewel' (1 Tim. 2:9f.; 1 Pet. 3:3f.). The cup the great harlot holds and offers is all the more attractive for being gold, but its contents, **abominations** and **impurities**, are vile and deadly, the wine of her fornication with which she makes the dwellers on earth drunk (verse 2). By drinking from her cup they indulge their lust for power and pleasure, but in doing so they inevitably drink their own judgment and destruction, for it is the Lord's hand, not the woman's, that determines the final consequence of their ungodly intoxication. Jeremiah, indeed, speaks of Babylon as 'a golden cup in the Lord's hand, making all the earth drunken', and then adds that 'the nations drank of her wine, therefore the nations went mad' (Je. 51:7).

> *And on her forehead a name was written, Mystery: Babylon the great, the mother of harlots and of earth's abominations (17:5).*

The **name** that is seen **on her forehead** is the equivalent of the mark of the beast (*cf.* 13:16f.; 14:11). It is, moreover a **mystery**, that is, a name of cryptic significance, like the name 'Sodom and Egypt' previously mentioned (11:8). In other words, the appellation **Babylon** is not to be taken literally, but symbolically – just as 'the mystery' of the seven golden lampstands and the seven stars in 1:20 is interpreted as signifying the seven churches and their angels. The significance of the designation 'Babylon' in the visions of St. John has already been discussed (see comments on 11:8 above). Here Babylon the great is called **the mother of harlots and of earth's abominations** because she is the symbol of all that corrupts and degrades human society, all its lust and lechery, its graft and deceit, its violence and tyranny, its hatred and squalor and injustice. The children of the other woman, however, of whom the harlot Babylon is the implacable enemy, bear the seal of the living God, the Lord's new name, on their foreheads (3:12; 7:2f.; 9:4; 12:17; 14:1; 22:4).

> *And I saw the woman drunk with the blood of the saints and with the blood of the martyrs of Jesus. And when I saw her I wondered with a great wonder. And the angel said to me, Why do you wonder? I will tell you the mystery of the woman and of the beast with the seven heads and ten horns that carries her (17:6–7).*

Driven by frenetic hatred of the other woman, Christ's bride the church, the harlot Babylon is the fierce persecutor of those who refuse to drink the abominations from her golden cup. She who makes others drunk with the excesses of her harlotry is herself **drunk** with the innocent blood of the saints and martyrs. If, as seems likely, a distinction is intended between **the blood of the saints** and **the blood of the martyrs of Jesus**, the former will represent the suffering of affliction in living and witnessing for Jesus and the latter the suffering of the death of martyr-dom for Jesus. Here again, as in 2:13 where the Lord calls Antipas 'my witness (Greek, *martyr*), my faithful one who was killed among you', we may discern the transition in meaning of the term *martyr* from witness in general to witness in the more particular sense of one who lays down his life for the gospel.

The seer **wondered with a great wonder**, not only because the spec-tacle of this ornate drunken harlot seated on the scarlet seven-headed and ten-horned beast was so extraordinary, but also because the sym-bolical significance of all that he saw was unclear to him. The angel, however, promises to explain to him **the mystery of the woman and of the beast**, and this he now proceeds to do.

> **The beast that you saw was, and is not, and is about to come up from the abyss and go to perdition; and the dwellers on earth whose names have not been written in the book of life from the foundation of the world will wonder as they behold the beast because it was and is not and is to come (17:8).**

As we have already remarked, **the beast** is the antichristian monster that was seen coming up out of the sea invested with the power and authority of the dragon Satan (13:1f.) – the sea being representative of the restless mass of unregenerate humanity (see comments on 12:17 and 13:1 above). **The abyss** is the beast's proper habitat, so to speak, and its point of departure. The assertion that it **was, and is not, and is about to come up**, or will reappear, from the abyss we understand as meaning that it is characteristic of the beast to appear and disappear and then appear again in a sequence of would-be world conquests which are essentially anatagonistic to God and his sovereignty. Its ultimate des-tiny, however, is to **go to perdition** in company with the devil and the false prophet (20:10).

Throughout the course of history **the dwellers on earth whose names have not been written in the book of life from the foundation of the world,** that is to say, the unregenerate among mankind (as also in 13:8 above), are filled with wonder and admiration at the beast's resilience and venerate its power as though it were the supreme power. The feats of despotic empire builders who aspire to world dominion always evoked the wonder and the worship of the citizens of Babylon the great.

It was, indeed, with the vision of world dominion and all the power and glory commonly associated with it that the devil vainly imagined he might entice Jesus to bow the knee in homage to him (Mt. 4:8f.), knowing that by so doing the incarnate Son, instead of gaining all, would instantly have lost all. This is the temptation by which those who are hungry for worldly power and glory are repeatedly deceived. They never gain the world, but the devil gains them, though he himself is but a finite creature subject to the dominion and judgment of him who is the Creator of all. That is why the empires of this fallen world, no matter how strong and dominant in their day they may appear to be, are rotten structures which rise only to fall, and are succeeded by other empires equally corrupt and fleeting. The resurgence of Babylon is always a doomed resurgence. As Rudyard Kipling wrote: 'Lo, all our pomp of yesterday is one with Nineveh and Tyre'. So it is that the world wonders at the beast *because it was and is not and is to come*.

> *Here is understanding with wisdom: the seven heads are seven mountains on which the woman is seated, and they are seven kings, five of whom have fallen, one is, the other has not yet come, and when he comes he must remain a little while* (17:9–10).

When the angel says to St. John, *Here is understanding with wisdom*, he means 'I am now going to give you the wise interpretation of the things you see'. The sense is identical with that in 13:18 concerning the number of the beast, 'Here is wisdom; let him who has understanding reckon . . .' This does not necessarily ensure that all that is mysterious will become clear; it is rather a signpost that points to the reality implicit in the symbolism of the vision. The Apostle receives the explanation that *the seven heads* of the beast are *seven mountains on which the woman is seated*, and, further, that *they are seven kings*. The attempts that have been made to demonstrate that the reference is to the world-power of Rome, the city of seven hills, and a sequence of Roman emperors or caesars are far from satisfactory. More acceptable is the postulation of a succession of powerful kingdoms, *five* of which *have fallen*, namely, Egypt, Assyria, Babylon, Persia, and Greece, *one is*, namely, Rome, and *the other has not yet come*, that is a kingdom yet future which *must remain a little while*. This also, however, is unsatisfactory, most of all with respect to the centuries that have followed the fall of Rome, for in them too dominions have arisen and fallen and been replaced by others. Among more modern names, it is sufficient to mention Napoleon and Hitler and Stalin to be reminded of this.

To treat the number seven here as symbolical in its significance is more consistent with the tenor of this apocalyptic book. Seven being the number of divine authority, it may be taken here to indicate the desire of the empire-builders of this fallen world to dethrone God and to exercise authority that is universal and absolute. The six empires mentioned above provide notable examples of this lust for world dominion. But a significant change has been introduced by the coming of Christ, in that Satan, who is intent on deceiving the nations, is now under restraint and will continue so until the fullness of time, when he will be loosed for a little while (see comments below on 20:1–3). This 'little while' will coincide, in our judgment, with the 'little while' of the appearance of the seventh of the kings represented by the heads of the beast. The last and fiercest mobilization of the world's anti-God forces will take place under this seventh king and will be quelled by the utter destruction of final judgment (20:7–10).

> *And the beast that was and is not is itself an eighth, and is of the seven, and it goes to perdition. And the ten horns you saw are ten kings who have not yet received a kingdom; but they receive authority as kings for one hour together with the beast. These are of one mind and they give their power and authority to the beast (17:11–13).*

The description of the monster on which the harlot is seated as *the beast that was and is not* is resumed from verse 8, but now the cryptic assertion is added that it *is itself an eighth* (king), and yet *is of the seven* (kings). That is to say, it has an intimate relationship with the seven kings, but, though of them, is not one of them or an additional king in series with them. It is an eighth, rather, in the sense that the seven kings are of it, just as the seven heads by which the seven kings are signified are the seven heads of the beast. In the nature of the case, the heads and the beast belong together: the mind and purpose by which they are animated are the mind and purpose of the beast. As the source of their kingship, then, the beast is an eighth, of them as they are of it, but not one of them.

This distinction applies in a similar manner to the *ten kings* symbolized by the ten horns *who have not yet received a kingdom*, for it is *together with the beast* that *they receive authority as kings*. These horns, like the heads, are of the beast; their kingly authority flows from their integral connection with the beast. This explains, too, why they are *of one mind*. Moreover, *they give their power and authority to the beast*, not in the sense that they are the source of the beast's power and authority, but that they give or ascribe to the beast the credit for the power and authority they wield. These ten kings stand for, as another way of expressing, 'the kings of the whole world' who, animated by the unclean spirits of satanic origin, mobilize their forces in warfare against God (16:13f.).

As the number ten symbolizes completeness, the ten kings yet to come to power may be intended to indicate the grasping after total dominion over all the world's peoples by the leaders of the forces of ungodliness. They hold sway, however, together with the beast, just *for one hour*; they and their kingdom pass away rapidly, both because they are finite and mortal and also because, despite their overweening arrogance, God is in control of his world. The period of their apparent authority is the period between the sixth and seventh kings of verse 10, namely, the present era between the two comings of Christ, which, however prolonged it may seem to us, is but a brief hour in the light of eternity (*cf.* 2 Pet. 3:8f.). Thus St. John could speak of these last days or this last time in which we are living as 'the last hour' (1 Jn. 2:18; *cf.* 2 Tim. 3:1; Heb. 1:2; 1 Pet. 1:5, 20). Though the kings are controlled by the beast and the beast in turn is controlled by the dragon, yet the sovereign control over all belongs to Almighty God who orders the course of history in accordance with his will and has set the time of the end of this age to coincide with the fulfilment of the immutable purpose for which he brought the world into being (*cf.* Eph. 1:11).

These will make war on the Lamb, and the Lamb will overcome them, for he is Lord of lords and King of kings, and those who are with him are called and chosen and faithful (17:14).

Driven by the demonic spirits that issue from the dragon and the beast and the false prophet, the ten kings, who represent the leadership of the world forces that are hostile to God, *make war on the Lamb*. This warfare leads up to the climactic conflict described in the chapters that follow, but in the meantime it is prosecuted not merely by afflicting the Lamb's followers with oppression and violence but also, and more damagingly, by the dissemination of falsehood and hostile propaganda – as is to be expected when we recall that the foul spirits by which they are possessed come *from the mouth* of their satanic overlords (16:13f.). Thus they wage war on the Lamb by seeking to destroy his credentials. With their hostile indoctrination they attack the Lamb's eternal sonship, his incarnation and sinless life, his atoning death and resurrection, his ascension and glorification, and his uniqueness as the Saviour of mankind.

Their assault on the truth, however, in no way alters the truth; their warfare against the Lamb is no threat to his reality and his survival. It is not they who will overcome him, but he who *will overcome them*, and the simple reason for this is that *he is Lord of lords and King of kings*: his lordship is absolute and his sovereignty invincible, and their doom is inescapable. But *those who are with him*, for 'they follow the Lamb wherever he goes' (14:4), participate in the blessings of his victory; *called* by him whose calling is never ineffective, *chosen* by him whose election is the consequence of inexhaustible grace, and *faithful* to him by virtue of the strength he supplies, there is no power in the universe that can separate them from the Lamb (*cf.* Rom. 8:28–39).

And he said to me, The waters that you saw, where the harlot is seated, are peoples and multitudes and nations and tongues (17:15).

When the angel reminds St. John of *the waters* he had seen *where the harlot is seated* the reference is to the spectacle mentioned in verse 1 of 'the great harlot who is seated on many waters'. Now the waters are explained as symbolizing *peoples and multitudes and nations and tongues*. Here, as elsewhere, the fourfold designation denotes human society throughout the length and breadth of the world, lost and unregenerate, and for that reason restless like the waters of the ocean. That in this same vision the harlot is seen sitting on many waters (verse 1), on the scarlet beast (verse 3), and on the beast's seven heads which are seven mountains is not indicative of confusion or inconsistency. The truth is conveyed by a variety of scenes, each of which portrays a particular aspect of symbolical significance. This consideration should persuade us, if persuasion is needed, of the important part that symbolism plays in the structure of St. John's account of his Patmos visions.

> *And the ten horns that you saw and also the beast will hate the harlot and will make her desolate and naked, and will devour her flesh and burn her up with fire (17:16).*

'And all men hate the thing they love', wrote Oscar Wilde; and this, poetic overstatement though it is, applies with particular force to those who are driven by an ungodly lust for power or pleasure, for they become sated and then nauseated with their excesses which always, after promising everything, leave them disillusioned and unfulfilled. The euphoria of being drunken with the wine of the harlot's fornication (verse 2) turns to disgust and hatred. The mad addiction to luxury and licentiousness of her citizens destroyed the grandeur of Rome, the 'great Babylon' of their day. And so it happens with the followers of tyrant after tyrant: they kill the thing they have loved. The fate of the harlot is to be hated by the very ones who have avidly drunk from the cup of her abominations and impurities, to be made *desolate and naked* by those who have wallowed in the voluptuousness of her company, and to be destroyed by the lovers who have wanted unending existence for her. Thus, over and over again in history, the great Babylons of this world rise only to fall by their own internal rottenness.

> *For God put it into their hearts to carry out his purpose and with one mind to give their kingly power to the beast, until the words of God should be fulfilled. And the woman you saw is the great city which has dominion over the kings of the earth (17:17–18).*

St. John is given further evidence that God is in control of all that takes place. His will is not frustrated but is actually, though unwillingly and unwittingly, set forward by the kingdoms that are in alliance with the beast. The handling over of their power to the beast is preparing the way for the fulfilment of *the words of God*. All history is ceaselessly moving on towards the ultimate accomplishment of God's declared purpose for his creation; and to this end, as the psalmist declared, 'Surely the wrath of men shall praise thee' (Ps. 76:10). It is explained to St. John again that *the woman* seen in his vision is *the great city which has dominion over the kings of the earth*, already named as 'Sodom and Egypt' and 'Babylon', 'the mother of harlots and of earth's abominations' (11:8; 14:8; verse 5 above), and as such the manifestation of the world-power of ungodliness. It is the fall of this woman that is now proclaimed.

> *After this I saw another angel coming down from heaven who had great authority, and the earth was made bright with his glory. And he cried with a loud voice, saying, Fallen, fallen is Babylon the great, and has become a dwelling place of demons, a haunt of every unclean spirit, and a haunt of every unclean and hateful bird (18:1–2).*

This angel, so replendent and authoritative in appearance, confirms the fall and desolation of Babylon the great already announced in 14:8 and 17:16. The language used here is reminiscent of the doom prophesied for Babylon in Isaiah 13:19–22 and in Jeremiah 50:39f. and 51:37, and also of the judgment proclaimed against Edom in Isaiah 34:8–15 and against Nineveh in Zephaniah 2:14f. ('Herds shall lie down in the midst of her, all the beasts of the field; the vulture and the hedgehog shall lodge in her capitals; the owl shall hoot in the window, the raven croak on the threshold. . . . This is the exultant city that dwelt secure, that said to herself, "I am and there is none else." What a desolation she has become!') The scene is one of utter devastation.

> *For all the nations have drunk the wine of the wrath of her fornication, and the kings of the earth committed fornication with her, and the merchants of the earth grew rich through the power of her arrogance (18:3).*

There is a repetition here of assertions previously made in 14:8 and 17:2 (see comments in those places). In the passage now introduced special attention is paid to the disastrous judgment that overtakes *the merchants of the earth* who *grew rich through the power* of the *arrogance* of Babylon the great (see especially verses 11–20). Through the fortunes they have unscrupulously accumulated these merchants were treated as the great men of the earth (verse 23). They are the equivalent of those who in our day amass millions by exploiting the weak, dealing in drugs, and trafficking in pornography – in short, who make money their god. (*Cf.* the destruction of Tyre, the great merchant centre of the ancient world, prophesied in Ezk. 27:25ff. and 28:1ff.)

189

> *And I heard another voice from heaven saying, Come out of her,*
> *my people, lest you take part in her sins and lest you receive her*
> *plagues; for her sins are heaped high as heaven and God has*
> *remembered her iniquities (18:4–5).*

The call to God's people to separate themselves from the abominable wickedness of the great world-city of ungodliness was sounded by the prophets of the Old Testament (*cf.* Is. 48:20; 52:11; Je. 50:8; 51:6ff., 45); and St. Paul admonished the members of the Corinthian church to the same effect: 'Do not be unequally yoked with unbelievers: for what agreement is there between righteousness and iniquity? or what fellowship has light with darkness? what accord has Christ with Belial? or what has a believer in common with an unbeliever? what point of contact has the temple of God with idols?' (2 Cor. 6:14–16). So here the **voice from heaven** is heard: **Come out of her, my people.** They are to keep themselves free from contamination and judgment by dissociating themselves from the evil practices and perversions of global ungodliness. Piling sin on sin, Babylon's wickedness has reached its limit, **for her sins are heaped high as heaven** and now stand in condemnation against her. Defiant to the end and scornful of the grace freely available to her, the last hour has now struck and it is too late for repentance. She has refused to embrace the mercy of God and to pray penitently, as Ezra prayed: 'O my God, I am ashamed and blush to lift my face to thee, my God, for our iniquities have risen higher than our heads, and our guilt has mounted up to the heavens' (Ezr. 9:6). Instead she is now judged by the grace she has rejected and condemned by the mountain of her sins: 'We would have healed Babylon,' the Lord declared, 'but she was not healed. Forsake her, . . . for her judgment has reached up to heaven and has been lifted up even to the skies' (Je. 51:9). To the same purpose St. Paul warned the impenitent and hard-hearted that they were 'storing up wrath' for themselves 'on the day of wrath when God's righteous judgment will be revealed' (Rom. 2:5).

Nothing could be more wrong-headed than to interpret the patience and longsuffering of God to mean that he is powerless or forgetful (*cf.* 2 Pet. 3:1ff.). God, by his very nature, cannot be inconstant or neglectful; his purpose to purge his creation entirely of evil is firm and cannot fail of fulfilment. It is only by virtue of the fact that the incarnate Son bore our sins on the cross and in our place endured our judgment there that, by the grace of the new covenant, God promises to all who repent and believe: 'I will remember their sins and their iniquities no more' (Heb. 10:17; Je. 31:34). But of the Babylonian harlot, who has thrust grace away that she may continue in evil, the voice from heaven announces, **God has remembered her iniquities** (*cf.* 16:19).

Render to her even as she herself has rendered, and double to her the double according to her deeds; mix double for her in the cup she mixed (18:6).

Now the voice from heaven addresses God, whose righteous judgment is implicit in his remembrance of the iniquities of Babylon the great. The punishment demanded is entirely in accord with the principles of justice: **Render to her even as she herself has rendered**. This is the logic of retribution. There is a balance between cause and consequence, as St. Paul so clearly stated: 'Do not be deceived; God is not mocked; for whatever a man sows that he will also reap. For he who sows to his own flesh will from the flesh reap corruption; but he who sows to the Spirit will from the Spirit reap eternal life' (Gal. 6:7f.; *cf.* Mt. 7:2). The principle is identical with the pronouncement of divine judgment on Babylon in Jeremiah's prophecy: 'Requite her according to her deeds, do to her according to all that she has done; for she has proudly defied the Lord, the Holy One of Israel' (Je. 50:29; *cf.* 51:24; Ps. 28:4).

The petition that God should **double to her the double** is not a contradiction of this principle of just retribution, as the qualification **according to her deeds** shows. The term 'double' here does not mean a twofold amount, as though the punishment were twice as much as the offence, but an exact equivalent, in the same way as a person who looks exactly like someone else is called his double; thus the retribution is 'the double' of the Babylonian harlot's sins. The assertions of Isaiah 40:2, that Jerusalem 'has received at the Lord's hand double for all her sins', and Jeremiah 16:18, that God 'will doubly recompense their iniquity and their sin', convey the same sense. So here, again, to **mix double** for the Babylonian harlot is to mix the double or exact equivalent of the draught **in the cup she** had **mixed** for others. This interpretation is confirmed by the demand that immediately follows.

To the extent that she glorified herself and played the wanton, give her the same amount of torment and mourning; for she says in her heart, I sit a queen and am no widow, and I will never see mourning. Therefore in a single day her plagues will come, pestilence and mourning and famine, and she will be burned up with fire; for the Lord God who judges her is mighty (18:7–8).

A balanced correspondence between her arrogance and wantonness on the one hand and the **torment and mourning** that will be hers on the other is clearly intended: it is **the same amount** (see comments on the preceding verse). Proudly imagining herself to be permanently enthroned as **queen** and, god-like, to be far above all loss and the sorrow that accompanies it, the harlot Babylon will learn **in a single day**, the Day of the Lord, how finite and insecure she is. The very disasters from which she persuaded herself she was immune will overwhelm her. As she meets with destruction she has perforce to acknowledge that **the Lord God who judges her is mighty**. What she now experiences is the culmination of divine judgment that has been pronounced against the pretension of every would-be world power to usurp the place of God. We remember, for example, how Ezekiel prophesied against the prince of Tyre:

> Thus says the Lord God: Because your heart is proud, and you have said, 'I am a god, I sit in the seat of the gods, . . .' yet you are but a man, and no god, though you consider yourself as wise as a god; . . . therefore thus says the Lord God: Because you consider yourself wise as a god, . . . you shall die the death of the slain . . . Will you still say, 'I am a god,' in the presence of those who slay you? *(Ezk. 28:2–9).*

What Babylon *says in her heart* she has persuaded herself to believe. The *heart* denotes the centre of one's being, the will and motivation by which one's attitudes and actions are determined. To set oneself up as God is the greatest folly, for it is to suppress the truth about the Lord God (*cf.* Rom. 1:18). Thus it is the mark of extreme wickedness and folly to think or say in one's heart, 'There is no God. . . . God has forgotten, . . . he will never see it, . . . Thou wilt not call to account' (Pss. 10:4, 11, 13; *cf.* 14:1; 53:1). The judgment of the harlot Babylon now heard by St. John is the ultimate fulfilment of the denunciation of ancient Babylon spoken through the prophet Isaiah:

> You shall no more be called the mistress of kingdoms. . . . You said, 'I shall be mistress for ever,' . . . Now therefore hear this, you lover of pleasures, who sit securely, who say in your heart, 'I am, and there is no one besides me; I shall not sit as a widow or know the loss of children': These two things shall come to you in a moment, in one day; . . . in spite of your many sorceries and the great power of your enchantments *(Is. 47:5–9; cf. Ob. 3f.; Zp. 2:15).*

All the judgments of history are but types and warnings of the final and total judgment of the last day.

2. LAMENTATION OVER BABYLON'S FALL, 18:9–24

And the kings of the earth who committed fornication and behaved wantonly with her will weep and wail over her when they see the

smoke of her burning, standing far off through fear of her torment,
saying, Alas, alas, the great city, Babylon the mighty city! for in one
hour has your judgment come! (18:9–10).

The kings of the earth who have been licentiously associated with the
harlot Babylon (see verse 3 above and 17:1f.) will **weep and wail**, and will
tremble for themselves, as they watch her destruction, for it is the
destruction of all that they have held dear. Suddenly, **in one hour** (which
signifies the same as 'in a single day', verse 8), the might of her humanistic sway, and with it all their pleasure and treasure, has been dissolved
by the divine judgment. For them, the loss of her is the loss of everything.
Hence their bitter lamentation.

And the merchants of the earth weep and mourn over her, because
no one buys their cargo any more, cargo of gold and silver and
precious stone and of pearls and fine linen and purple and silk and
scarlet, every kind of scented wood and every object of ivory and
every object of most costly wood and of bronze and iron and marble,
and cinnamon and spice and incense and myrrh and frankincense
and wine and oil and fine flour and wheat and cattle and sheep and
horses and chariots and bodies and persons of men (18:11–13).

This is in effect a summary of Ezekiel 27 concerning Tyre and her
merchandise. The list of this merchandise is a catalogue of the things that
this world holds dear and for which the ungodly are prepared to barter
their souls. The trading, moreover, is not merely in things but also in
persons, whom they treat without compunction as marketable commodities to be bought and sold; and in their lust for pleasure and lucre
and power they are in fact trading away their own lives, for to gain the
world is to lose one's own self (*cf.* Mt. 16:26) – and, as the next verse
declares, it is to lose also what one thought to have gained.

And the fruits your soul lusted after have gone from you, and all
your dainties and luxuries are lost to you, never to be found again
(18:14).

This statement is addressed to the world-city Babylon (the pronoun **you** is
singular here in the Greek). All the **dainties and luxuries**, such as those
mentioned in the preceding verses, which contributed to the materialistic
extravagance and carnal voluptuousness of her existence, and for which
she had sold her soul, are now suddenly and irretrievably lost. Before the
Judge of all the world she is empty and naked.

The merchants of these wares, who gained their wealth from her,
will stand far off through fear of her torment, weeping and

mourning as they say, Alas, alas, for the great city that was clothed in fine linen and purple and scarlet, and adorned with gold and precious stones and pearls, for in one hour such great wealth has been laid waste! And every shipmaster and every seafaring man, sailors and all whose trade is on the sea, stood far off and cried out as they watched the smoke of her burning, What city was like the great city? And they threw dust on their heads and cried out as they wept and mourned, saying, Alas, alas, for the great city where all who had ships at sea grew rich by her wealth, for in one hour she has been laid waste (18:15–19).

The lamentations of the merchants of the earth as they gaze in horror on the spectacle of Babylon's destruction matches that of the kings of the earth (verses 9f.). While the kings bewail the collapse of their power and prestige, the merchants bewail the loss of the trade in costly and luxurious commodities that has been the source of their wealth. The owners and navigators of the ships in which the merchandise of Babylon was carried across the sea likewise bemoan bitterly the dashing of their prosperity. As with the merchants and mariners of Tyre, who with their expensive cargoes 'sink into the heart of the seas' on the day of their ruin (Ezk. 27:27), the loss of their worldly wealth is the loss of their all. This explains the frantic demonstration of utter despair, weeping, mourning, and throwing dust on their heads (as in Ezk. 27:30ff.). The greatness of the great city had seemed so permanent and so impregnable, and her pleasures so inexhaustible, but now nothing remains but the smoking ashes of her devastation.

Rejoice over her, O heaven, together with saints and apostles and prophets, for God has exacted your judgment from her (18:20).

The Lord's own people, whose citizenship is in heaven (Phil. 3:20), do not share the grief of the kings, merchants, and seafarers of the world-city Babylon; on the contrary, for them the destruction of Babylon is cause for rejoicing and celebration, for it vindicates the justice of Almighty God. He has rendered to her even as she had rendered (verse 6 above). And thus the prophecy of Jeremiah is fulfilled: 'Then the heavens and the earth, and all that is in them, shall sing for joy over Babylon. . . . Babylon must fall for the slain of Israel, as for Babylon have fallen the slain of all the earth' (Je. 51:48f.). The execution of this righteous judgment coincides with the sounding of the seventh trumpet and its consequences, when the worshippers of the true God welcome the arrival of 'the time for the dead to be judged and to reward thy servants the prophets and saints and those who fear thy name, both small and great, and to destroy the destroyers of the earth' (11:15–18).

And a mighty angel took up a stone like a great millstone and threw it into the sea, saying, So shall Babylon the great city be violently thrown down, and shall be found no more. And the sound of harpers and minstrels and flute-players and trumpeters shall be heard in you no more; and a craftsman of any craft shall be found in you no more; and the sound of the millstone shall be heard in you no more; and the light of a lamp shall shine in you no more, and the voice of bridegroom and bride shall be heard in you no more; for your merchants were the great ones of the earth, and all the nations were deceived by your sorcery. And in her the blood of prophets and saints and of all who have been slain on earth was found (18:21–24).

The greatness of Babylon in the eyes of the world is symbolized by the taking up of **a great millstone** by **a mighty angel**, and the supreme greatness of God by the casting of this millstone **into the sea**, where it sinks out of sight, thus indicating the devastating judgment that overtakes Babylon. The message of this vision is comparable to that of the dramatized parable in Jeremiah 51:59–64, where it is recounted that 'Jeremiah wrote in a book all the evil that should come upon Babylon', and then told Seraiah, the king of Judah's quartermaster, first to read what was written in the book on his arrival in Babylonia, and then to 'bind a stone to it and cast it into the midst of the Euphrates', saying, 'Thus shall Babylon sink, to rise no more'.

The vision then returns to the scene of total devastation: no music, no industry, no light, no love, no life. This is the passing away of the world with all its ungodly lust (1 Jn. 2:17): what was formerly a hive of self-seeking activity has become a place of death and desolation. The prophecy of Isaiah is fulfilled: 'The earth shall be utterly laid waste and utterly despoiled; for the Lord has spoken this word' (Is. 24:3); and also the prophecy spoken through Jeremiah: 'I will banish from them the voice of mirth and the voice of gladness, the voice of the bridegroom and the voice of the bride, the grinding of the millstones and the light of the lamp. This whole land shall become a ruin and a waste' (Je. 25:10f., *cf.* 7:34; 16:9; Ezk. 26:12f.). All such judgments pronounced in the course of history against Babylon and other arrogant world-powers, and also against apostate Israel, are, as we have said previously, preliminary judgments which are at the same time the harbingers of final judgment. They declare with unmistakable clarity that God scatters the proud in the imagination of their hearts, puts down the mighty from their thrones, and sends the rich empty away (Lk. 1:51–53).

In Babylon, moreover, **the blood of prophets and saints ... was found**, so much so that she was 'drunk with the blood of the saints and the blood of the martyrs of Jesus' (17:6); and also found was the blood of **all who have been slain on earth.** That is to say, this harlot of anti-God secular power is guilty of all the bloodshed that has disgraced and defiled the history of mankind, starting with the blood of Abel shed by his brother Cain. To shed the blood of one's fellow man whose distinguishing mark and unique dignity is that he has been created in the image of God is the greatest contempt of one's brother and rebellion against the Creator. To take another person's life is fratricide; it is also the sin of acting as though one were the Creator and not his creature. It is thanks entirely to the redeeming grace of God that the blood of Christ, the Lamb, shed for us on the cross affords pardon for our blood-guiltiness, speaking as it does 'more graciously than the blood of Abel', which is the prototype and the paradigm of all the blood shed by man in his fallenness and insurgence against the Creator (1:5; 5:9; 7:14; 12:11; Heb. 12:24).

3. REJOICING OVER BABYLON'S FALL, 19:1–5

After this I heard what was like the loud voice of a great multitude in heaven, saying, Hallelujah! Salvation and glory and power belong to our God; for his judgments are true and righteous; for he has judged the great harlot who corrupted the earth with her fornication, and he has avenged the blood of his servants at her hand. And again they cried, Hallelujah! And her smoke goes up for ever and ever (19:1–3).

The **great multitude in heaven** whom St. John now hears loudly praising God is probably the angelic host rather than the great multitude of the redeemed whom he has also heard praising God with a loud voice (7:9f.). The invitation to all God's human servants to praise him follows in verse 5 below, and then comes the thunderous praise of all, men and angels, in unison (verse 6). The exclamation **Hallelujah** is a Hebrew expression which means 'Praise God!' In the Psalms it occurs 24 times, but only in this place (verses 1, 3, 4, 6) in the New Testament. Its use here, however, suggests that it was naturally retained in Christian worship; but to keep it from becoming a mindless cry it is important to have in mind its meaning. In accordance with the symbolical significance of the numbers three and seven in this apocalyptic book, God is praised in threefold or sevenfold terms, the former here: **Salvation and glory and power** are joyfully ascribed to him (*cf.* 4:9, 'glory and honour and thanks', and 4:11, 'glory and honour and power'; for the sevenfold usage see 5:12 and 7:12). The true reality is now absolutely plain to all: salvation and glory and power do not belong to the pseudo-divine world-city Babylon, though the nations of the earth have been deceived into thinking otherwise, but to God, and to God alone.

The *judgments* of God are no less to be praised than his salvation. Indeed, the two belong together. The love of God for us manifested at Calvary is inseparable from the satisfaction of his justice; for there, in infinite love, God himself endured, as the incarnate Son, the just punishment of our sins so that we might by faith be clothed with his righteousness (2 Cor. 5:21). The final judgment of the impenitent rejecters of divine grace is the purgation of the world, the elimination of all that is discordant with the will of God, the blessedness of redeemed mankind, and the harmony of the universe. The renewed creation will be the kingdom of perfect peace and righteousness because it will be the realm of loving holiness. So here the heavenly multitude praises God, whose judgments are *true and righteous*, because *he has judged the great harlot who corrupted the earth* and spilled the blood of his servants (*cf.* 16:5–7). Her destruction is complete and irreversible. As with God's judgment of Sodom and Gomorrah (Gn. 19:28) and of Edom (Is. 34:10), which portended this ultimate judgment, *her smoke goes up for ever and ever.* Her doom is one with the doom of the worshippers of the beast and his image (14:11), for they are at the same time the lovers of the harlot Babylon.

> *And the twenty-four elders and the four living creatures fell down and worshipped God who is seated on the throne, saying, Amen, Hallelujah! And a voice came forth from the throne, saying, Praise our God, all his servants, you who fear him, small and great (19:4–5).*

As we have indicated, *the twenty-four elders* represent the redeemed of mankind and *the four living creatures* represent the restored creation (see comments above on 4:4, 6f.). These now contribute their praise of Almighty God and his justice. Their *Amen* expresses their agreement with the angels' adoration of God for his salvation and glory and power (verse 1; see comments on 3:14 above regarding the meaning of 'Amen'), and their *Hallelujah* takes up the 'Hallelujah' of the angelic host (verses 1 and 3). There follows the voice *from the throne*, that is, from the divine presence, summoning the whole company of the redeemed, *all his servants*, who truly are those *who fear him*, to unite their voices in the praise of their Creator and Redeemer. They are to do so without exception or discrimination, both *small and great*, as the world once regarded them, but no longer, for now all the fallen distinctions of race, class, and culture are a thing of the past.

The marriage of the Lamb, 19:6–16

1. THE BRIDE PREPARED, 19:6–10

And I heard what was like the sound of a great multitude and like the sound of many waters and like the sound of mighty thunders, saying, Hallelujah! for the Lord our God the Almighty reigns (19:6).

This **great multitude**, whose voice is now lifted in praise to **the Lord our God the Almighty**, we understand to be the entire company of God's servants, angelic as well as human, the doubly 'great multitude', so to speak, of the spiritual hosts (verse 1 above) and of redeemed humanity (7:9). The sound has the majestic beauty of **many waters** and **mighty thunders** (*cf.* 14:2), and the hymn of praise, whose theme is one of triumph and joy as God's creatures are brought into the unending perfection of his kingdom, is introduced by **Hallelujah** to become a stupendous Hallelujah Chorus.

Let us be joyful and exultant and give him the glory, for the marriage of the Lamb has come and his bride has made herself ready. And it was given to her to be clothed with fine linen, bright and pure; for the fine linen is the righteous deeds of the saints (19:7–8).

There is good reason to **be joyful and exultant**, to give expression to a superabundance of joy, because the inauguration of the everlasting kingdom coincides with **the marriage of the Lamb**. The imagery emphasizes in a striking way the intense love of the Lord for his own. In the Old Testament God speaks of himself as the husband of his people (Is. 54:5; Ho. 2:19f., *etc.*); and in the New Testament the church is depicted as the bride of Christ whose advent as the Bridegroom to take her to himself she eagerly awaits (Eph. 5:25, 32; Mt. 25:1ff.; Mk. 2:19; Jn. 3:29; 2 Cor. 11:2). Now the long desired moment has arrived when love blends with love in a union of everlasting perfection.

For this climactic moment **his bride has made herself ready**: the **fine linen, bright and pure**, in which she is arrayed for the marriage is **the** *righteous deeds of the saints*. These righteous deeds are indeed performed by the bride, but they do not make up a gown of self-righteousness; for that would be cause for them in their rejoicing to give themselves the glory, whereas they are exhorted to *give him the glory*. The whole of their salvation, from beginning to end, is from God (2 Cor. 5:18), and therefore all the praise belongs to God. The oneness of the saints in Christ Jesus is owed entirely to God, thanks to whom Christ has become not only their redemption but also their wisdom and righteousness and sanctification. Accordingly, their glorying is not at all in themselves, but only and altogether in the Lord (1 Cor. 1:29f.; *cf*. Eph. 2:8–10).

The righteous deeds of the saints, then, do not constitute or contribute to their justification before God, which would be self-justification; as the deeds *of the saints* they are performed by those who are already redeemed and justified in Christ. They are evidence of the bride's sanctification and at the same time of her serious concern to prepare herself for the marriage of the Lamb. This preparedness is effected through the sanctifying work of the Holy Spirit transforming her progressively into the likeness of her Bridegroom (*cf*. 2 Cor. 3:18; 1 Jn. 3:2f.). It is the fulfilment of the obligation of the redeemed 'to live no longer for themselves, but for him who for their sake died and was raised' (2 Cor. 5:15). St. Paul's concern for the Christ-centred holiness of the church as the bride of the Lamb is expressed in his admonition to the Christians in Corinth: 'I am jealous over you with a godly jealousy, for I betrothed you to Christ to present you as a pure virgin to her one husband' (2 Cor. 11:2; *cf*. Tit. 2:11–14). Thus it is *given* to the bride to be clothed with fine linen for the marriage. The responsibility to live the life of pure holiness to the glory of God is not removed but is intensified by the very givenness of the Holy Spirit.

When it is said, in 7:9, 14, that the great multitude of the redeemed had washed their robes and made them white in the blood of the Lamb, the reference is to their justification before God through faith in the reconciling death of Christ on the cross. The fine linen in which they are seen, in this vision, to be clothed, and which is explained as representing the righteous deeds of the saints, relates, as we have observed, to their sanctification. This double concept points to the truth that in principle justification is naturally followed by, because it is productive of, sanctification. The spotless righteousness of Christ which is graciously reckoned to us in our justification should increasingly be approached as in our daily conduct we walk in the Spirit; and the two will coincide at the Lord's appearing when believers will be brought to total conformity to his likeness, which will be their glorification. As St. John writes in his First Epistle: 'We know that when he appears we shall be like him, for we shall see him as he is', while in the meantime 'every one who thus hopes in him purifies himself as he is pure' (1 Jn. 3:2f.). At the Lamb's marriage the bride's robes will at last be as the Bridegroom's, white and dazzling as the light (*cf.* Mt. 17:2; Lk. 9:29). This is the fulfilment of the prophetic declaration of Isaiah 61:10: 'I will greatly rejoice in the Lord, my soul shall exult in my God; for he has clothed me with the garments of salvation, he has covered me with the robe of righteousness, as a bridegroom decks himself with a garland, and as a bride adorns herself with her jewels.'

> *And he said to me, Write: Blessed are those who are invited to the marriage banquet of the Lamb. And he said to me, These are the true words of God (19:9).*

If, as seems probable, the angel who makes these pronouncements is the same as the one who previously said, 'Write: Blessed are the dead who die in the Lord' (14:13), what is declared here is the consummation of that blessedness, namely, participation in **the marriage banquet of the Lamb**. Here, too, is the fulfilment of Christ's expectation, as expressed at the institution of his Supper: 'I tell you', he said to his apostles, 'I shall not drink again of this fruit of the vine until that day when I drink it new with you in my Father's kingdom' (Mt. 26:29; *cf.* Lk. 22:28–30).

The universal scope of the invitation to be present at the Lamb's marriage banquet is repeatedly implied in this book, for his bride consists of those who are ransomed 'from every tribe and tongue and people and nation' (see, for example, 5:9; 7:9; 14:6); and this accords with Christ's statement that 'many will come from east and west and sit at the table with Abraham, Isaac, and Jacob in the kingdom of heaven' (Mt. 8:11).

The angel's further assertion, **These are the true words of God**, refer most naturally to the beatitude he has just uttered. Comparable assertions are made in 21:5 and 22:6 below, and there is also an affinity with the 'faithful sayings' of 1 Timothy 1:15, 3:1, 4:9, 2 Timothy 2:11, and Titus 3:8.

> *And I fell down at his feet to worship him; and he said to me, You must not do that! I am a fellow servant with you and your brethren who maintain the testimony of Jesus. Worship God! For the testimony of Jesus is the spirit of prophecy (19:10).*

Awed, no doubt, by the resplendent dignity of the angel (*cf.* the appearance of the angel in 18:1) and moved by the glorious reality of the truth communicated to him, St. John prostrates himself at the feet of the heavenly messenger in order to worship him; but he is immediately and peremptorily forbidden to do so. The angel explains that he is *a fellow servant* with John and with all other believers, not a divine being, and that God alone is to be worshipped. A lonely exile on the isle of Patmos, and all too plainly not yet glorified, the Apostle will give way a second time, on the spur of the moment, to this same impulse in a similar situation, and will meet with the same reproof (see 22:8f. below).

Repeatedly in the New Testament any temptation to worship the creature, whether angelic or human, meets with the rejoinder that God alone is to be worshipped. Satan himself is an angel who, by disguising himself as an angel of light, attracts the attention of men and sets himself up as the god of this world to divert their worship from the true God (2 Cor. 4:4; 12:14). He even presumed to invite the incarnate Son to fall at his feet and worship him at the time of the temptation in the wilderness, but the invitation evoked the stern rejection: 'Begone Satan! for it is written, You shall worship the Lord your God and him only shall you serve' (Mt. 4:8–10). Angel-worship was evidently a temptation to be firmly resisted by the members of the Colossian church (Col. 2:18). The temptation to allow themselves to be worshipped as though they were superhuman beings was likewise entirely repugnant to the apostles. Thus St. Peter lifted up Cornelius, who had prostrated himself at his feet in an attitude of worship, and said, 'Stand up! I too am a man' (Acts 10:25f.); and Paul and Barnabas were appalled when they realized that the inhabitants of Lystra were about to worship and offer up sacrifice to them: 'Men', they cried, 'why are you doing this? We are also men, of like nature with you', and they directed them to the worship of the living God (Acts 14:11ff.).

In the statement that follows this repudiation of worship by the angel, *For the testimony of Jesus is the spirit of prophecy*, the conjunction *for* indicates a close logical connection with what has just been said. (Whether the statement was uttered by the angel or is a comment by the Apostle is debatable; but in either case the logical connection holds good.) The point is this: prophecy here is the declaration of the message entrusted by God to his servant. It is a function of servanthood, as the angel has just said, *I am a fellow servant with you and your brethren who maintain the testimony of Jesus*. The ministry of the servant is to bear witness to Jesus, not to oneself. Therefore any element of self-glory or worship offered to the servant is entirely incongruous with this ministry, the spirit or heart of which is witness to Jesus.

It is certainly not St. John's intention to dishonour the Creator by offering worship to a creature or to put an angel in the place of God. He was simply overawed by the presence of this angel and gave way to an impulse that was ill-considered. The essential humility of the angel, who claimed no more than to be the Apostle's fellow servant, is striking. Their common mission is the testimony of Jesus. This gives perspective to the witness of all God's servants, whether angelic or human. And so it is that the testimony of Jesus is St. John's dominant motivation in the composition of this book (1:2). It was for the testimony of Jesus that he was an exile on the isle of Patmos (1:9), it is for the word of their testimony to Jesus that his servants suffer persecution and martyrdom (12:11), and it is against those who bear testimony to Jesus that the dragon makes war (12:17); for the testimony of Jesus is the hallmark of all God's true prophets, well known and little known, who declare the message of the gospel to those who worship the creature instead of the Creator (Rom. 1:16, 25).

2. THE RIDER ON THE WHITE HORSE, 19:11–16

And I saw the heaven opened, and behold, a white horse, and he who sat on it is called Faithful and True, and in righteousness he judges and makes war (19:11).

A new vision is granted to St. John as he sees **the heaven opened** and a rider seated on **a white horse** who is called, because he is, **Faithful and True**. The rider is the incarnate and now glorified Son leading his hosts against the mass concentration of the enemy forces of evil. Rightly, and in contrast to those adversaries, he is known as 'Faithful and True', for he has already been designated as 'the Amen, the faithful and true witness' (3:14; *cf.* 1:15) and as 'he who is holy, he who is true' (3:7; *cf.* 5:10; 15:3), and of him alone can it be said that he is absolutely the Truth (Jn. 14:6). Moreover, it is because he is faithful and true that *in righteousness he judges and makes war* (*cf.* Is. 11:3–6).

And his eyes are like a flame of fire, and on his head are many diadems, and he has a name written which no one knows but himself; and he is clothed with a robe dipped in blood; and his name by which he is called is The Word of God (19:12–13).

The description of the rider's **eyes** as **like a flame of fire** further confirms his identity as the incarnate Son in glory, for his eyes were described thus in 1:14 and 2:18. The ardent intensity of his gaze is the shining forth of his absolute truth and righteousness. The diadems betoken kingly power and authority. The diadems that St. John has seen on the heads of the dragon (12:3) and on the horns of the beast (13:1) signify the rebellious design of the enemy to dethrone God and usurp his royal supremacy. But the **many diadems** on the rider's head are a symbol of his unassailable sovereignty which is now about to be exercised in final judgment. His absolute supremacy is indicated, further, by the **name written which no one knows but himself**. Where it is written is not said; but it is his own unique name, 'the name which is above every name' in his high exaltation (Phil. 2:9), a name which can belong to no creature and to no worldly power, no matter how formidable it may for the time appear to be.

The information that the rider on the white horse is **clothed with a robe dipped in blood** recalls the description in Isaiah's prophecy of one who comes 'in crimsoned garments . . . glorious in his apparel, marching in the greatness of his strength'. In answer to the question regarding the identity of this person and the reason for the redness of his apparel, 'like his that treads in the wine press', he replies:

> It is I, announcing vindication, mighty to save [the statement of one who is divine] . . . I have trodden the wine press alone, and from the peoples no one was with me; I trod them in my anger and trampled them in my wrath; their lifeblood is sprinkled upon my garments, and I have stained all my raiment. For the day of vengeance was in my heart, and my year of redemption has come (*Is. 63:1–4*).

This graphic portrayal of the coming Judge and Redeemer affirms the expectation that the Day of the Lord will be the day on which judgment and redemption coincide. There will be final judgment for the enemies of God and redemption in the sense of consummating deliverance and glorification for his long-suffering people. Those who have gratefully welcomed the salvation that flows from the cross on which the blood of Christ was shed for them will enter into the fullness of the blessing of that blood-shedding, while the blood of those who have despised that blood-shedding will flow from the winepress that is trodden by the Son (see verse 15 below; *cf.* 14:19f.). The symbolism is that of the execution of justice that is as awesome as it is thorough.

The identity of the rider is now disclosed: **his name by which he is called is The Word of God**. It is a name that provides corroborating evidence of the Johannine authorship of Revelation, for in the prologue of John's Gospel the Son is called the Word, who is God, through whom all things were created, and who as the incarnate Son dwelt among us (Jn. 1:1ff., 14). As the Word of God the Son is both the revealer of the divine mind and also the agent of the divine will. Since the word of God never fails to effect what it decrees (*cf.* Is. 55:11), it is through him who is the eternal Word that the will of God is brought to pass not only in creation but also in re-creation (2 Cor. 4:6) and in judgment (Acts 17:31). Clearly, the name 'The Word of God' recorded here is not the same as the 'name written which no one knows but himself' and which therefore is not made known.

> **And the armies in heaven, arrayed in fine linen, white and pure, followed him on white horses** (19:14).

Mounted, like their leader, on white horses (*cf.* verse 11), and arrayed, like the Lamb's bride, in fine white and gleaming linen (*cf.* verse 8), the heavenly hosts, who have already appeared as Michael and his angels (12:7), follow the Son to participate in this final encounter.

> *And a sharp sword with which to smite the nations proceeds from his mouth, and he will rule them with a rod of iron; and he treads the winepress of the fury of the wrath of Almighty God* (19:15).

In the earliest of the visions recorded in this book St. John had seen a sharp two-edged sword proceeding from the mouth of the exalted Son (1:16; see comments there), and in the letter to the church in Pergamum the warning was given that the Lord would make war against the unrepentant with the sword of his mouth (2:12, 16). Now the prophecy of Isaiah is fulfilled, that 'he shall smite the earth with the rod of his mouth, and with the breath of his lips he shall slay the wicked' (Is. 11:4; *cf.* 2 Thes. 2:8). The assertion that he will **rule** the nations **with a rod of iron** implies the overthrow of the ungodly in this final judgment, and is practically a quotation from Psalm 2:9 ('You shall break them with a rod of iron'; see 2:27 and 12:5 above). For **the winepress of the fury of the wrath of Almighty God** see comments on 14:19f. above. The threefold imagery here of sword, rod, and winepress signifies warfare, subjugation, and destruction: the ultimate demonstration to the impenitent that God is indeed almighty.

> *And on his robe and on his thigh he has a name written: King of kings and Lord of lords* (19:16).

This is the fourth name assigned in this vision to the Son in his glory: first, 'Faithful and True' (verse 11); second, the name 'which no one knows but himself' (verse 12); third, 'The Word of God' (verse 13); and now **King of kings and Lord of lords**, a name which declares the eternal reality of his absolute power and authority over all, as we have already seen in 17:14, where the all-conquering Lamb is so described. The location of the name **on his robe and on his thigh** most probably means that the name was inscribed on the robe at the place where it was draped over his thigh.

The enemies of the Word of God
destroyed, *19:17 – 20:15*

1. THE DOOM OF THE BEAST AND THE FALSE PROPHET AND THEIR FOLLOWERS, 19:17–21

> *And I saw an angel standing in the sun, and he cried with a loud voice to all the birds that fly in midheaven, saying, Come, gather together for the great banquet of God, to eat the flesh of kings and the flesh of captains and the flesh of mighty men and the flesh of horses and their riders and the flesh of all men, both free and bond, both small and great (19:17–18).*

This **angel standing in the sun**, resplendent and, as it were, from the very height of heaven, summons **all the birds that fly in midheaven** (*cf.* 8:13; 14:6) to feast themselves on the flesh of the slain. Ezekiel 39:17ff. is a comparable passage, where the prophet is instructed to call together every kind of bird and beast to eat flesh and drink blood at the great sacrificial feast that God is preparing, with the promise that they will be filled 'with horses and riders, with mighty men and all kinds of warriors'. To the same purpose is the epigrammatic saying of Christ in his discourse regarding the end of the age: 'Wherever the carcase is, there the eagles will be gathered together' (Mt. 24: 28; Lk. 17:37; *cf.* 1 Sa. 17:44, 46; Is. 18:6). The scene envisaged is one of total carnage in which all the hosts of ungodliness perish, the small as well as the great, the followers as well as the leaders (*cf.* 6:15 and 13:16 above; 20:12 below).

> *And I saw the beast and the kings of the earth and their armies gathered together to make war against him who is seated on the horse and against his army. And the beast was captured together with the false prophet who performed the signs in its presence by which he deceived those who had received the mark of the beast and those who worshipped its image; and they were both thrown alive into the lake of fire that burns with brimstone; and the rest were slain with the sword that proceeds from the mouth of him*

who is seated on the horse; and all the birds were gorged with their flesh (19:19-21).

The battle-lines are arrayed for the climactic conflict. The warfare is total as antichrist leads the armies of earth's kings (*cf.* 16:14; 17:2, 18) in this global assault on the Lamb and his throne. But the victory of the Lamb is assured (17:14), for his is the supreme power over the kings of the earth, and the authentic kings are those who have been freed from their sins by his blood (1:5, 6). Here *the beast* is the first of the two beasts that appeared in an earlier vision and stands for the antichrist (13:1ff.; see comments there), and *the false prophet* is the second of the two beasts (see comments on 13:11ff.). Their positions, under the headship of the dragon, who is Satan (12:3, 7ff.), are second and third respectively in the hierarchy of evil. Their seizure and consignment to *the lake of fire that burns with brimstone*, which is also known as the second death (20:10, 14, 15; *cf.* Mt. 18:9), symbolizes the purging of their defiling hostility and antichristianity from creation. Satan, whose agents they are, meets with the same doom (20:10). *The rest* who are *slain with the sword that proceeds from the mouth of him who is seated on the horse* (*cf.* verse 15 above) are the whole company of disobedient and impenitent mankind. The word of grace they have rejected becomes the word of judgment by which they are condemned. This is precisely as Christ himself forewarned: 'If any one hears my sayings and does not keep them, I do not judge him; for I did not come to judge the world but to save the world. He who rejects me and does not receive my sayings has a judge: the word that I have spoken will judge him on the last day' (Jn. 12:47f.). Thus, tragically, because of their blind folly and hardness of heart, the means of their salvation is transformed into the means of their damnation. The horror of their self-invited doom is intensified by the spectacle of the birds gorging themselves on the flesh of their carcases. The graphic imagery is a solemn reminder that 'it is a fearful thing to fall into the hands of the living God' (Heb. 10:31).

2. INTERVENING VISION, 20:1-10

A. Satan bound for a thousand years, 20:1-6

And I saw an angel coming down from heaven with the key of the abyss and a great chain in his hand; and he seized the dragon, the ancient serpent, who is the Devil and Satan, and bound him for a thousand years, and threw him into the abyss, and shut it up and sealed it over him, so that he should no longer deceive the nations, until the thousand years were completed. After that he must be loosed for a little while (20:1–3).

The concluding section of the Apocalypse, which is now introduced, depicts the doom of Satan and his retinue and the renewal of creation as it is brought to the glory for which it was always destined. Whether the *angel* now seen by St. John *coming down from heaven with the key of the abyss* is the same as the angel with great authority in 18:1 or the angel who was given the key of the abyss in 9:1 we are not told. He certainly seems to be a formidable figure, for with the *great chain in his hand* he binds the devil, who is the angel of the abyss, also known as Abaddon or Apollyon (9:11). The binding of Satan with this chain, his being cast into the abyss, and the closing and sealing of the abyss over him plainly indicate that the power over him and the abyss belongs to One who is his superior, that is, to Almighty God against whose authority he has rebelled. The key of the abyss, as indeed the key to the destiny of all things, is held by God, or the angel to whom he gives it, not by Satan.

The period of *a thousand years* is symbolical (in a manner consistent with the use of numbers in this book) of a relatively long and complete age or time. It is long from man's point of view and complete in accordance with the timetable predetermined by God. That it is a limited period of time is evident from the information that at the end of the thousand years Satan *must be loosed for a little while*, which will be the short duration of his final insurrection culminating in final judgment (as described in 19:17ff.).

The purpose of this restraint of the devil is *that he should no longer deceive the nations*. If, during this thousand-year period, he is 'no longer' to be free to do this, it follows that prior to the exercise of this restraining power it is what he had been busy doing. Thus in 12:9, as we have seen, the devil is described as 'the deceiver of the whole world'. The account there of his being cast down from heaven with his angels, having been decisively defeated by Christ's self-offering at Calvary, has important connections with the spectacle here of his being bound and cast into the abyss. (See the comments on 12:7–9 above.) It is interesting, too, that his designation here as *that ancient serpent, who is the Devil and Satan*, is a repetition of his designation there. He who deceived and defeated the first Adam has met his match, and more than his match, in the person of the incarnate Son, who is the Second Adam. The point is that the advent of Christ brought about a change in the relationship between Satan and the nations.

Prior to the incarnation, the nations had been permitted to remain in the darkness and ignorance induced by Satan's deception. They had 'walked in their own ways' (Acts 14:16). In striking contrast to this, Israel alone of all the peoples on earth had been entrusted with the oracles of God (Rom. 3:2); they had the knowledge and the enlightenment that God's revelation brings; and therefore it was required of them to maintain their distinctness from the surrounding heathen nations by walking in God's ways (*cf.* Dt. 5:32f.; 10:12; 12:1ff., *etc.*). 'You are a people holy to the Lord your God,' Moses reminded them, 'and the Lord has chosen you to be a people for his own possession, out of all the peoples that are on the face of the earth' (Dt. 14:2). The purpose of this choosing of Israel, however, was to bring worldwide blessing to all earth's nations through the incarnate Son who is the promised seed of Abraham, the first father of the people of Israel (Gn. 22:18; Gal. 3:16).

No longer, then, are the nations left in the shadows of superstition; for God's salvation has been 'prepared in the presence of all peoples', and Christ is the light of divine revelation to the nations as well as the glory of God's people Israel (Lk. 2:30–32). And no longer are the people of God to keep themselves separate; for their commission is now to proclaim the gospel message to the farthest parts of the earth so that the fullness of the nations may be brought in (Mt. 24:14; 28:19f.; Rom. 10:12f.; 11:25). The power of Satan over the nations is broken by the power of the gospel. The darkness of the devil's deception is dispelled by the glory of him who declared, 'I am the Light of the world' (Jn. 8:12; 9:5). Thus the presence of Jesus in 'Galilee of the nations' is seen by St. Matthew as the fulfilment of the words spoken by the prophet Isaiah: 'The people who sat in darkness have seen a great light, and for those who sat in the region and shadow of death light has dawned' (Mt. 4:13–16; Is. 9:1f.).

The illumination of the nations with the light of the gospel is effected both by the coming of Christ and by the binding of Satan. The coming and the binding are interconnected. Thus when Jesus was accused by the scribes of casting out demons by the prince of demons he responded by pointing out the absurdity of suggesting that Satan was casting out Satan and was divided against himself; and then he added that 'no one can enter a strong man's house and plunder his goods unless he first binds the strong man' (Mk. 3:22ff.; Mt. 12:24ff.). The implication is plain: Christ's casting out of demons was an evidence not only that the house of 'the strong man', who is the prince of demons, was being plundered, but also that 'the strong man' Satan had been bound.

The casting of the dragon into the abyss, therefore, we understand as coinciding with his being cast down from heaven as previously recorded in 12:7–9. This accords with the statement made by Christ when the seventy whom he had sent out returned with the joyful news that in his name even the demons were subject to them: 'I saw Satan fall like lightning from heaven. Behold, I have given you authority over all the power of the enemy' (Lk. 10:17–19). This assertion indicates that 'the strong man' is bound and confined, as also does the declaration of Jesus as he approached the ordeal and the victory of the cross: 'Now is the judgment of this world, now shall the ruler of this world be cast out; and I, when I am lifted up from the earth, will draw all men to myself' (Jn. 12:31f.). So, too, the risen Lord commissioned his apostles with these words of encouragement: 'All authority in heaven and on earth has been given to me. Go therefore and make disciples of all nations' (Mt. 28:18f.). No longer is 'the deceiver of the whole world' (12:9) able to deceive the nations. It is Christ who wields the power and the authority throughout the universe, who draws all men to himself, and who sends out his servants to make disciples of all nations; for it is he, not the devil, whose destiny is 'to rule all the nations' (12:5). That Christ is the one who is stronger than Satan is plainly seen also in the Epistle to the Hebrews, where we read that in his incarnation the Son of God partook of our human nature, 'in order that through death he might render ineffective him who has the power of death, that is, the devil, and deliver all those who through fear of death were subject to lifelong bondage' (Heb. 2:14f.).

This evidence leads to the conclusion that the thousand years during which Satan is bound and confined had their beginning with the incarnation of the eternal Son, and in particular with the achievement of the purpose of the incarnation, namely, the conquest of Satan and his realm on the cross of Calvary and the redemption of man by the grace that flows from that cross – a conquest confirmed and assured by Christ's resurrection from the dead and his ascension and enthronement in glory at the right hand of the Majesty on high (Heb. 1:3; 12:2).

> *And I saw thrones, and judgment was given to those who were seated on them. And I saw the souls of those who had been beheaded for the testimony of Jesus and for the word of God, and those who had not worshipped the beast or its image and had not received its mark on their forehead or on their hand. And they lived and reigned with Christ a thousand years (20:4).*

As this vision unfolds, St. John sees **thrones** and records that **judgment was given to those who were seated on them**. We are informed that it is **souls** that are thus enthroned, that is to say, persons in the disembodied state which prevails between death and resurrection. These souls are classified in two categories. Firstly, there are **those who had been beheaded for the testimony of Jesus and for the word of God**, or, in other words, those who had suffered the death of martyrdom, 'beheading' being a cover-term for every kind of violent death endured by the martyrs. And secondly, there are **those who had not worshipped the beast or its image and had not received its mark on their forehead or on their hand**, or, in other words, faithful witnesses who had honoured Christ in their lives without being called to seal their testimony with martyrdom (the reference is to what has been written in 13:11f.). This

211

distinction repeats, in effect, the distinction between the blood of the martyrs and the blood of the saints in 17:6 above; and it corresponds with the experience of the brothers James and John. The former died the death of a martyr (Acts 12:1f.), while the latter lived on into old age, yet both were assured by Jesus that they would drink the cup that he would drink and be baptized with the baptism with which he would be baptized (Mk. 10:38f.). The souls in view, then, are the souls of all who, whether their lives have been shortened by the cruel death of martyrdom or they have died, so to speak, in their beds, belong to the company of those who persevere to the end in following their Lord while here on earth.

These are the souls whom St. John saw seated on thrones and of whom it is said that *they lived and reigned with Christ a thousand years*. They are the persons who have suffered death in their bodies but not in their souls. They have not feared 'those who kill the body but cannot kill the soul' (Mt. 10:28), and now it is as souls that they live and reign with Christ. Faithful unto death, they have received the crown of life (Rev. 2:10; *cf.* 3:21) and they experience the blessedness of the dead who die in the Lord (14:13). St. Paul taught the same truth when he declared that the Christian who has died is 'away from the body and at home with the Lord' (2 Cor. 5:8), and that 'to die is gain' because it means 'to depart and be with Christ' (Phil. 1:21, 23).

The thousand years may be defined as the period between the two comings of Christ, or, more strictly, between the return of the ascended Son to glory, his mission to earth completed, and the loosing of Satan 'for a little while' (verse 3 above). The latter, however, is the final event of this period and it ends, as we have seen, in the conclusive defeat of Satan and his hosts at Christ's second coming. This is the perspective clearly delineated in the assertion of Hebrews 10:12f., that 'when Christ had offered for all time a single sacrifice for sins, he sat down (enthroned) at the right hand of God, then to wait until his enemies should be made a stool for his feet' (*cf.* Ps. 110:1); and this is precisely what St. Paul affirms when he writes that 'he must reign until he had put all his enemies under his feet' (1 Cor. 15:25). For Christ, it is the meantime as he awaits the final assault and total subjugation of the enemy. For the Christian who has departed this life, it is the meantime between death and resurrection as he awaits the reinvestment of the soul with his body that, sown in weakness, will be raised in glory and power (1 Cor. 15:42–44). And this is the meantime of 'a thousand years' within which the souls of the faithful live and reign with Christ.

> *The rest of the dead did not live until the thousand years were ended. Blessed and holy is he who has a part in the first resurrection! Over such the second death has no power, but they shall be priests of God and of Christ, and they shall reign with him during the thousand years (20:5–6).*

The rest of the dead are those who, in contrast to Christian believers who have died and whose souls live and reign with Christ within this span of ***the thousand years***, end their present life in a state of impenitence and unbelief. There is no comfort or blessedness for them in the interval between death and resurrection, for they have no part in ***the first resurrection***. Christian believers, however, are pronounced ***blessed and holy*** even while they themselves are dead and unresurrected because of their participation in the first resurrection; indeed, it is by virtue of this participation that they are ***priests of God and of Christ*** and ***reign with him during the thousand years***. This priestly and kingly status, which derives from the believer's union with the incarnate Son who is the Priest-King (Heb. 7:1ff.), continues through death into the intermediate state and beyond into the everlasting perfection of the new creation. Hence the doxology uttered by St. John in the opening part of this work: 'To him who loves us and freed us from our sins by his blood and made us a kingdom, priests to his God and Father, to him be the glory and the dominion for ever and ever. Amen' (1:6; *cf.* 1 Pet. 2:9, 'a royal priesthood'). Theirs are the souls that live and reign with the ascended and enthroned Redeemer during the thousand years.

That the Apostle is writing about Christ's servants who have died is obvious: they are referred to as souls, living and reigning indeed with Christ, but as such awaiting their own resurrection. This separation from their bodies is not permanent, but only for this interim period of one thousand years; and in this state they are distinct from 'the rest of the dead'. As those who have ***a part in the first resurrection*** they have the assurance that ***the second death has no power*** over them. Just as mention of 'the second death' plainly implies that there is a first death, so also the mention of 'the first resurrection' plainly implies that there is a second resurrection. The second death and the second resurrection are future realities yet to be experienced by the dead. We must now inquire into the significance of this terminology regarding first and second deaths and first and second resurrections.

We may conveniently start with the second resurrection, even though in chronological order it follows the first, for (while the precise designation 'second resurrection' does not occur) it is evident that it is one and the same with what is customarily known as the general resurrection of the dead which, as affirmed in the creeds, will take place at the end of this age ('At [Christ's] coming all men shall rise again with their bodies', Athanasian Creed). Thus St. Paul taught that 'there will be a resurrection of both the just and the unjust' (Acts 24:15), and Christ himself instructed his disciples that 'the hour is coming when all who are in the tombs will hear his voice and come forth, those who have done good to the resurrection of life, and those who have done evil to the resurrection of judgment' (Jn. 5:28f.; see also the similar teaching in Dn. 12:2).

In the nature of the case, resurrection means *bodily* resurrection: if it is not resurrection of the body, it is not resurrection. Accordingly, Christian believers are assured that the Saviour whose advent from heaven they await will transform their lowly body into the likeness of his glorified body (Phil. 3:20f.), while those who persist in unbelief will face God 'who can destroy both soul and body in hell' (Mt. 10:28).

The same considerations apply to the first resurrection in which the living souls of Christians who have died have a part. It is quite commonly supposed that what is intended is a notion of resurrection in a merely spiritual and analogical sense. Christ declared, it is true, that the believer has passed from death to life (Jn. 5:24), and St. Paul was saying the same thing when he taught that God makes alive those who were dead through trespasses and sins (Eph. 2:1). But to spiritualize or allegorize the first resurrection in such a way as to leave it a mere theological concept unconnected with bodily resurrection (except for the future second or general resurrection at the end of this age – and it is the first resurrection that is our present concern) is incommensurate with the requirements of the context. If the second resurrection is bodily, in other words, truly a resurrection, then the first resurrection must also be bodily.

In the whole of the New Testament there is only one resurrection of such central importance that it qualifies without rival to be designated the first resurrection, and that is the bodily resurrection of Jesus from the dead. This particular resurrection, indeed, is determinative of the general or second resurrection. The relation of the first to the second resurrection is that of the firstfruits to the full harvest, for, as St. Paul affirms, 'Christ has been raised from the dead, the firstfruits of those who have fallen asleep' (1 Cor. 15:20). The supreme significance of this resurrection impels the apostle to insist that 'if Christ has not been raised, then our preaching is in vain and your faith is in vain . . . and you are still in your sins' (1 Cor. 15:14, 17). The unique bond between the first resurrection and the person of the incarnate Son is that of identity, so much so that he declared of himself: 'I am the resurrection and the life: he who believes in me, though he die, yet shall he live, and whoever lives and believes in me shall never die' (Jn. 11:25).

This is the first resurrection in which the Christian believer has a part because through its power, even though he died, he in soul lives and reigns with the incarnate Son who is now risen, ascended, and glorified. The first resurrection of which he partakes is not in himself but in Christ. His participation is entirely due to his union with Christ, and his union with Christ is a reality because the human nature which the Son took to himself in the incarnation is one with the human nature of those he came to redeem. Their living and reigning with him is interpreted by their incorporation into him. What happened to him happened to our human nature. His rising is our rising; his ascending is our ascending; his glorification is our glorification. Hence St. Paul's assertion that 'even when we were dead through our trespasses God made us alive *together with Christ* . . . and raised us up *with him* and made us sit *with him* in the heavenly places' (Eph. 2:5f.). And so it is that in this period between the first resurrection and the second resurrection the souls of those who have died in the Lord (Rev. 14:13) live and reign **with him**, precisely because they have a part in the first resurrection, which is not their resurrection but the true bodily resurrection of the incarnate Son.

Our intimate union with Christ as those whose whole standing before God is in him is also portrayed in the profound symbolism of our baptism, which proclaims our dying to the old life and our rising to newness of life in Christ. 'You were buried with him in baptism', St. Paul instructs the members of the Colossian church, 'in which you were also raised with him through faith in the working of God, who raised him from the dead' (Col. 2:12); and to the Christians in Rome he writes: 'We were buried therefore with him by baptism into death, so that as Christ was raised from the dead through the glory of the Father we too might walk in newness of life' (Rom. 6:4). The destiny of the incarnate Son is thus shown to be the destiny of all who are his. They are 'blessed and holy' because 'the first resurrection' in which they have a part is his resurrection.

Moreover, it is because of their participation in the resurrection of Jesus that **the second death** has no power over them, for the death of Jesus was once for all, as his resurrection to life confirms: there is no second death for him, and therefore no second death for those who by grace are one with him. 'The second death' is defined symbolically in verse 14 below as 'the lake of fire' into which the devil, the beast, and the false prophet, and with them all who are not found written in the book of life, are cast (verse 10, 14, 15 below). Thus the second death is total death, the utter destruction of final judgment executed against the obdurate enemies of God (*cf.* 2:11; 21:8).

What, then, is the first death that, by implication, precedes the second death (though the expression 'the first death', like 'the second resurrection', is not actually used)? The simple answer to this question might seem to be that the first death is the death that ends the life of every person in the course of human history and is the inescapable evidence of man's mortality (as in Heb. 9:27, 'it is appointed for men to die once, and after this the judgment'); and this is correct so far as individual experience goes.

But there is a deeper understanding of the significance of the first death which shows that the death of the individual is a consequence of the death and mortality by which humanity as a whole is pervaded. There is, indeed, a definite correlation between the first death and the first resurrection. The focal point of both is a person with whom in a particular sense humanity is united. In the case of the first resurrection, as we have seen, that person is the incarnate Son; in the case of the first death, as we shall see, that person is Adam. This perception is summed up in St. Paul's statement that 'as in Adam all die, so also in Christ shall all be made alive' (1 Cor. 15:22). In other words, since our human nature was concentrated in the person of the first man, Adam's fall was our fall and his dying was our dying; and this is counteracted by the dying and rising again of Christ, who, by taking to himself our human nature as Adam first received it, is the second man or the Last Adam (see 1 Cor. 15:45ff.). The first death is radically connected with Adam, as also the first resurrection is radically connected with Christ. To imagine that one can isolate oneself from either is to be dangerously in error. If Christ by virtue of his resurrection, 'the first resurrection', is the firstfruits of the harvest of all who fall asleep in him (1 Cor. 15:20); Adam is by virtue of his death, 'the first death', the firstfruits of the harvest of all who remain in union with him (cf. Mt. 13:24ff., 36ff.).

St. Paul expounds his argument regarding the first death more fully in his letter to the Christians in Rome. 'As sin came into the world through one man', he writes, 'and death through sin, so also death passed into all men, for the reason that all sinned'. On the one hand, many died through the trespass of one man, and, on the other, and much more so, the grace of God that flows freely to us from the one man Jesus Christ abounds to many. 'If, because of one man's trespass, death reigned through that one man', St. Paul continues, 'much more will those who receive the abundance of grace and the free gift of righteousness reign in life through the one man Jesus Christ' (Rom. 5:12ff.). Accordingly, all men are either in Adam or in Christ. To be in Adam is to partake of his death, the first death, of which one's own death on earth is the entail, and which leads on to the second death of final judgment. To be in Christ is to partake of his life and resurrection, which is the first resurrection, and which has its culmination in the transfiguration of our bodies into the likeness of the body of his glorification. Those who experience the second death are strangers to the grace and power of the first resurrection. Over those who have a part in the first resurrection the second death has no power. For the former the second or general resurrection is the resurrection of judgment; for the latter it is the resurrection of life (Jn. 5:28f.).

B. Satan loosed. His final assault, 20:7–10

> And when the thousand years are completed Satan will be loosed from his prison and will come forth to deceive the nations which are at the four corners of the earth, Gog and Magog, to gather them together for war, whose number is as the sand of the sea (20:7–8).

As the thousand years are concluded there comes the 'little while' (verse 3) during which **Satan** is **loosed** for the enactment of the closing scene prior to the renewal of the whole creation. Once more Satan sets out *to deceive the nations*, which he has been inhibited from doing during the thousand years; and he deceives them with the vain promise that their mobilization for one massive climactic onslaught against God of global proportions (*at the four corners of the earth*) will enable them to seize control of the world. Their *number is as the sand of the sea* and this is the uprising to end all uprisings.

The designation of this vast host under Satan's leadership as *Gog and Magog* indicates a connection with the prophecies of Ezekiel 38 and 39, where 'Gog, of the land of Magog' is presented as God's opponent. It is declared that 'after many days' (the equivalent of 'when the thousand years are completed' here) Gog and his battalions will be mustered 'in the latter years' to go to war against God's people who have been 'brought out from the nations', and that they will come on 'like a storm' and will be 'like a cloud covering the land' (Ezk. 38:1–9). But it is God who will prevail as he overwhelms Gog and his hordes with the wrath of his judgment. 'So', the All-Holy and Almighty Creator proclaims, 'I will show my greatness and my holiness and make myself known in the eyes of many nations. Then they will know that I am the Lord' (38:18–23; cf. 39:7f.). In this prophecy too, as we observed in the comments on 19:17–21 above, the birds and beasts are invited to feast on the flesh of Gog's fallen army (Ezk. 39:17ff.). The affinity between Ezekiel's vision and that of St. John is unmistakable, and the latter in fact helps to interpret the former by showing that its fulfilment belongs to the end of history as we now know it.

> *And they went up over the breadth of the earth and surrounded the camp of the saints and the beloved city, and fire came down from heaven and consumed them. And the devil who deceived them, was thrown into the lake of fire and brimstone where the beast and the false prophet were, and they will be tormented day and night for ever and ever (20:9–10).*

The warfare is worldwide, *over the breadth of the earth*. Its target *the camp of the saints and the beloved city*, is not a geographical location or a specific city but God's faithful people who constitute the church of Jesus Christ and are the authentic citizens of the city of the living God (Heb. 12:22), and as such totally distinct from the great city called Sodom and Egypt and Babylon (11:8; 18:10). The design of the hosts of Gog and Magog is to obliterate from the face of the earth the faith and fear of Jesus Christ. But it is they who are *consumed* by the *fire* of God's holy indignation *from heaven* (cf. Dt. 4:24; Heb. 12:29). The doom of the devil and his agents is both certain and irreversible. Their elimination from God's creation, renewed in Christ Jesus, will be *for ever and ever*. Thus, as Christ taught, all causes of offence and all evildoers will be gathered

217

out of his kingdom and thrown into the furnace of fire where there will be weeping and gnashing of teeth; and 'then the righteous will shine like the sun in the kingdom of their Father' (Mt. 13:36–43).

3. THE LAST JUDGMENT, 20:11–15

And I saw a great white throne and him who was seated on it, from whose presence earth and heaven fled away, and no place was found for them. And I saw the dead, great and small, standing before the throne; and the books were opened. And another book was opened which is the book of life. And the dead were judged by what was written in the books, according to their works (20:11–12).

The awesome scene depicted here is that of the last judgment of unregenerate mankind. The **throne** is the seat of absolute authority and justice: it is **great** by reason of its majestic and formidable appearance; it is **white** because of the perfect purity and holiness that radiate from it; and it is one throne, not many, by virtue of the sole and supreme sovereignty of **him who is seated on it** as the Judge before whom all must stand. The cataclysmic terror of this climactic day of judgment towards which all history in its fallenness has been moving is conveyed by the portrayal of the fleeing away and displacement of **earth and heaven**, convulsed in the rebirth of all things preparatory to the appearance of the new heaven and new earth (21:1). The spectacle graphically described in the parallel passage 6:12ff. is recapitulated here. In this judgment there is no respect of persons (*cf.* 1 Pet. 1:17), no distinction of class and caste, no hierarchial discrimination, nor is physical death an escape from this assize – **the dead**, that is, specifically all whose status is still in Adam, both **great and small**, are found **standing before the throne**, and **the books** are **opened** to disclose incontrovertible evidence of guilt (*cf.* the judgment scene in Dn. 7:9f.).

The celestial book-keeping observed in this vision is a pictorial representation of the truth that 'all things are open and laid bare to the eyes of him to whom we have to render account' (Heb. 12:13). The judgment of all is **according to their works**, that is to say, according to the principle of the strictest justice. The confidence in the complete integrity of the divine justice expressed, for example, in the affirmation of the psalmist that the Lord will 'judge the world with righteousness, and the peoples with his truth' (Pss. 96:13; 98:9) and in Abraham's rhetorical question, 'Shall not the Judge of all the earth do right?' (Gn. 18:25), is dramatically confirmed to the Apostle on the isle of Patmos. But there is also **another book** which is **opened**, namely, **the book of life** (see comments above on 3:5). It is those who are 'in Christ' whose names are written in this book, and those who are 'in Adam' whose names are missing from it; and it is the latter who stand condemned before Almighty God (verse 15 below). There are no absentees and there are no exemptions; nor is there any place for self-justification; every mouth is stopped as the whole world is held accountable to God (Rom. 3:10–20).

Those, indeed, whose names are written in the book of life are sinners and in themselves guilty before God. They belong, however, to the company of those who have washed their robes and made them white in the blood of the Lamb (7:14); for their faith is in the Lamb who received their condemnation and endured their punishment on the cross, the innocent for the guilty (1 Pet. 3:18). Forgiven and reconciled, they stand before the Judge justified, not in themselves but in Jesus Christ the righteous who is the propitiation for their sins and their advocate with the Father (1 Jn. 2:1f.; Rom. 3:22–26; 5:1). The last judgment, then, has no terrors for those who, thanks to the grace that flows from the cross, are no longer in Adam but in Christ (Jn. 3:36; 5:24).

> And the sea gave up the dead that were in it, and Death and Hades gave up the dead that were in them, and all were judged according to their works. And Death and Hades were thrown into the lake of fire. This, the lake of fire, is the second death. And every one who was not found written in the book of life was thrown into the lake of fire (20:13–15).

The giving up of the dead by *the sea* and by *Death and Hades* signifies that all the dead are raised and brought to judgment. The manner and place of their dying make no difference; it matters not whether they were drowned at sea or consumed by fire or devoured by wild beasts, or whether they succumbed through illness or old age; all are given up to judgment (*cf.* Heb. 9:27). In these verses there is a personification of Death and Hades, as though having hitherto held all in their rebellious grip they are now compelled to hand over all for judgment. Christ has already liberated the redeemed from their thraldom, and now he demonstrates conclusively that it is he who holds the keys of Death and Hades (as declared in 1:18) as they are *thrown into the lake of fire*, which is *the second death*, and with them all who have chosen death instead of life and thus are *not found written in the book of life* (see on 3:5 above; *cf.* Dt. 30:19; Jn. 5:40; 8:24; 1 Jn. 5:12). This final judgment clears the scene for the establishment of the new heaven and earth from which sin and imperfection and death are banished for evermore, as the vision that follows reveals.

The new heaven and new earth,
21:1 – 22:5

1. CREATION RENEWED. THE HOLY CITY, 21:1–8

And I saw a new heaven and a new earth, for the first heaven and the first earth had passed away; and the sea was no more. And I saw the holy city, new Jerusalem, coming down from God out of heaven, prepared as a bride adorned for her husband (21:1–2).

St. John is now given a view, as it were, of the dawn of the everlasting day of God's rule of peace and righteousness. The judgment is past, the world is purged, and universal joy and harmony prevail. But what is the meaning of the **new heaven** and **new earth** that he sees? In what sense are they new? And what are we to understand by the information that **the first heaven and the first earth** have **passed away**? Does this terminology imply the annihilation of the present world and the introduction in its place of a completely new creation? The prophets of the Old Testament spoke of the dissolution of heaven and earth (see, for example, Ps.102:26; Is. 34:4; 51:6); St. Peter foretold a conflagration or holocaust of the world to be succeeded by 'new heavens and a new earth in which righteousness dwells' (2 Pet. 3:7, 10–13); and Christ declared: 'Heaven and earth will pass away, but my words will not pass away (Mt. 24:35). On the face of it, such statements could certainly denote the discarding of the old and its replacement by a totally new creation.

There are weighty considerations, however, which lead us to conclude that this is an incorrect interpretation. For one thing, as we have noticed earlier, St. Paul speaks of the present creation as 'waiting with eager longing for the revealing of the sons of God' when it 'will be set free from its bondage to decay' (Rom. 8:19–22). This indicates that the new heaven and new earth will be creation renewed and brought to the glorious consummation for which it was always intended. This is the sense, too, of the new birth or new creation of a person in Christ: 'If any one is in Christ he is a new creation; the old things have passed away; behold, they have become new' (2 Cor. 5:17). The terminology is the same as in the passage before us, but it is obvious that the man-in-Christ who as such is a new creature or creation has not passed away with the old, but is the same creature as before, only now renewed and set free. He is now 'created in Christ Jesus' (Eph. 2:10). The transition from being 'in Adam' to being 'in Christ' is the transformation of the old into the new.

For another thing, for God to discard or annihilate the present creation would testify to the failure of his purpose in bringing it into being, and this in turn would contradict the doctrine of the being of God, whose purposes, by definition, are incapable of meeting with failure. God's purpose as Creator is seen in the fact that all things were created in the Son and through him and for him (Col. 1:16), and consequently all things have the purpose of their creation fulfilled in the Son, through whom God 'reconciles to himself all things, whether on earth or in heaven, having made peace through the blood of his cross' (Col. 1:20). Accordingly, by the new heaven and new earth we understand the realization of 'the time of restoration of all that God spoke by the mouth of his holy prophets from of old', as proclaimed by St. Peter (Acts 3:21) – or the achievement, in a word, of what Christ called the *palingenesia*, the 'rebirth' or 'regeneration', 'when the Son of Man shall sit on the throne of his glory' (Mt. 19:28).

As the vision unfolded St. John observed that **the sea was no more.** The disappearance of the sea does not imply that it was regarded as evil in itself, but rather that its aspect was one of hostility to man. It held in its depths the bodies of unnumbered persons who had perished in its waters (hence the concept of the sea giving up its dead at the last judgment, 20:13). Its calms were deceptive. Its restless turbulence was a picture of the instability of the wicked (Is. 57:20f.). And because its expanses separated men and peoples from each other, its removal may symbolize the harmonious unification as well as the security of all mankind in the renewed creation.

In contrast to the world-city known as 'Sodom and Egypt' and 'Babylon' (11:8; 18:10), which has perished in the wrath of divine judgment (14:8; 18:2), **the holy city, new Jerusalem**, seen **coming down from God out of heaven** is the city with foundations, lasting and free, the city of the living God. It is holy because its inhabitants are the saints, a holy nation (3:12; Heb. 11:10, 16; 12:22; 13:14; Gal. 4:26; 1 Pet. 2:9), and new because it belongs to the new heaven and new earth. A city has no vital identity apart from its citizens, and it is because the great company of the redeemed comprises the authentic citizens of this holy city from heaven (Phil. 3:20) that its appearance is that of **a bride adorned for her husband.** The Lamb is the great Bridegroom with whom his bride the church is now united in a state of everlasting blessedness (see 19:7–9 above; *cf.* Eph. 5:23–32). The saints are the vibrant components of the new Jerusalem in the same way as they are the living stones that form the spiritual temple of which the incarnate Son is himself the chief cornerstone (1 Pet. 2:4ff.).

> *And I heard a great voice from the throne saying, Behold, the dwelling of God is with men, and he will dwell with them, and they will be his peoples; and God himself will be with them; and he will wipe away every tear from their eyes, and death will be no more, nor will there be mourning or crying or pain any more; for the former things have passed away (21:3–4).*

The announcement made by the **great voice from the throne** now heard by St. John is, in effect, the announcement of the fulfilment of all God's covenant promises; for the central message of these promises is that God's presence and dwelling will be with mankind in a relationship of perfect and joyful harmony between the Creator and his creatures. 'I will make my abode among you, and my soul shall not abhor you', the Lord God declared to his people of old; 'And I will walk among you, and will be your God, and you shall be my people' (Lv. 26:11f.). So also in the terms of the new covenant the assurance is given: 'I will make a covenant of peace with them; it shall be an everlasting covenant with them; . . . and [I] will set my sanctuary in the midst of them for evermore. My dwelling place shall be with them; and I will be their God, and they shall be my people' (Ezk. 37:26f.; also Je. 24:7; 30:22; 31:33; 32:38; Zc. 8:8). Now, in this proclamation heard by the Apostle on Patmos, it is said that **they will be his peoples**: there is a change from the singular 'people' to the plural 'peoples'. Yet this, too, is a fulfilment rather than a change, for the ancient promise to Abraham was that in his seed all the nations or peoples of the world would be blessed (Gn. 12:3; 18:18; 22:18) – a promise which signified, as we have seen, the blessing of all mankind through Christ, who in a unique sense is the seed of Abraham (Gal. 3:8, 16, 26–29). The choosing of a people was in order that the promised blessing should come through the person and work of the incarnate Son to all peoples. St. John sees this actualized in the manifestation of the new Jerusalem.

God's presence with his peoples is itself the guarantee that the paradise lost is now restored and more than restored in Christ. The announcement to the redeemed from every nation that **God himself will be with them** carries within itself the implication that **he will wipe away every tear from their eyes**, that **death will be no more**, and likewise **mourning** and **crying** and **pain** (*cf.* 7:17; 20:14). In fulfilment of Isaiah's prophecy, 'the ransomed of the Lord shall return and come to Zion with singing; everlasting joy shall be upon their heads; and they shall obtain joy and gladness, and sorrow and sighing shall flee away' (Is. 35:10; 51:11; *cf.* 65:19). **For**, the great voice explains, **the former things have passed away**; all that has disfigured and debased the work

223

of creation and the society of mankind, all sorrow and suffering and death itself, the last enemy (1 Cor. 15:26), will cast no shadow in that holy city, for they will be known no more.

> *And he who was seated on the throne said, Behold, I make all things new! And he said, Write, for these words are faithful and true. And he said to me, They have come to pass! I am the Alpha and the Omega, the beginning and the end. To him who thirsts I will give freely of the fountain of the water of life. He who overcomes will inherit these things, and I will be his God and he shall be my son (21:5–7).*

In announcing '*Behold, I make all things new!*' the Lord God, who is *seated on the throne*, is declaring the consummation of the revitalizing power of divine grace which is even now active in the hearts of believers, and which caused St. Paul to exclaim that everyone who is in Christ is a new creation and that old things have become new (2 Cor. 5:17). The renewal of creation in its totality (*all things*) is the fulfilment of the old prophetic assurance: 'Remember not the former things, nor consider the things of old. Behold, I am doing a new thing!' (Is. 43:18f.). *These words* heard by the Apostle *are faithful and true* (a statement repeated in 22:6) both because it is impossible for God who spoke them to lie (Heb. 6:18; 2 Tim. 2:13; *cf.* 1 Cor. 1:9; 10:13; 1 Thes. 5:24; 2 Thes. 5:3; also 3:14; 19:9, 11 above), and also because, as this preview of the renewal of all things testifies, *They have come to pass* (*cf.* the 'faithful sayings' in 1 Tim. 1:15; 4:9; 2 Tim. 2:11; Tit. 3:8). They are faithful and true, moreover, not only because of the integrity and trustworthiness of the speaker, but also because of his sovereign control of all things which is implicit in the assertion, '*I am the Alpha and the Omega, the beginning and the end'*. What he starts he brings to fulfilment. His purpose as the Creator of all things cannot fail of realization. The end is implanted in the beginning. The divine Alpha guarantees the attainment of the divine Omega (see comments above on 1:8).

From this scene of the glory yet to be revealed (Rom. 8:18) the Lord God now addresses those to whom, together with the Apostle on Patmos, this glory is still future, and in particular those who are perishing from soul-thirst because they have not drunk from the pure stream of his redeeming grace. He promises to give *to him who thirsts*, and to *give freely of the fountain of the water of life*, for the price has been paid by the incarnate Son (*cf.* Jn. 4:10; 7:37; 1 Cor. 6:19f.; 1 Pet. 1:18f.; the invitation is repeated in 22:17 below). To drink from this source is to drink from the inexhaustible source of the river of God, which is always full of water (Ps. 65:9). It is to turn away from the broken cisterns of our fallenness that can hold no water and to return to him who is 'the fountain of living waters' (Je. 2:13; 17:13). It is to experience the truth of the Saviour's promise: 'Whoever drinks of the water that I shall give him will never thirst; but the water that I shall give him will become in him a spring of water welling up to eternal life' (Jn. 4:14). That is why it is called the water of life.

There is also a word of encouragement for the Christian who is suffering affliction because of his faithful witness: the Lord God assures such that *he who overcomes will inherit these things*, that is, all the unclouded blessings of the new heaven and new earth; and, he adds, '*I will be his God and he shall be my son*', that is to say, the harmonious personal fellowship with his Creator for which the believer was formed will be an unbroken reality. The sonship and the inheritance belong inseparably together. But it is only in him who is uniquely the Son and therefore uniquely the heir of all things (Heb. 1:2), and not at all in himself, that the believer is both son and heir. The ancient promise given to David regarding his Son, the throne of whose kingdom would be established for ever, together with the assurance, 'I will be his father, and he shall be my son' (2 Sa. 7:14), attains its fulfilment in Christ (Heb. 1:5). And the same applies to the covenant promise given to Abraham concerning his seed, which again, as we have seen, is realized, in a unique manner, in Christ (Gal. 3:16). Our sonship is through incorporation into him and his unique sonship. Accordingly, St. Paul instructs the Galatian Christians. 'In Christ Jesus, through faith, you are all sons of God; . . . and if you are Christ's, then you are Abraham's seed, heirs according to the promise' (Gal. 3:26, 29); and to the Christians in Rome he writes: 'All who are led by the Spirit of God are sons of God. . . . The Spirit himself bears witness with our spirit that we are children of God, and if children, then heirs, heirs of God, and fellow heirs with Christ' (Rom. 8:14, 16f.). In the renewed creation the Christian believer enters into the fullness of that sonship and that inheritance in and through the incarnate Son, God's only beloved Son, with whom alone he is well pleased (Mt. 3:17; 17:5; Jn. 1:14).

> *But as for the craven and unbelieving and abominable and mur-*
> *derers and fornicators and sorcerers and idolaters and all liars, their*
> *lot will be in the lake that burns with fire and brimstone, which is*
> *the second death (21:8).*

This statement makes it plain that there is no part or inheritance in the holy city for the types of persons who are named. The *craven* are those who fear and serve men rather than God. The *unbelieving* are the rejecters of the gospel with its invitation to put their faith in Christ. The *abominable* are those who have given themselves over to the practice of unnatural vices. The *murderers* are those who count human life cheap and whose hands are stained with innocent blood. The *fornicators* indulge their lust in promiscuity without respect for the sanctity of the marriage bond. The **sorcerers** allow their lives to be governed by potions and the stars and demonic magic instead of by God and his wisdom. The **idolaters** worship the creature rather than the Creator (Rom. 1:25). And **all liars** have committed themselves to falsehood instead of truth, loving darkness rather than light and turning their backs on him who is the Truth and the Light of the world (Jn. 3:19; 8:12; 14:6).

Such persons are excluded, and indeed exclude themselves, from the new heaven and new earth (*cf.* verse 27 below and 22:15). They are unrepentant and wholly given over to their ungodly ways (*cf.* 9:21; Rom. 1:24, 26, 28). It is those who deliberately and impenitently persist in the practice of evil who are in view here. There is no justification for anyone to conclude that because he has told lies or practised idolatry or engaged in carnal lusts or even committed murder he has shut himself off from the grace of God's forgiveness and redemption. It is sinners of every kind whom Christ came to redeem (Mk. 10:45; 1 Tim. 1:15) and the blood of the incarnate Son cleanses from all sin (1 Jn. 1:7). That is the point of the gracious promise in verse 6: 'To him who thirsts I will give freely of the fountain of the water of life'. And thus St. Paul wrote to the members of the Corinthian church:

> Do you not know that the unrighteous will not inherit the kingdom of God? Do not be deceived; neither fornicators nor idolaters nor adulterers nor catamites nor sodomites nor thieves nor exploiters nor drunkards nor revilers nor extortioners will inherit the kingdom of God. *And such were some of you*; but you were washed, you were sanctified, you were justified in the name of the Lord Jesus Christ and in the Spirit of our God (*1 Cor. 6:9–11*).

Those who impenitently and incorrigibly persist in the practice of evil have their inheritance: it is **the lake** of fire, **which is the second death** (see comments above on 2:11 and 20:6).

2. THE LAMB'S BRIDE, 21:9–27

And one of the seven angels who had the seven bowls that were full of the seven last plagues came and spoke to me, saying, Come, I will show you the bride, the wife of the Lamb. And he carried me away in the Spirit to a great and high mountain, and showed me the holy city Jerusalem coming down out of heaven from God (21:9–10).

Regarding **the seven angels** with **the seven bowls** filled with **the seven last plagues** see 15:1 and 16:1ff. above. The angel seen here may be the same angel who in 17:1 spoke to St. John and showed him the judgment of the great harlot. Now the Apostle is shown *the bride* who is *the wife of the Lamb*, and who, as in verse 2 above, is seen as *the holy city Jerusalem coming down out of heaven from God.* Transported *in the Spirit* (or *in spirit,* cf. 2 Cor. 12:2ff.), he looks on this magnificent spectacle from the top of *a great and high mountain,* a necessary vantage-point for him to see in its right perspective the glorious city he is now about to describe.

> *Having the glory of God, its radiance like a most precious jewel, resembling a jasper, clear as crystal (21:11).*

The glory of the holy city, populated with the innumerable company of the redeemed, is *the glory of God* – glory which human language is inadequate to describe. Yet St. John is required to write down what he sees (1:19), and here, once again, he can but resort to the use of analogy. The transcendental *radiance* of the city, he says, is *like a most precious jewel,* whose resemblance is that of *a jasper, clear as crystal* – an analogy that belongs to him who gloriously rules over all on the throne of his majesty (4:3), and appropriately so, for, as we are told in verse 23 below, 'the glory of God gives it light and its lamp is the Lamb'. The scene is one of ineffable beauty and splendour.

> *Having a great and high wall, with twelve gates, and at the gates twelve angels, and inscribed on the gates the names of the twelve tribes of the sons of Israel, on the east three gates and on the north three gates and on the south three gates and on the west three gates. And the wall of the city had twelve foundations, and on them the twelve names of the twelve apostles of the Lamb (21:12–14).*

The *great and high wall* indicates the magnitude and impregnability of the city. In a manner comparable to the city of Ezekiel's vision (Ezk. 48:30ff.), which had twelve gates, three on each side, and each one connected with one of the twelve tribes, the holy city seen by St. John has twelve gates in its four walls with *the names of the twelve tribes of the sons of Israel* inscribed on them. In addition to this, he notices that the wall of the city has *twelve foundations,* on which he observed *the twelve names of the twelve apostles of the Lamb.* Added together, the twelve patriarchs of Israel and the twelve apostles of the Lamb make up the number of the twenty-four elders (see on 4:4 above; also 4:10; 5:8; 11:16), who represent symbolically the totality of believers in both Old and New Testaments and the perfection of the church (cf. Heb. 11:39f.). This signifies, further, that the holy city is a structure of redeemed persons, not inanimate blocks of stone and other substances.

And he who spoke to me had a golden measuring rod to measure the city and its gates and its wall. And the city lies foursquare, and its length is the same as its breadth. And he measured the city with the rod, twelve thousand stadia; its length and breadth and height are equal. He also measured its wall, a hundred and forty-four cubits, by a man's, that is, an angel's measure. And the wall was built of jasper, and the city was pure gold, like pure crystal. The foundations of the wall of the city were adorned with every kind of precious stone: the first foundation was jasper, the second sapphire, the third chalcedony, the fourth emerald, the fifth sardonyx, the sixth cornelian, the seventh chrysolite, the eighth beryl, the ninth topaz, the tenth chrysoprase, the eleventh jacinth, the twelfth amethyst. And the twelve gates were twelve pearls: each of the gates formed from a single pearl; and the street of the city was pure gold, like transparent crystal (21:15–21).

The measuring of the holy city with *a golden measuring rod* is in itself an indication that its dimensions are in full accord with the plan and purpose of God. The whole scene is essentially symbolical. Its structure as a cube signifies the perfect harmony of its symmetry. Its massive magnitude and capacity are denoted by the figure *twelve thousand stadia*, that is, some fifteen hundred miles, for *its length and breadth and height* are *equal*. The meaning is present in the number twelve thousand, which is three, representing the Trinitarian God, times four, representing the four quarters of the earth, times a thousand, representing, especially as a multiple, the great concourse of its population. There is a correspondence with the 144,000 who are sealed as the Lord's own people (the factors are the same) and who are otherwise described, as we have said, as the 'great multitude which no one could number, from every nation and from all tribes and peoples and tongues', clothed in the white robes of their Redeemer's righteousness (7:3–14). These measurements, then, demarcate the eternal city as the habitation of the vast company of mankind of every generation and from every country who have been redeemed by the regenerating grace of God in Christ Jesus.

The height of the wall, given as *a hundred and forty-four cubits*, that is, two hundred and sixteen feet, could be regarded as disproportionately low in view of the measurements of the city; but, again, the number, as the square of twelve with three and four as its factors, is symbolical of the worldwide harvest among mankind of God's redeeming grace. The comment that this measurement of the wall is *by a man's, that is, an angel's measure* would seem to indicate that this is but a *creaturely* calculation, with the implication that the numbers bear a significance deeper than that of mere mathematical cyphers. Indeed, it is an observation that applies equally to the measurement of the city in verse 16.

To describe the walls and the foundations and the gates and the street of the holy city is to attempt something that is indescribable in merely human terms. Their composition of crystalline gold and precious stones can but give an impression of the transcendental beauty and radiance of the spectacle on which the Apostle gazed; for the true splendour of the new Jerusalem and its citizenry is, as the verses that follow show, the glory of God, nothing less. The fullness of that glory will be seen and known only hereafter by those for whom that city is prepared (*cf.* Phil. 3:20; 1 Cor. 13:12; Heb. 11:10, 13, 16; 13:14). Then there will be no further need for earthly symbols and analogies.

> *And I saw no temple in it, for its temple is the Lord God the Almighty and the Lamb. And the city has no need of the sun or of the moon to shine upon it, for the glory of God gives it light and its lamp is the Lamb* (21:22–23).

There is **no temple**, or sanctuary in the holy city, for, in one respect, it is itself all sanctuary. Its structure, as seen in the vision, in the form of a cube recalls the fact that the dimensions of the Holy of Holies, the inner sanctuary of the presence of God in the Mosaic tabernacle of old, were those of a cube, and that that sanctuary was 'a copy and shadow of the heavenly sanctuary' (Heb. 8:5). Moreover, the construction of this true sanctuary is not from material blocks, not even precious stones and metals, but the persons of the redeemed multitude, who, 'like living stones', are 'built into a spiritual temple, to be a holy priesthood, to offer spiritual sacrifices acceptable to God through Jesus Christ' (1 Pet. 2:5) – 'Christ Jesus himself being the chief cornerstone' of this 'holy sanctuary in the Lord, in whom', St. Paul tells the believers in Ephesus, 'you are being built into a dwelling place of God in the Spirit' (Eph. 2:20–22). Yet, in the ultimate perspective, it is not they who are God's dwelling place but God who is their dwelling place (Ps. 90:1). The city is not a holy sanctuary because the redeemed are its inhabitants, except in a secondary sense, but because it is pervaded by the presence of God himself and thus is absolutely holy, and because all blessedness and all grace come from him who is Lord over all both as Creator and as Redeemer. It is because God is *all in all* (1 Cor. 15:28) that St. John says that the city's **temple is the Lord God the Almighty and the Lamb.**

And the immediate presence of God removes any need of light as it were from outside. The uncreated light that is inseparable from God himself will ceaselessly illumine that city; consequently, there will be **no need of** the light of **the sun or of the moon to shine upon it.** His **glory** provides its light, and **its lamp is the Lamb** whose life is the light of men (Jn. 1:4), and whose glory is one with the eternal glory of the Father (Jn. 17:5) – a foreglimpse of which was seen by the privileged apostles on the mount of transfiguration (Mt. 17:2). No wonder St. John testified: 'We have beheld his glory, glory as of the only Son from the Father' (Jn.

1:14), and St. Peter remembered to his dying day that 'we were eyewitnesses of his majesty . . . when he received honour and glory from God the Father and the voice was brought to him from the Majestic Glory, "This is my beloved Son with whom I am well pleased"' (2 Pet. 1:16f.).

> *And the nations will walk by its light, and the kings of the earth will bring their glory into it, and its gates will never be shut by day, for there will be no night there, and they will bring into it the glory and the honour of the nations; and there will in no wise enter into it anything unclean or that practises abomination or falsehood, but only those who are written in the Lamb's book of life (21:24–27).*

This assertion regarding the holy city that *the nations will walk by its light, and the kings of the earth will bring their glory into it*, announces the fulfilment of the ingathering of a worldwide harvest of the gospel, as predicted in Isaiah 60:3 ('nations shall come to your light, and kings to the brightness of your rising'). The scene will be one of rejoicing and splendour as the citizens of the new Jerusalem *bring into it the glory and the honour of the nations*, for in this multitude of the redeemed assembled in everlasting blessedness and harmony the wonderful potential of man's giftedness by virtue of his creation in the divine image will, in the renewal of creation, blossom forth in unimpaired fullness. Thus the glory and honour with which the nations are endowed will be ascribed entirely and gratefully to the glory and honour of Almighty God their Creator and their Redeemer.

The assurance that the city's *gates will never be shut by day* conveys the sense of the perfect freedom of the saints in glory resulting from the perfect attunement of their wills to the will of God, in whose image they are formed and to which they are now fully conformed. There is no suggestion, however, that the gates will be closed at night, as is necessary in the state of our fallenness, for in fact, as St. John adds, *there will be no night there*, since its light is the glory of the Lord God and the Lamb (verse 23), which means that its day is eternal day. Moreover, as the new heaven and new earth will have been purged of all evil and ungodliness, there will be no hostile power to threaten the peace of the city and cause the closing of its gates. This, once again, will be the coming to pass of the situation envisaged in Isaiah's prophecy: 'Your gates shall be open continually. . . . The sun shall be no more your light by day, nor for brightness shall the moon give light to you by night; but the Lord will be your everlasting light, and your God will be your glory' (Is. 60:11, 19f.).

That the gates of the city will be perpetually open does not mean that they will be open to evil and ungodliness. How could it be *the holy city* (verse 2) if it were all-inclusive in this sense? That there is indeed exclusion is plain from the declaration that *there will in no wise enter into it anything unclean or that practises abomination or falsehood* – that is to say, there will be absolutely no place in it for unholiness and perversion and untruthfulness, which are the hallmarks of Satan and his followers (*cf.* Jn. 8:44). But there will also be no danger of evil things and those who practise them entering in through the ever-open gates, since they will have been eternally excluded and indeed eliminated by the purgation of the world in final judgment (see verse 8 above, also 22:15). The inhabitants of the holy city will be *only those who are written in the Lamb's book of life* (see on 3:5 above), and as such have been called, justified, and glorified by the grace of God who predestined them to be conformed to the image of his Son (Rom. 8:29f.). Thus yet another promise of the ancient prophecy is brought to realization: 'Your people shall all be righteous' (Is. 60:21).

3. THE WATER OF LIFE AND THE TREE OF LIFE, 22:1-5

And he showed me a river of water of life, bright as crystal, flowing from the throne of God and of the Lamb in the middle of its street, and on either side of the river the tree of life, bearing twelve kinds of fruit, yielding its fruit month by month, and the leaves of the tree for the healing of the nations (22:1-2).

What the Apostle sees in this vision is Paradise regained: all that was lost in Adam is restored, and more than restored, in Christ. The river that flowed in Eden (Gn. 2:10) reappears now as the *river of water of life*, so pure and wholesome that it is *bright as crystal*. There are affinities also with the vision of Ezekiel, who saw a river that issued from the temple sanctuary bringing life to every living creature, with all kinds of trees on its banks that bear fresh fruit for food every month and whose leaves are for healing (Ezk. 47:1-12). In the scene described by St. John the life-giving river flows through the holy city, *in the middle of its street*, and only one tree, *the tree of life*, grows on its banks, *on either side of the river* overshading and within reach of all, as it yields its *fruit month by month*, that is to say, ceaselessly, for there is now no death to cut short the abundant life associated with the tree (20:14; 21:4). Moreover, as with the leaves of Ezekiel's trees, *the leaves of the tree are for the healing of the nations.* It is, in short, a picture of total peace and well-being.

The single tree here (in contrast to the many trees of Ezekiel's vision), specifically designated *the tree of life*, plainly indicates its direct connection, indeed identity, with the tree of life of Genesis 2:9 from which fallen Adam was driven. In Christ man is brought back to the paradise he had lost and forward to the destiny in glory for which he was created.

The river with its water of life symbolizes the inexhaustible grace of God (*cf*. Ps. 65:9). It is the reality of which the Psalmist wrote: 'There is a river whose streams make glad the city of God, the holy habitation of the Most High' (Ps. 46:4), and the fountain which Joel foresaw would come forth from the house of the Lord (Joel 3:18), and the living water to which, as we have seen, the Lamb leads his people (7:17; 21:6). And it flows *from the throne of God and of the Lamb.* While this signifies that the Lamb, who is the incarnate Son, his redeeming mission to earth accomplished, is now exalted to the highest glory and is seated with his Father on his throne (3:21), and thus is 'in the midst of the throne' (7:17), it does not mean that, though there is certainly a distinction between the person of the Father and the person of the Son, we should envisage two separate entities seated on the one throne; for God is one (1 Tim. 2:5; Gal. 3:20) and the Father and the Son are one (Jn. 10:30). The problem is the inadequacy of the finite mind and language of man to comprehend and describe the infinite being of the Triune God. The threefoldness of the divine being naturally requires distinctions to be made between the Father and the Son and the Holy Spirit (distinctions which are essential to our understanding, limited though it is, of the economy of our redemption) but never at the cost of dissolving the oneness of the Godhead. As there is none to whom God can be compared and 'his understanding is unsearchable' (Is. 40:25, 28), we must be content with the mystery (and indeed grateful for it, for if there were no mystery and all were comprehensible to us we should not be talking about God, but about a mere projection of ourselves); and the mystery of the divine unity yet diversity is preserved by St. John as he speaks of 'the throne of God and the Lamb'. But, most significantly, the fact that it is the throne of God *and of the Lamb* instructs us that our Sovereign God who is the Creator of all is also the Redeemer of his fallen creatures, and that the river which flows from his throne is indeed the river of the living water of his grace. In the Lamb the Creator-God is the Reconciling God (Gal. 5:19); hence the anthem of the hosts in glory: 'Worthy is the Lamb who was slain . . . To him who is seated on the throne and to the Lamb be the blessing and the honour and the glory and the might for ever and ever!' (5:11–13).

> *And there will no longer be any curse, and the throne of God and the Lamb will be in it, and his servants will worship him, and they will see his face, and his name will be on their foreheads; and there will be no more night, and they need neither light of lamp nor light of sun, for the Lord God will be their light, and they will reign for ever and ever* (22:3–5).

Another link with the account of the creation and fall of man in the opening chapters of Genesis is the declaration that in the holy city *there will no longer be any curse*, for this implies the removal of the curse which man brought upon himself through his sin (Gn. 3:17ff.) and the fulfilment of Zechariah's prophecy: 'There shall be no more curse; Jerusalem shall dwell in security' (Zc. 14:11). This, again, is due entirely to the Lamb's propitiatory self-offering of himself for us on the cross, itself the symbol of the curse; for, as St. Paul wrote, 'Christ redeemed us from the curse of the law, having become a curse for us' (Gal. 3:13). And that, further, is why **the throne of God and the Lamb** (see comments on preceding section) will be in the new Jerusalem, and be there as the inexhaustible fount of grace and blessing to its citizens who have been saved from the curse and condemnation. These are **his servants** who **will worship him** as they perform his will, and in doing so joyfully fulfil the purpose of their creation in the divine image. Clothed in robes of holiness that have been washed and made white in the blood of the Lamb, they are before the throne of God and serve him ceaselessly in his temple (7:14f.).

Moreover, **they will see his face.** This is the height and summation of all blessedness, not only to be in God's presence but actually to see his face, that is, to know the perfection of harmony and fellowship with their Creator and, thanks to his redeeming grace, to stand before him with unhesitating confidence and commune with him in total love. This relationship of blissful immediacy will everlastingly fulfil the longing expectation of the Lord's faithful servants in all generations. In his long distant time Job believed that with his own eyes he would hereafter behold God, his living Redeemer (Jb. 19:25–27). David's heart was filled with the same assurance: 'As for me,' he wrote, 'I shall behold thy face in righteousness; when I awake, I shall be satisfied with beholding thy form' (Ps. 17:15). Seeing the Lord's face means also the dispelling of all doubt and uncertainty and ignorance: 'Now we see in a mirror dimly', St. Paul declared, 'but then face to face; now I know in part, but then I shall know fully, even as I am fully known' (1 Cor. 13:12). Though Christian believers are the children of God, yet, as St. John says, we are not yet what we shall be hereafter, knowing as we do that 'when he appears we shall be like him, for we shall see him as he is' (1 Jn. 3:2). To see his face indicates a personal relationship of absolute trust and openness. This is confirmed by the assertion that **his name will be on their foreheads** (see comments above on 3:12; 7:3; 14:1), for this signifies not only their preciousness to him, to whom they gladly belong (*cf.* 1 Cor. 6:19f.) but also that in the multitude of the redeemed who populate the holy city there will be none who are unknown and unloved, none whose identity is lost in the crowd, and none who miss seeing him face to face.

The statement that **there will be no more night** and that **they need neither light of lamp nor light of sun** because **the Lord God will be their light** repeats what has already been said in 21:23, 25. It is more than a mere repetition, however, for here the information that the Lord's servants will see his face takes us more deeply into the reason why there will be no more night and no more need of light from lamp or sun: this will be the full and unveiled experience of what St. Paul meant when he wrote that 'God has shined in our hearts to give the light of the knowledge of the glory of God in the face of Christ' (2 Cor. 4:6). This is the light that is absolute. In this light the Lord's redeemed *will reign for ever and ever.* But this reigning is no more their own independent reigning than the light in which they serve is light they themselves generate. It is the Lord who reigns supreme over all; their reigning is by virtue of the grace that has united them to the Lord. He alone is King of kings and Lord of lords (17:14; 19:16); their kingship is in and through him who loves them and freed them from their sins by his blood (1:6; 5:10). Their reigning is *reigning with him* (2 Tim. 2:12; *cf.* Rom. 8:17; Lk. 22:28–30), and that explains why it is for ever and ever.

Conclusion, 22:6–21

ADMONITIONS, INVITATIONS, BENEDICTION

> *And he said to me, These words are faithful and true. And the Lord, the God of the spirits of the prophets, sent his angel to show his servants the things that must soon come to pass. And behold, I am coming soon. Blessed is he who keeps the words of the prophecy of this book* (22:6–7).

The preceding section with its promise that the company of the redeemed will reign for ever and ever in the resplendent light of the Lord God is to all intents and purposes the conclusion of St. John's visions on Patmos. The angel who has been speaking to him and revealing to him the glorious consummation of the new heaven and earth (*cf.* 21:9, 15; 22:1) assures him that *these words*, all that he has seen and heard and recorded, *are faithful and true.* This is an assurance already given in 21:5 by the Lord himself, together with the evidential affirmation 'They have come to pass', because what St. John saw there was a proleptic vision of future glory as though it was already an accomplished reality. Here, however, the perspective is from the present to the future; hence the declaration that *the Lord . . . sent his angel to show his servants the things that must soon come to pass.* This forms an obvious link with the opening statement of the book, namely: 'The revelation of Jesus Christ, which God gave him to show to his servants the things which must soon come to pass' (1:1).

The description of the Lord as *the God of the spirits of the prophets* is an affirmation that the prophets and their teaching are under the control of God. The expression 'the spirits of the prophets' is indeed an idiom characteristic of St. John in the New Testament (in 1 Cor. 12:10 St. Paul seems to have 'spirits' by itself with the same connotation, but 'the spirits of the prophets' in 1 Cor. 14:32 is not a parallel usage), for in his First Epistle he writes:

> Beloved, do not believe every spirit, but test the spirits to see whether they are of God, for many false prophets have gone

out into the world; . . . every spirit which confesses that Jesus Christ has come in the flesh is of God, and every spirit which does not confess Jesus is not of God: this is the spirit of antichrist *(1 Jn. 4:1–3).*

By the spirits of the prophets the cognitive faculties of the prophets are intended, particularly as revealed in their teaching. The testing of spirits is necessary in order to discern between the true and the false prophets. The Lord, of course, is the God only of the spirits of those who are true prophets.

The implication that St. John himself belongs to the number of the true prophets is confirmed by the assertion, **Blessed is he who keeps the words of the prophecy of this book,** which, together with the Lord's admonition, **Behold, I am coming soon,** is another link with the opening passage of the Revelation, where we read: 'Blessed is he who reads and those who hear the words of the prophecy, and who keep the things written in it; for the time is near' (1:3).

> *And I John am he who heard and saw these things; and having heard and seen I fell down to worship at the feet of the angel who showed them to me. And he said to me, You must not do that! I am a fellow servant with you and your brethren the prophets and with those who keep the words of this book. Worship God! (22:8–9).*

St. **John,** who identified himself three times in the beginning of this work, now names himself again, and testifies that it was **he who heard and saw these things.** This is true of all that is recorded in this book, but here seems to apply more particularly to the spectacle of the holy city, new Jerusalem, the most recent of the revelations granted to him. Profoundly moved by the splendour of the scene and awed by the dignity of the angel present with him, the Apostle, without stopping to consider what he was doing, falls down to worship before this angelic being. This was a well intentioned but improper impulse and it was the second time he had given way to it; and the rebuke he received was almost identical with the one he had evoked on the first occasion: **You must not do that! I am a fellow servant with you and your brethren and with those who keep the words of this book.** And again he is told that his worship must be offered to God alone, not to any creature, whether man or angel, however exalted he may seem to be (see comments above on 19:10). This whole book makes it absolutely plain that in the renewed creation the worship of all will be offered constantly and solely to God, and this incident reminds us again that as our worship will be hereafter so it should be here and now.

> *And he said to me, Do not seal up the words of the prophecy of this book, for the time is near. Let the evildoer still do evil, and let the*

filthy still be filthy, and let the righteous still do right, and let the holy still be holy (22:10–11)

In contrast to the command given to Daniel to seal up the vision he had been given, 'because it pertains to many days hence' (Dn. 8:26), St. John is told that he should **not seal up the words of the prophecy of this book** and for the reason that **the time is near**, that is to say, the time of fulfilment is imminent. This interval between the comings of Christ is the time of the last days, and the last of these last days is always impending. The Lord is always coming soon (verses 7, 12, 20; 3:11), but at an unrevealed hour, and those who are wise will live their lives in the expectation of his coming. Hence this book with its promises and warnings and exhortations is to remain unsealed and open for all to read. Those who impenitently and obdurately refuse to heed its message will persist in their ungodly ways, but they do not thereby separate themselves from the sovereign rule of God. **The evildoer** may **still do evil** and **the filthy** may **still be filthy**, but it is a course that leads to final judgment and death. Conversely, those who keep the words of the prophecy of this book (verse 7) must persevere in their service of the Lord, undeterred by the wickedness and hostility of others; **the righteous** should **still do right** and **the holy** should **still be holy**, pressing on toward their imperishable inheritance in glory (*cf.* 1 Pet. 1:3ff.).

Behold, I am coming soon, and my recompense is with me, to render to every one according to his work. I am the Alpha and the Omega, the first and the last, the beginning and the end (22:12–13).

These are the words of the Lord, addressed to those referred to in the preceding verse – that is, to every one, regenerate and unregenerate. The day of his coming will be the day of reckoning: he will **render to every one according to his work** (*cf.* Mt. 16:27; Rom. 2:6; 14:12; 2 Cor. 5:10). The principle as we have said (see on 20:12 above), is that of strict justice. The distinction is between those who practise evil and those who practise righteousness; but it would be a serious mistake to conclude that it is by good works that we will be justified. Such a conclusion would be in conflict with the plain teaching that the sinner is justified by grace through faith, which is God's gift, and not because of works he has done (Eph. 2:8f.; Rom. 3:20ff.; Tit. 3:4ff.). It would be in conflict with the whole tenor of this book, in which all the worthiness of our justification is ascribed to the Lamb who was slain and with his blood 'purchased men for God from every tribe and tongue and people and nation' (5:9); and with the immediate context, which (in verse 14 that follows) announces the blessedness of 'those who wash their robes' – wash them, that is to say, and make them white in the blood of the Lamb (as in 7:14 above). At the same time, however, the Christian believer has died to the old life of sin and been raised to newness of life in Christ. That is the significance of his baptism (Rom. 6:1–4). He becomes what his Creator intended him to be, for by the new birth he is 'created in Christ Jesus for good works, which God prepared beforehand that he should walk in them' (Eph. 2:10).

By identifying himself as *the Alpha and the Omega, the first and the last, the beginning and the end* the Lord is, by implication, warning the ungodly that his will be the last word of final judgment and assuring his faithful servants that the glorious consummation of their salvation is secure in his hands. What the Lord starts he completes (*cf.* Phil. 1:16; Heb. 12:2; and see comments above on 1:8, 17; 21:6).

> *Blessed are those who wash their robes that they may have the right to the tree of life and enter the city by the gates. Outside are the dogs and the sorcerers and the fornicators and the murderers and the idolaters and every one who loves and practises falsehood (22:14–15).*

Blessed are those who wash their robes is the last of the beatitudes of this book (for the others see 1:3; 14:13; 16:15; 19:9; 20:6; 22:7). That what is intended is not self-purification (see the preceding comment on verse 12), is evident from 7:14 where the multitude of the redeemed is composed of those who have washed their robes and made them white in the blood of the Lamb; that is to say, their cleansing is by virtue of the grace that flows to mankind from the cross of Christ. Reconciled to God by the death of his Son (Rom. 5:10), they have *the right to the tree of life*, access to which had been barred because of their sinfulness (see comments on verse 2 above), and they are free to *enter the city by the gates*, which stand open for them to pass through (21:25). The gates are not open, however, to permit the entry of evildoers who persist in their ungodly and unbelieving ways. The redeemed society is purged of all such, classified here as *the dogs and the sorcerers and the fornicators and the murderers and the idolaters and every one who loves and practises falsehood.* All evil is false and opposed to the truth, and it is those who obdurately *love and practise* evil that are excluded from the holy city in which there is no place for unholiness (see comments above on 21:8). They are *outside.* Together with the devil and the beast and the false prophet, and together with Death and Hades, they are consigned to the lake of fire, which is the second death (20:10, 13–15; 21:8). The end of the falsehood they love to practise is death (Rom. 6:21). They have cut themselves off from all right of access to the tree of life. No end could be more calamitous than that.

> *I Jesus have sent my angel to testify to you these things concerning the churches. I am the root and the offspring of David, the bright morning star (22:16).*

The Lord who speaks to St. John is the risen, ascended, and glorified **Jesus.** Here, and throughout the New Testament, there is no suggestion of a distinction between 'the historic Jesus' and 'the risen Christ', as though some kind of discontinuity were involved – a distinction invented by some who disavow the bodily resurrection of Jesus. The assertion *I Jesus have sent my angel to testify to you these things concerning the churches* relates back to the information given in the opening paragraph of this book, namely, that Jesus Christ made known the things that must soon take place by sending his angel to his servant John (1:1). The seven churches that were then addressed (1:4, 20 and chs. 2 and 3) are, as we have said before, representative in their various ways of the churches in every place and in every generation. But 'the things that must soon come to pass' mentioned at the beginning refer to all that is to follow in this record of St. John's Patmos vision, and the expression *these things* here at the end refers to all that has preceded.

Jesus describes himself as *the root and offspring of David*, and in doing so indicates that he is not only after David but also before him. This designation is essentially the same as that already encountered in 5:5, where he is called 'the Lion of the tribe of Judah' and 'the Root of David' (see comments there). Not only is Jesus David's descendant or shoot, he is also his root, the cause of his existence. As the root he is David's God and Creator; as the shoot he is, by virtue of his incarnation, the Son of David, the promised royal Deliverer, 'descended from David according to the flesh' (Rom. 1:3; Heb. 7:14). In other words, the incarnate Son is a theanthropic person: he is both truly God and truly man, and therefore truly the 'one Mediator between God and men, who gave himself a ransom for all' (1 Tim. 2:5f.).

As we have seen, in the letter to the church in Thyatira Jesus promised to give 'the morning star' to him who overcomes (see comments there); and now he tells his Apostle that he himself is *the bright morning star.* Implicit in this self-description is the assurance that the darkness of the long night will soon end and that the day without shadows and without end is about to dawn, for his brightness is the brightness of God himself (*cf.* Jn. 1:4, 5, 9, 14; 17:5). The shining of him who is our bright Morning Star continues, and will continue, intense and constant, until the eternal day dawns and the shadows flee away (Song 2:17; 4:6); and then there will be no need of light or lamp because the glory of the Lord God and the Lamb will be our light for ever (21:23; 22:5).

> *And the Spirit and the bride say, Come! And let him who hears say, Come! And let him who is thirsty come, let him who wishes take the water of life freely (22:17).*

In the great visions of ultimate reality revealed to the Lord's servant suffering for the gospel on the isle of Patmos, the end has been disclosed as the glorious fulfilment of all that was there in the beginning of creation, and he has seen that, for all whose names are written in the Lamb's book of life, it is an end that is all future, an end without end. Meanwhile, as the Morning Star with its firm promise shines brightly, it is still the night of this present age; and that means that it is still the age of the gospel, still the season for the Lord's ambassadors to appeal to men and women throughout the world: 'We beseech you on behalf of Christ, be reconciled to God' (2 Cor. 5:20). The Lord of all still bestows his riches on all who call upon him, and faith comes by hearing the message of redemption proclaimed (Rom. 10:12–17). So the gracious gospel invitation is repeated, simply and clearly here: *the Spirit and the bride say, Come!* – that is to say, the Holy Spirit whose energizing presence is in the bride, Christ's church, the company of all who are united to him by faith (19:7–9; 21:2, 9; 2 Cor. 11:2; Eph. 5:25ff.; Jn. 14:17), issues the invitation, through and with the bride, to come to him who is the world's Redeemer and Lord. The responsibility of evangelization, moreover, belongs not just to the church as a corporate entity or organization, but to every single member of the church. To issue the gospel invitation is the privilege and the debt or obligation of each individual believer (*cf.* Rom. 1:14). Accordingly, the exhortation is added: *And let him who hears say, Come!*

The gospel invitation is then spoken for all to hear and respond to: *And let him who is thirsty come, let him who wishes take the water of life freely.* This confirms the promise already uttered by the glorified Saviour: 'To him who thirsts I will give freely of the fountain of the water of life' (21:6; see comments there). To *wish* for the water of life is to have the will to receive it, indeed a will that is intent on receiving it and earnestly seeks it (*cf.* Je. 29:13; Mk. 7:6). It was those who had the will to be healed that Jesus made whole (*cf.* Mk. 10:51f.; Jn. 5:7, *etc.*). Even the strong will for the healing of the gospel is a gift of divine grace, for, as St. Paul says, it is God who causes us to will what is pleasing to him (Phil. 2:13). And the water of life that he gives to the thirsty is an ever-full, ever-flowing river of grace (verse 1; *cf.* Jn. 4:10; 6:35). There is nothing in the whole universe that should be so earnestly willed as that.

> *I testify to every one who hears the words of the prophecy of this book: if any one adds to them God will add to him the plagues written in this book; and if any one takes away from the words of the book of this prophecy God will take away his part from the tree of life and from the holy city, which are written about in this book (22:18–19).*

This solemn warning may be said to be the obverse side of the blessing pronounced at the beginning of the book on every one who reads and hears and keeps what is written in it (1:3; also 22:7). The warning is no doubt directed primarily against false teachers who pervert the book's message either by adding their own fantasies to it or by subtracting from it what they find inconvenient. There is an appropriate balance or symmetry in its construction: to the person who adds *God will add*, by a condign judgment, *the plagues written in this book*; from the person who subtracts or takes away *God will take away*, no less justly, *his part from the tree of life and from the holy city* (*cf.* 21:2, 10; 22:2, 14). In effect, of course, the retributive 'addition' amounts to the same thing as the retributive 'taking away', total perdition. The point is that such perverters of the book's message will experience to their irreparable cost the truth of what is written in this book. In much the same manner Moses had admonished the Israelites: 'You shall not add to the word which I command you, nor take from it; that you may keep the commandments of the Lord your God which I command you', while reminding them that God had destroyed their fellows who had been faithless and disobedient (Dt. 4:2–4). St. John's warning indeed may be seen as a claim that this book of Revelation belongs to the canon of Holy Scripture.

> *He who testifies to these things says, Surely I am coming soon. Amen: Come, Lord Jesus!* (22:20).

The Lord repeats the declaration already made in verses 7 and 12 and in 3:11 that he is *coming soon.* The hour of his coming remains undisclosed, but, as we have said, it is an event that is always imminent; hence the need always to live in the expectation of his appearing (*cf.* 1 Jn. 2:28, and see comments above on 1:1, 'the things that must soon come to pass', and on 3:11). His coming, moreover, should not only be looked for but also longed for by the believer, for it will bring the consummation of our salvation and the completion of our conformity to his likeness (*cf.* 1 Jn. 3:2; 2 Cor. 3:18; Phil. 3:20f.), indeed, the renewal of all things (21:5). And so the fervent response of the Bride, longing for the appearance of the beloved Bridegroom, is *Amen: Come, Lord Jesus!*

> *The grace of the Lord Jesus be with all the saints. Amen* (22:21).

This concluding wish or prayer is commonly added at the end of a letter (see Rom. 16:20; 1 Cor. 16:23; Gal. 6:18; Phil. 4:23, *etc.*). The literary form of this composition, however, is not that of a letter, though it is addressed 'to the seven churches that are in Asia' with a salutation in a manner comparable to the opening of a letter (1:4; *cf.* Rom. 1:7; 1 Cor. 1:1–3). The so-called letters to the seven churches in chapters 2 and 3 are not so much letters as messages. St. John's book, none the less, was a communication intended to be read and heard in the different churches (see 1:3), and in the light of this fact the ending is entirely appropriate as a prayerful and affectionate wish from the Apostle to his fellow believers.

There can be no higher desire for others than that the grace of God should be with them, grace which is identical with *the grace of the Lord Jesus*, the eternal and incarnate Son, who, himself the fulness of divine grace, is risen from the dead and exalted to glory as Lord over all (17:14; 19:16; Phil. 2:6–10). His absolute lordship is the guarantee of the everlasting security of *all the saints*, the believers of every generation, the innumerable multitude cleansed through the shedding of his redeeming blood (7:9, 14). This wonderful conclusion, the Lord of grace with his saints redeemed by that grace, is also the beginning of the day without cloud or night or ending in which the redeemed multitude, themselves purified and conformed to the likeness of the incarnate Son, ceaselessly praise God by worshipping and serving him in the created realm that, purged from all defilement, is forever new.